T0178322

Lecture Notes in Business Information Processing 438

More information about this series at https://link.springer.com/bookseries/7911

Adam Przybyłek · Aleksander Jarzębowicz ·
Ivan Luković · Yen Ying Ng (Eds.)

Lean and Agile Software Development

6th International Conference, LASD 2022
Virtual Event, January 22, 2022
Proceedings

 Springer

Editors
Adam Przybyłek 🔟
Gdańsk University of Technology
Gdańsk, Poland

Aleksander Jarzębowicz 🔟
Gdańsk University of Technology
Gdańsk, Poland

Ivan Luković 🔟
University of Belgrade
Belgrade, Serbia

Yen Ying Ng 🔟
Nicolaus Copernicus University
Toruń, Poland

ISSN 1865-1348   ISSN 1865-1356 (electronic)
Lecture Notes in Business Information Processing
ISBN 978-3-030-94237-3   ISBN 978-3-030-94238-0 (eBook)
https://doi.org/10.1007/978-3-030-94238-0

This Springer imprint is published by the registered company Springer Nature Switzerland AG
The registered company address is: Gewerbestrasse 11, 6330 Cham, Switzerland

Preface

In 2020, the world changed. In just a few months, COVID-19 transformed our lives on an unprecedented scale, impacting individuals, communities, organizations, and countries. The pandemic had an immediate effect on the software community. As omnipresent agile methods emphasize the importance of collocation and face-to-face communication to coordinate the work, the sudden transition to a remote virtual environment has challenged the well-established approach to delivering product increments. Fortunately, the agile mindset and principles have allowed agile teams to implement ad-hoc actions to smoothly shift to a remote setting. Unfortunately, more than two years since COVID-19 broke out, we are still in pandemic mode and experts predict that the virus will be a part of our daily life. Therefore, the agile community is responsible for elaborating systematic solutions and best practices for remote agile teams and reporting the lessons learned. In this setting, the LASD conference series and the community feel particularly proud of their contributions to research and practice investigating how to stay agile while working remotely.

This volume contains the papers presented at LASD 2022, the 6th International Conference on Lean and Agile Software Development, held online on 22 January 2022. As everyone involved in LASD 2022 worked voluntarily, the conference was fully free of charge. LASD 2022 received 29 submissions. After a rigorous review process, which included at least three reviews per submission, nine high-quality full papers, one short paper, and one position paper were selected. The accepted papers were presented to a well-focused audience, thus the discussion provided the authors with new ideas and directions for further research. Topics discussed in this volume range from teams under COVID-19 through agile testing to agile effort estimation and an agile approach to model-driven development.

Corresponding authors of all accepted papers received a complimentary one year membership of Agile Alliance. Agile Alliance is a nonprofit global member organization dedicated to promoting the concepts of agile software development as outlined in the Agile Manifesto. With more than 75,000 members and subscribers around the globe, Agile Alliance is driven by the principles of agile methodologies and the value delivered to developers, business, and end users. Agile Alliance organizes and supports events to bring the agile community together on an international scale.

The high quality of the LASD 2022 technical program was enhanced by two keynote lectures delivered by outstanding guests: Markus Borg ("Agility in Software 2.0—Notebook Interfaces and MLOps with Buttresses and Rebars") and Raman Ramsin ("Promises of Model-Driven Development in an Agile Context").

We would like to express our gratitude to everyone who made LASD 2022 successful. First of all, we thank all authors for their contributions, the members of the Program Committees for taking the time and effort to provide insightful remarks, and both keynote speakers for their impressive speeches. We are also deeply grateful to Mirjana Ivanović and Marjan Mernik for the opportunity to publish an extended version of the best papers in Computer Science and Information Systems (ComSIS) and the Journal of Computer

Languages (COLA), respectively. Furthermore, we acknowledge Michał Jakubowicz and Szymon Żebrowski for developing our conference website. Finally, we would like to thank the team at Springer for making this volume possible.

We hope that you find this monograph useful for your professional and academic activities, and we wish you a stimulating read. We also cordially invite you to visit our conference website at https://lasd.pl, and to join us for the upcoming edition.

January 2022

Adam Przybyłek
Aleksander Jarzębowicz
Ivan Luković
Yen Ying Ng

Organization

Conference and Program Committee Chair

Adam Przybyłek   Gdańsk University of Technology, Poland

Program Committee

Ibrahim Akman	Atilim University, Turkey
Fernando Almeida	University of Porto and INESC TEC, Portugal
Mohammad Alshayeb	King Fahd University of Petroleum and Minerals, Saudi Arabia
Alessandra Bagnato	SOFTEAM R&D Department, France
Woubshet Behutiye	University of Oulu, Finland
Mario Bernhart	Vienna University of Technology, Austria
Vikram Bhadauria	Texas A&M University-Texarkana, USA
Miklós Biró	Software Competence Center Hagenberg and Johannes Kepler University Linz, Austria
Jan Olaf Blech	Aalto University, Finland
Markus Borg	SICS Swedish ICT AB, Sweden
Alena Buchalcevova	Prague University of Economics and Business, Czech Republic
Jim Buchan	Auckland University of Technology, New Zealand
Luigi Buglione	Engineering Ingegneria Informatica SpA, Italy
Shariq Aziz Butt	University of Lahore, Pakistan
Daniela Cruzes	Norwegian University of Science and Technology, Norway
Wiktor Bohdan Daszczuk	Warsaw University of Technology, Poland
Igor Dejanović	University of Novi Sad, Serbia
Anna Derezinska	Warsaw University of Technology, Poland
Philipp Diebold	Bagilstein GmbH, Germany
Arpita Dutta	National University of Singapore, Singapore
Maria Jose Escalona Cuaresma	Universidad de Sevilla, Spain
Imane Essebaa	Hassan II University of Casablanca, Morocco
Fernando Marques Figueira Filho	Universidade Federal do Rio Grande do Norte, Brazil
Gabriel Alberto García-Mireles	Universidad de Sonora, Mexico
Bartłomiej Gawin	University of Gdańsk, Poland
Javad Ghofrani	University of Lübeck, Germany
Krzysztof Goczyła	Gdańsk University of Technology, Poland

Arne Noyer	Ostfalia University of Applied Sciences, Germany
Hanna Oktaba	National Autonomous University of Mexico, Mexico
Tosin Daniel Oyetoyan	Western Norway University of Applied Sciences, Norway
Necmettin Özkan	Kuveyt Türk Participation Bank, Turkey
Subhrakanta Panda	Birla Institute of Technology and Science, Pilani, India
Rui Humberto R. Pereira	Instituto Politécnico do Porto, Portugal
Aneta Poniszewska-Maranda	Lodz University of Technology, Poland
Alexander Poth	Volkswagen AG, Germany
Michał Przybyłek	University of Warsaw, Poland
Sandra Ramłrez Mora	Universidad Nacional Autónoma de México, Mexico
Raman Ramsin	Sharif University of Technology, Iran
Andreas Riel	Grenoble Alpes University, France
Sonja Ristić	University of Novi Sad, Serbia
Bruno Rossi	Masaryk University, Czech Republic
Zdenek Rybola	Charles Technical University in Prague, Czech Republic
Dina Salah	Sadat Academy for Management Sciences, Egypt
Mattia Salnitri	University of Trento, Italy
Wylliams Barbosa Santos	University of Pernambuco, Brazil
Eva-Maria Schön	University of Seville, Spain
Jorge Sedeno	University of Seville, Spain
Mali Senapathi	Auckland University of Technology, New Zealand
Álvaro Soria	ISISTAN Research Institute, Argentina
Maria Spichkova	RMIT University, Australia
Tor Stålhane	Norwegian University of Science and Technology, Norway
Christoph Johann Stettina	Leiden University, The Netherlands
Ayca Tarhan	Hacettepe University, Turkey
Adel Taweel	Birzeit University, Palestine
Sven Theobald	Fraunhofer IESE, Germany
Jörg Thomaschewski	University of Applied Sciences Emden/Leer, Germany
Carlos Torrecilla Salinas	University of Seville, Spain
Michael Unterkalmsteiner	Blekinge Institute of Technology, Sweden
Jan Werewka	AGH University of Science and Technology, Poland
Dominique Winter	University of Applied Sciences Emden/Leer, Germany

Promises of Model-Driven Development in an Agile Context (Abstract of Keynote Talk)

Raman Ramsin (ID)

Department of Computer Engineering, Sharif University of Technology,
Azadi Avenue, Tehran, Iran
ramsin@sharif.edu

Abstract. Model-Driven Development (MDD) has always been considered as a promising means for automatic code generation. Although MDD has come a long way in achieving its objectives, its potential has yet to be fulfilled. Recent advances in low-code development have given new hope to old MDD-inspired dreams; integrating MDD with agile development is one of these old dreams. The MDD community has long been striving to convince the agile community of the potential merits of this integration. However, the general agile mindset tended to value simplicity over rigor, and modeling seemed too rigorous to be useful and affordable from an agile perspective.

As MDD approaches have evolved over the years, so have agile methodologies: the model-phobia frequently seen in older agile methodologies is no longer prevalent, and modeling activities have become an essential part of newer agile processes. This seems to signify an invaluable opportunity to reinvigorate the integration efforts. In this talk, a brief overview will be provided of the recent developments in the two fields, and the new opportunities for fusing MDD into agile processes will be explored.

Contents

Short Paper

Position Paper

Keynote Paper

Agility in Software 2.0 – Notebook Interfaces and MLOps with Buttresses and Rebars

Markus Borg[1,2(✉)]

[1] RISE Research Institutes of Sweden, Lund, Sweden
markus.borg@ri.se
[2] Department of Computer Science, Lund University, Lund, Sweden

Abstract. Artificial intelligence through machine learning is increasingly used in the digital society. Solutions based on machine learning bring both great opportunities, thus coined "Software 2.0," but also great challenges for the engineering community to tackle. Due to the experimental approach used by data scientists when developing machine learning models, agility is an essential characteristic. In this keynote address, we discuss two contemporary development phenomena that are fundamental in machine learning development, i.e., notebook interfaces and MLOps. First, we present a solution that can remedy some of the intrinsic weaknesses of working in notebooks by supporting easy transitions to integrated development environments. Second, we propose reinforced engineering of AI systems by introducing metaphorical buttresses and rebars in the MLOps context. Machine learning-based solutions are dynamic in nature, and we argue that reinforced continuous engineering is required to quality assure the trustworthy AI systems of tomorrow.

1   Introduction

No one has missed the AI surge in the last decade. There is an ever-increasing number of AI applications available as enterprises across domains seek to harness the promises of AI technology. Enabled by the growing availability of data, most of the AI success stories in recent years originate in solutions dominated by Machine Learning (ML) [1]. Where human programmers previously had to express all logic in source code, ML models can now be trained on huge sets of annotated data – for certain tasks, this works tremendously well. Andrej Karpathy, AI Director at Tesla, somewhat cheekily refers to development according to the ML paradigm as "Software 2.0"[1]. For many applications seeking mapping from input to output, it is easier to collect and annotate high-quality data than to program a mapping function in code explicitly.

Agile software development has become the norm in the software engineering industry. Flexibly adapting to change has proven to be a recipe to ripe some of the benefits of software – significant changes can often occur at any time, both

---

[1] https://bit.ly/3dKeUEH.

© Springer Nature Switzerland AG 2022
A. Przybyłek et al. (Eds.): LASD 2022, LNBIP 438, pp. 3–16, 2022.
https://doi.org/10.1007/978-3-030-94238-0_1

during a development project and post-release. Quickly adapting to shifting customer needs and technology changes is often vital to survival in a competitive market. In this light, the concept of DevOps has emerged as an approach to minimize time to market while maintaining quality [2]. While agile development is particularly suitable for customer-oriented development in the Internet era, it is also increasingly used in embedded systems development of more critical nature [3] with adaptations such as SafeScrum [4]. Moreover, while agile software development is flexible, we argue that ML development iterates even faster – and thus necessitates "agility on steroids."

Data scientists often conduct the highly iterative development of ML models. Data scientists, representing a new type of software professionals, often do not have the software engineering training of conventional software developers [5]. This observation is analogous to what has been reported for developers of scientific computing in the past, e.g., regarding their familiarity with agile practices [6]. Instead of prioritizing the crafts of software engineering and computer science, many data scientists focus on mastering the art of taming data into shapes that are suitable for model training – typically using domain knowledge to hunt quantitative accuracy targets for a specific application. The ML development process is experimental in nature and involves iterating between several intertwined activities, e.g., data collection, data preprocessing, feature engineering, model selection, model evaluation, and hyperparameter tuning. An unfortunate characteristic of ML development is that nothing can be considered in isolation. A foundational ML paper by Google researchers described this as the CACE principle "Changing Anything Changes Everything" [7]. When developing ML models in Software 2.0, no data science activities are ever independent.

In this keynote address, we will discuss two phenomena that have emerged to meet the characteristics of ML development. First, **Notebook interfaces** to meet the data scientists' needs to move swiftly. Unfortunately, the step from prototyping in Notebook interfaces to a mature ML solution is often considerable – and cumbersome for many data scientists. In Sect. 2, we will present a solution by Jakobsson and Henriksson that bridges the gap between the data scientists' preferred notebook interfaces and standard development in Integrated Development Environments (IDE). Second, analogous to DevOps in conventional agile software development, in Sect. 3, we will look at how **MLOps** has emerged to close the gap between ML development and ML operations. More than just an agility concept, we claim that it is required to meet the expectations on the trustworthy AI of the future – illustrated in the light of the recently proposed Artificial Intelligence Act in the European Union. We refer to our concept of reinforcing the development and operations of AI systems, afflicted by the CACE principle, using two metaphors from construction engineering: buttresses and rebars.

2   Connecting Notebook Interfaces and IDEs

Many data scientists are not trained software engineers and thus might not be fully aware of available best practices related to various software engineering activities [5]. Moreover, even with awareness of software engineering best practices, data science introduces new challenges throughout the engineering lifecycle [8,9] – from requirements engineering [10] to operations [7]. Due to the intrinsically experimental nature of data science, practitioners seek development environments that allow maximum agility, i.e., high-speed development iterations.

The go-to solution for many data scientists is to work iteratively in cloud-based notebook interfaces. While this allows rapid experimentation, it does not easily allow the application of the various tools available in a modern IDE [11]. The first part of this keynote address presents a solution developed as part of a MSc thesis project by Jakobsson and Henriksson at Backtick Technologies [12] that enables data scientists to easily move between notebook interfaces and an IDE thanks to a networked file system. The idea is to let data scientists work in their favorite editor and use all the tools available for local development while still being able to use the cloud-based notebook interface for data exploration – and reaping its benefits of easy access to distributed cloud computing. Jakobsson and Henriksson integrated and evaluated the solution as part of Cowait Notebooks, an experimental cloud notebook solution developed by Backtick Technologies. Cowait[2] is an open-source framework for creating containerized distributed applications with asynchronous Python.

2.1 Agility Supported by Notebook Interfaces

A substantial part of today's data science revolves around notebook interfaces, also known as computational notebooks. Notebook interfaces are typically cloud-based and consist of environments with interactive code interpreters accessible from web browsers that allow raöid, iterative development. The notebooks themselves usually run on a remote machine or a computer cluster, allowing the user easy access to compute resources available in data centers. While the notebook interfaces gradually mature, i.e., more features become available, the environments are still far from as capable as the IDEs software developers run locally. Consequently, the support for version control software, static analysis, linting, and other widely used development tools is limited in notebook interfaces [11].

The implementation of a notebook interface differs from a conventional IDE. A notebook runs an interpreter in the background that preserves the state for the duration of a programming session. A user observes a notebook as a sequence of cells that are either textual (allowing data scientists to document the process) or containing code. These two different types of cells are interwoven in the notebook. Notebook interfaces usually excel at presenting plots and tables that support data exploration. A code cell contains one or more statements and can be executed independently from any other code cell. Users can execute code cells in any order, but the cells all mutate the shared state of the background interpreter. This freedom of execution order greatly supports the agility of data science as users can re-run portions of a program while keeping other parts of the previously generated state. While this enables fast iterations toward a useful

---

[2] https://cowait.io.

solution, it also makes it difficult to trace the path of execution that led to a specific result. Even worse, subsequent executions of the notebook may yield different results.

The concept of computational notebooks was envisioned by Knuth already in 1984 [13]. Knuth proposed the *literate programming* paradigm and showed how the idea could support program comprehension by mixing snippets of source code and natural language explanations of its embedded logic. As elaborated in Knuth's seminal book on the topic [14], the key point is that literate programming explicitly shifts who is the most important reader of the programming artifact. In literate programming, source code is primarily written for *humans* instead of computers – and the artifact can be seen as a piece of literature. Many developers of scientific computing follow this paradigm to develop maintainable software artifacts [15].

A more general version of literate programming is *literate computing*, where the source code cells and natural language explanations are accompanied by visual content such as tables, graphs, and images. Today's widely used notebook interfaces, such as the popular Jupyter Notebook[3] and Databrick's Collaborative Notebook[4], are examples of literate computing. For a recent overview of the notebook landscape, we refer the curious reader to an article by Vognstrup Fog and Nylandsted Klokmose [16]. Their summary presents both a historical perspective and a discussion of design decisions for future notebook interfaces.

Notebook interfaces have certainly evolved substantially since Knuth first envisioned them. However, there are still certain impediments for data scientists working in notebooks. Chattopadhyay *et al.* analyzed contemporary issues with notebook interfaces and reported nine pain points [11]. According to the authors, the most pressing pain points for developers of notebook interfaces to tackle are 1) code refactoring, 2) deployment to production, 3) exploring notebook history, and 4) managing long-running tasks. Notebook interfaces constitute a highly active research topic, and researchers have proposed several solutions to address their limitations [17–19]. However, while notebook interfaces are a prominent medium for software development, there is still a substantial need for research and development [20].

This talk will introduce a solution proposal by Jakobsson and Henriksson that bridges the benefits of notebook interfaces and local IDEs. Lau *et al.* examined 60 different notebook interfaces and categorized them according to 10 dimensions of analysis: 1) data sources, 2) editor style, 3) programming language, 4) versioning, 5) collaboration, 6) execution order, 7) execution liveness, 8) execution environment, 9) cell outputs, and 10) notebook outputs. In the MSc thesis project by Jakobsson and Henriksson, the authors focused on the dimensions of *execution environment* and *data sources* for Cowait Notebooks. Their solution allows Cowait Notebooks to execute code in a remote multi-process execution environment using local files as data sources. This solution contrasts with Jupyter Notebook for which both code execution and data is local. The solution is also different

---

[3] https://jupyter.org.

[4] https://databricks.com/product/collaborative-notebooks.

from Databrick's Collaborative Notebook, where code is executed in a remote multi-process execution environment, but the data sources cannot be local. In the next section, we present the open-source Cowait framework.

2.2 Cowait – A Framework for Simplified Container Orchestration

Cowait is a framework that simplifies the execution of Python code on the container orchestration system Kubernetes. The two main constituents of Cowait are 1) a workflow engine built on top of Docker and Kubernetes and 2) a build system to easily package source code into containers. Together, the workflow engine and the build system form an abstraction of containers and container hosts that helps developers leverage the power of containerization through Docker and cluster deployment using Kubernetes without knowing all technical details. Backtick Technologies designed Cowait to hide the intrinsic complexity of Docker and Kubernetes behind simple concepts that are familiar to general software developers. Cowait is developed under an Apache License and the source code is available on GitHub[5].

Cowait provides four key features with a focus on user-friendliness, i.e., Cowait...

1. ...helps the development of distributed workflows on your local machine with minimal setup.
2. ...simplifies dependency management for Python projects.
3. ...allows developers to unit test their workflow tasks.
4. ...lowers the bar for users to deploy solutions on Kubernetes clusters.

In line with other workflow engines, Cowait organizes code into *tasks*. A task is essentially a function that can accept input arguments and return values. As for functions in general, a task can invoke other tasks—with one key difference: a call to invoke another task will be intercepted by the Cowait runtime environment and subsequently executed in a separate container. Cowait can also direct the execution of this separate container to a particular machine. The fundamental differentiator offered by Cowait is that tasks can interface directly with the underlying cluster orchestrator. In practice, this means that tasks can start other tasks without going through a central scheduler service. Instead, tasks create other tasks on demand, and they communicate with their parent tasks using web sockets. Further details are available in the Cowait Documentation[6].

The task management system in Cowait relies on containers and thus supports the execution of arbitrary software. Thanks to this flexibility, Cowait can execute notebook interfaces. In their MSc thesis project, Jakobsson and Henriksson demonstrate the execution of the open-source JupyterLab notebook interface in a Cowait solution – we refer to this as running a Cowait Notebook. JupyterLab is a popular notebook interface that is particularly suitable for this demonstration since it is implemented in Python. Once the JupyterLab task is started in a

---

[5] https://github.com/backtick-se/cowait.
[6] https://cowait.io/docs/.

cluster, it automatically gets a public URL that the users can connect to. Cowait Notebooks allow data scientists to host notebook interfaces in any Kubernetes cluster with minimal setup. Executing Cowait Notebooks within a Cowait task lets the notebook access Cowait's underlying task scheduler and allow sub-tasks to be launched directly from the notebook cells – data scientists can thus easily execute background tasks on the cluster. In the next section, we present Jakobsson and Henriksson's solution to allow access to local files – and thus enabling work with local IDEs.

2.3   Local Files and Cowait Notebooks Executing on Clusters

Jakobsson and Henriksson developed a proof-of-concept implementation of a general solution to file sharing between a data scientist's local computer and software running on a remote cluster. The key enabler is a custom networked file system implemented using File System in Userspace (FUSE)[7]. FUSE is an interface for userspace programs to export a file system to the Linux kernel. To make the solution compatible with as many different data science applications as possible, the network file system was implemented as a custom storage driver for Kubernetes. Kubernetes is the most popular cluster orchestration solution, available as a managed service from all major cloud providers. Furthermore, Kubernetes is an open-source solution that users can also deploy on-premise. Practically, Jakobsson and Henriksson ensured compatibility with Kubernetes by implementing the Container Storage Interface, an open standard for developing new Kubernetes storage options[8].

The goal of the MSc thesis project was to design a user-friendly, reliable, and widely compatible solution to file sharing for data scientists. The aim was to provide seamless access to files residing on a data scientist's local computer for other data scientists accessing the local files through cloud-based notebook interfaces executing on Kubernetes clusters. With such a solution in place, data scientists could collaborate online using the notebook interfaces they prefer while allowing state-of-the-art software engineering tools to operate in IDEs on local machines.

To evaluate the proof-of-concept, Jakobsson and Henriksson conducted two separate studies. First, a quantitative study was carried out to verify the solution's performance in light of requirements set by prior user experience research on human response times [21, p. 135]. The authors studied the performance as different numbers of files, of different sizes, where accessed under different network conditions. While details are available in the MSc thesis [12], the general finding is that the solution satisfied the requirement of file access within 1 s for reasonable file sizes and realistic network latency. We consider this a necessary but not sufficient requirement for the novel solution.

---

[7] File System in Userspace, https://github.com/libfuse/libfuse.
[8] https://kubernetes-csi.github.io/docs/.

Second, Jakobsson and Henriksson conducted a qualitative study to collect deep insights into the solution's utility. The authors recruited a mix of data scientists and software developers (with substantial ML experience) to perform a carefully designed programming task under a think-aloud protocol [22]. The purpose was to collect feedback on whether the novel file sharing solution could improve the overall experience of working with cloud-based notebook interfaces. The feedback displayed mixed impressions. Data scientists who were comfortable using managed cloud solutions expressed hesitation to use such a system due to reduced ease-of-use and potential collaboration issues. The group that was the most positive were developers with a software engineering background, who were excited to be able to use familiar tooling for local files. Despite the mixed opinions, we still perceive the proof-of-concept as promising – but more work is needed to bridge notebook interfaces and local IDEs.

3 MLOps – A Key Enabler for Agility in Software 2.0

Many organizations report challenges in turning an ML proof-of-concept into a production-quality AI system [23]. The experimental nature of ML development limits qualities such as reproducibility, testability, traceability, and explainability—which are needed when putting a trustworthy product or service on the market. On top of this, an AI system must be maintained until the product or service reaches its end-of-life. This holistic lifecycle perspective, i.e., what follows post-release, is often missing when novice data science teams develop AI proofs-of-concept in the sandbox. An organization must continuously monitor the ML models in operation and, in many cases, evolve the models according to feedback from the production environment – where phenomena such as distributional shifts can be game-changers [7]. Without designing for the operations phase and ensuring that ML model changes easily can be pushed to production, it will be tough to reach sustainably value-creating AI solutions. This attractive state is sometimes referred to as *Operational AI* [24]. In the next section, we will share our view on how the concept of MLOps can help organizations reach this state.

3.1 Continuous Engineering in the AI Era

In software development, continuous software engineering and DevOps emerged to reduce the lead time and remove the barriers between development, testing, and operations [2]. Workflow automation in pipelines is fundamental, as it enables approaches such as 1) continuous integration (integration of code changes followed by test automation), 2) continuous delivery (building software for an internal test environment), and 3) continuous deployment (delivery of software to actual users) [25]. Depending on the application, organizations can also add staging processes when human validation is needed. Thanks to the automation, development qualities such as traceability come at a substantially lower cost compared to a manual workflow [26]. DevOps has inspired a similar mindset within ML development in the form of *MLOps*, i.e., the standardization and streamlining of ML lifecycle management [27] – which is a recommended approach to tackle continuous engineering in Software 2.0 [28].

Just like DevOps is more than a set of tools, MLOps can be seen as a mindset on the highest level. As an engineering discipline, MLOps is a set of practices that combines ML, DevOps, and Data Engineering. Organizations adopting MLOps hope to deploy and maintain ML systems in production reliably and efficiently. Going beyond technology, MLOps involves embracing a culture with corresponding processes that an organization must adapt for the specific application domain. MLOps has emerged from the Big Tech Internet companies; thus, customization is required to fit smaller development organizations. Extrapolating from DevOps in conventional software engineering [2,26], MLOps relies on pipeline automation to remove the barriers between data processing, model training, model testing, and model deployment.

MLOps is not yet well-researched from an academic perspective. The primary reason is that MLOps is a production concept, i.e., the phenomenon must be studied in the field rather than in university labs. However, this does not mean that MLOps should not be targeted by academic research. On the contrary, it is critically important that software and systems engineering researchers initiate industrial collaborations to allow empirical studies of what works and what does not when developing and evolving AI systems. As always in software engineering research, we have to identify the most important variation points needed to provide accurate guidance given specific application contexts. Just like there are uncountably many ways to implement pipeline automation – the ML tools market is booming – there is not a one-size-fits-all way to adopt MLOps in an organization.

3.2   Reinforced AI Systems Using Buttresses and Rebars

Just as agile development enters regulated domains [3], Software 2.0 is gradually entering critical applications [29]. Examples include automotive software [30] and software in healthcare [31]. From a quality assurance perspective, AI systems using ML constitute a paradigm shift compared to conventional software systems. A contemporary deep neural network might be composed of hundreds of millions of parameter weights – such an artifact is neither applicable to code reviews nor standard code coverage testing. Development organizations have learned how to develop trustworthy code-based software systems through decades of software engineering experience. This collected experience has successfully been captured in different industry standards. Unfortunately, many best practices are less effective when developing AI systems. Bosch *et al.* and others argue that software and systems engineering must evolve to enable efficient and effective development of trustworthy AI systems [23]. One response to this call is that new standards are under development in various domains to complement existing alternatives for high-assurance systems [32].

Due to the growing reliance on AI systems, the European Union (EU) AI strategy stresses the importance of *Trustworthy AI*. EU defines such systems as lawful, ethical, and robust [33]. Unfortunately, we know that existing software engineering approaches such as requirements traceability [34] and verification &

validation [29] are less effective at demonstrating system trustworthiness when functionality depends on ML models. Due to its experimental nature, data science makes it hard to trace design decisions after-the-fact and the resulting ML models become less reproducible [11]. Moreover, the internals of ML models are notoriously difficult to interpret [35], and AI systems are difficult to test [43, 44].

Not only must developers of critical AI systems comply with emerging industry standards, but novel AI regulations are also expected in the EU. In April 2021, the European Commission proposed an ambitious *Artificial Intelligence Act* (AIA) [36]. AIA is a new legal framework with dual ambitions for turning Europe into the global hub for trustworthy AI. First, AIA aims to guarantee the safety and fundamental rights of EU citizens when interacting with high-risk AI systems. Second, AIA seeks to strengthen AI innovation by providing legal stability and instilling public trust in the technology. Many voices have been raised about the proposed legislation, in which especially the broad definition of AI has been criticized. However, all signs point to increased regulation of AI in the EU, in line with the now established General Data Protection Regulation [37] – including substantial fines defined in relation to annual global turnover.

ML is an increasingly important AI technology in the digitalization of society that receives substantial attention in the AIA. According to the proposal, any providers of high-risk solutions using ML must demonstrate AIA conformance to an independent national authority prior to deployment on the EU internal market. Demonstrating this compliance will be very costly – and how to effectively (and efficiently!) do it remains an important open research question.

We are currently exploring the topic of built-in trustworthiness through a metaphor of reinforced engineering: *buttresses and rebars*. Our fundamental position is that organizations must tackle quality assurance from two directions. Requirements engineering and verification & validation shall work together like two bookends supporting the AI system, including its development and operations, from either end. Figure 1 illustrates how the primary reinforcement originates in buttressing the development of the AI system with requirements engineering (to the left) and verification & validation (to the right). The metaphor, inspired by construction engineering, further borrows the concept of rebars, i.e., internal structures to strengthen and aid the AI system. In our metaphor, the rebars are realized in the form of so-called automation *pipelines* for data, training, and deployment, respectively. Pipeline automation allows continuous engineering throughout the lifecycle, i.e., data management, training, deployment, and monitoring in an MLOps context. Pipeline automation enables flexibly adding automated quality assurance approaches as pipe segments, e.g., Grad-CAM heatmaps for explainability [38], originating in the requirements engineering and verification & validation buttresses. The envisioned reinforcement allows organizations to continuously steer the development and operations toward a trustworthy AI system—in the context of highly agile data science, the CACE principle, and the ever-present risks of distributional shifts.

Numerous studies report that requirements engineering is the foundation of high-quality software systems. However, the academic community has only recently fully embraced the idea of tailored requirements engineering for AI

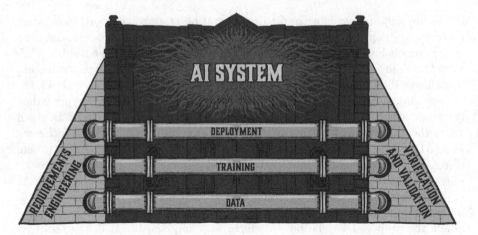

Fig. 1. Metaphorical buttresses and rebars. Robust requirements engineering and verification & validation support the engineering of an ever-changing AI system. Pipeline automation in an MLOps context constitutes the rebars that sustain trustworthiness by strengthening the AI system despite the dynamics involved.

systems. We argue that the particular characteristics of ML development in data science necessitate an evolution of requirements engineering processes and practices [10]. New methods are needed when development transitions to the generation of rules based on training data and specific fitness functions. Based on a 2020 Dagstuhl seminar, Kästner stressed requirements engineering as a particular ML challenge, Google researchers express it as underspecification [39], and several papers have been recently published by the requirements engineering research community [40–42].

Academic research on verification & validation tailored for AI systems has received a head start compared to requirements engineering for AI. New papers continuously appear, and secondary studies on AI testing [43,44] and AI verification [45] reveal hundreds of publications. As automation is close at hand for verification & validation solutions, the primary purpose of the pipelines in the metaphor is to stress that they shall reach all the way to the requirements engineering buttress. Aligning requirements engineering with verification & validation can have numerous benefits in software engineering [46] – and even more so, we argue, in AI engineering. Our planned next steps include exploring AIA conformant high-risk computer vision systems with industry partners reinforced by buttresses and rebars. Our ambition is to combine automated verification & validation with an integrated requirements engineering approach [47] in the continuous engineering of MLOps. Finally, we are considering introducing yet another metaphor from construction engineering, i.e., virtual plumblines as proposed by Cleland-Huang *et al.* to maintain critical system quantities [48]. We posit that reinforcement and alignment will be two key essential concepts in future AI engineering, supported by a high level of automation to allow agile development of Software 2.0.

4 Conclusion

Whether we endorse the term Software 2.0 or not, AI engineering inevitably brings novel challenges. The experimental nature of how data scientists perform ML development means that the work must be agile. However, this agility can be supported in various ways. In this keynote address, we discussed two contemporary phenomena in data science and ML. First, we presented notebook interfaces, weaknesses, and a solution proposal to lower the bar for them to coexist with modern IDEs. Second, we shared our perspective on MLOps and our ongoing work on providing reinforced engineering of AI systems in this context. Agility and continuous engineering are needed in AI engineering, as AI systems are ever-changing and often operate in dynamic environments. Finally, the EU AI Act further exacerbates the need for reinforced engineering and alignment between requirements engineering and verification & validation. As a guiding light toward this goal, we introduced our vision of metaphorical buttresses and rebars.

Acknowledgements. Martin Jakobsson and Johan Henriksson are the co-creators of the solution presented in Sect. 2 and deserve all credit for this work. Our thanks go to Backtick Technologies for hosting the MSc thesis project and Dr. Niklas Fors, Dept. of Computer Science, Lund University for acting as the examiner. This initiative received financial support through the AIQ Meta-Testbed project funded by Kompetensfonden at Campus Helsingborg, Lund University, Sweden and two internal RISE initiatives, i.e., "SODA - Software & Data Intensive Applications" and "MLOps by RISE."

References

1. Giray, G.: A software engineering perspective on engineering machine learning systems: state of the art and challenges. J. Syst. Softw. **180**, 111031 (2021)
2. Ebert, C., Gallardo, G., Hernantes, J., Serrano, N.: DevOps. IEEE Softw. **33**(3), 94–100 (2016)
3. Diebold, P., Theobald, S.: How is agile development currently being used in regulated embedded domains? J. Softw. Evol. Process **30**(8), e1935 (2018)
4. Hanssen, G.K., Stålhane, T., Myklebust, T.: SafeScrum®-Agile Development of Safety-Critical Software. Springer, Cham (2018). https://doi.org/10.1007/978-3-319-99334-8
5. Kim, M., Zimmermann, T., DeLine, R., Begel, A.: The emerging role of data scientists on software development teams. In: Proceedings of the 38th International Conference on Software Engineering, pp. 96–107 (2016)
6. Sletholt, M.T., Hannay, J.E., Pfahl, D., Langtangen, H.P.: What do we know about scientific software development's agile practices? Comput. Sci. Eng. **14**(2), 24–37 (2011)
7. Sculley, D., et al.: Hidden technical debt in machine learning systems. In: Proceedings of the 28th International Conference on Neural Information Processing Systems, pp. 2503–2511 (2015)
8. Amershi, S., et al.: Software engineering for machine learning: a case study. In: Proceedings of the 41st International Conference on Software Engineering, pp. 291–300 (2019)

9. Wan, Z., Xia, X., Lo, D., Murphy, G.C.: How does machine learning change software development practices? IEEE Trans. Software Eng. **47**(9), 1857–1871 (2021)
10. Vogelsang, A., Borg, M.: Requirements engineering for machine learning: perspectives from data scientists. In: Proceedings of the 27th International Requirements Engineering Conference Workshops, pp. 245–251 (2019)
11. Chattopadhyay, S., Prasad, I., Henley, A.Z., Sarma, A., Barik, T.: What's wrong with computational notebooks? Pain points, needs, and design opportunities. In: Human Factors in Computing Systems, pp. 1–12 (2020)
12. Jakobsson, M., Henriksson, J.: Sharing local files with Kubernetes clusters. MSc thesis, Lund University (2021). http://lup.lub.lu.se/student-papers/record/9066685/file/9066686.pdf
13. Knuth, D.E.: Literate programming. Comput. J. **27**(2), 97–111 (1984)
14. Knuth, D.E.: Literate Programming. Center for the Study of Language and Information, Stanford, US (1992)
15. Hannay, J.E., MacLeod, C., Singer, J., Langtangen, H.P., Pfahl, D., Wilson, G.: How do scientists develop and use scientific software? In: Proceedings of the ICSE Workshop on Software Engineering for Computational Science and Engineering, pp. 1–8. IEEE (2009)
16. Vognstrup Fog, B., Nylandsted Klokmose, C.: Mapping the landscape of literate computing. In: Proceedings of the 30th Annual Workshop of the Psychology of Programming Interest Group (2019)
17. Kery, M.B., John, B.E., O'Flaherty, P., Horvath, A., Myers, B.A.: Towards effective foraging by data scientists to find past analysis choices. In: Human Factors in Computing Systems, pp. 1–13 (2019)
18. Kery, M.B., Myers, B.A.: Interactions for untangling messy history in a computational notebook. In: Proceedings of the IEEE Symposium on Visual Languages and Human-Centric Computing, pp. 147–155 (2018)
19. Head, A., Hohman, F., Barik, T., Drucker, S.M., DeLine, R.: Managing messes in computational notebooks. In: Human Factors in Computing Systems, pp. 1–12 (2019)
20. Singer, J.: Notes on notebooks: is Jupyter the bringer of jollity? In: Proceedings of the ACM SIGPLAN International Symposium on New Ideas, New Paradigms, and Reflections on Programming and Software, pp. 180–186 (2020)
21. Nielsen, J.: Usability Engineering. Morgan Kaufmann Publishers, Burlington (1993)
22. Kuusela, H., Paul, P.: A comparison of concurrent and retrospective verbal protocol analysis. Am. J. Psychol. **113**(3), 387–404 (2000)
23. Bosch, J., Holmström Olsson, H., Crnkovic, I.: Engineering AI systems: a research agenda. In: Artificial Intelligence Paradigms for Smart Cyber-Physical Systems, pp. 1–19. IGI Global (2021)
24. Tapia, P., Palacios, E., Noël, L., et al.: Implementing Operational AI in telecom environments. Tupl White Paper 7 (2018)
25. Fitzgerald, B., Stol, K.J.: Continuous software engineering: a roadmap and agenda. J. Syst. Softw. **123**, 176–189 (2017)
26. Jabbari, R., Ali, N., Petersen, K., Tanveer, B.: Towards a benefits dependency network for DevOps based on a systematic literature review. J. Softw. Evol. Process **30**(11), e1957 (2018)
27. Treveil, M., et al.: Introducing MLOps. O'Reilly Media Inc., Sebastopol (2020)
28. Hummer, W., et al.: ModelOps: cloud-based lifecycle management for reliable and trusted AI. In: Proceedings of the International Conference on Cloud Engineering, pp. 113–120 (2019)

29. Borg, M., et al.: Safely entering the deep: a review of verification and validation for machine learning and a challenge elicitation in the automotive industry. J. Automot. Softw. Eng. **1**(1), 1–19 (2019)
30. Falcini, F., Lami, G., Costanza, A.M.: Deep learning in automotive software. IEEE Softw. **34**(3), 56–63 (2017)
31. Jiang, F., et al.: Artificial intelligence in healthcare: past, present and future. Stroke Vasc. Neurol. **2**(4), 230–243 (2017)
32. Vidot, G., Gabreau, C., Ober, I., Ober, I.: Certification of embedded systems based on machine learning: a survey. arXiv preprint arXiv:2106.07221 (2021)
33. High-Level Expert Group on Artificial Intelligence: Ethics guidelines for trustworthy artificial intelligence. Technical report, European Commission, Brussels, Belgium (2019)
34. Borg, M., Englund, C., Duran, B.: Traceability and deep learning-safety-critical systems with traces ending in deep neural networks. In: Proceedings of the Grand Challenges of Traceability: The Next Ten Years, pp. 48–49 (2017)
35. Gilpin, L.H., Bau, D., Yuan, B.Z., Bajwa, A., Specter, M., Kagal, L.: Explaining explanations: an overview of interpretability of machine learning. In: Proceedings of the 5th International Conference on Data Science and Advanced Analytics, pp. 80–89 (2018)
36. European Commission: Proposal for a Regulation of the European Parliament and of the Council laying down harmonised rules on artificial intelligence (Artificial Intelligence Act) and amending certain union legislative acts, 21 April 2021. https://eur-lex.europa.eu/legal-content/EN/TXT/?uri=CELEX
37. European Commission: Regulation (EU) 2016/679 of the European Parliament and of the Council on the protection of natural persons with regard to the processing of personal data and on the free movement of such data, and repealing Directive 95/46/ec (General Data Protection Regulation). Off. J. Eur. Union **119**, 1–88 (2016)
38. Borg, M., Jabangwe, R., Åberg, S., Ekblom, A., Hedlund, L., Lidfeldt, A.: Test automation with Grad-CAM heatmaps - a future pipe segment in MLOps for vision AI? In: Proceedings of the 14th International Conference on Software Testing, Verification and Validation Workshops, pp. 175–181 (2021)
39. D'Amour, A., et al.: Underspecification presents challenges for credibility in modern machine learning. arXiv preprint arXiv:2011.03395 (2020)
40. Ahmad, K., Bano, M., Abdelrazek, M., Arora, C., Grundy, J.: What's up with requirements engineering for artificial intelligence systems? In: Proceedings of the 29th International Requirements Engineering Conference, pp. 1–12 (2021)
41. Habibullah, K.M., Horkoff, J.: Non-functional requirements for machine learning: understanding current use and challenges in industry. In: Proceedings of the 29th International Requirements Engineering Conference, pp. 13–23 (2021)
42. Siebert, J., et al.: Construction of a quality model for machine learning systems. Softw. Qual. J., 1–29 (2021)
43. Zhang, J.M., Harman, M., Ma, L., Liu, Y.: Machine learning testing: survey, landscapes and horizons. IEEE Trans. Softw. Eng. (2020)
44. Riccio, V., Jahangirova, G., Stocco, A., Humbatova, N., Weiss, M., Tonella, P.: Testing machine learning based systems: a systematic mapping. Empir. Softw. Eng. **25**(6), 5193–5254 (2020)
45. Xiang, W., et al.: Verification for machine learning, autonomy, and neural networks survey. arXiv preprint arXiv:1810.01989 (2018)

46. Bjarnason, E., et al.: Challenges and practices in aligning requirements with verification and validation: a case study of six companies. Empir. Softw. Eng. **19**(6), 1809–1855 (2014)

47. Bjarnason, E.: Integrated Requirements Engineering - Understanding and Bridging Gaps in Software Development. Lund University, Sweden (2013). https://lucris.lub.lu.se/ws/portalfiles/portal/3427902/4117182.pdf

48. Cleland-Huang, J., Marrero, W., Berenbach, B.: Goal-centric traceability: using virtual plumblines to maintain critical systemic qualities. IEEE Trans. Software Eng. **34**(5), 685–699 (2008)

Full Papers

The Integrated List of Agile Practices - A Tertiary Study

Michael Neumann[(✉)]

Hochschule Hannover, Ricklinger Stadtweg 120, 30459 Hannover, Germany
`michael.neumann@hs-hannover.de`

Abstract. *Context:* Companies adapt agile methods, practices or artifacts for their use in practice since more than two decades. This adaptions result in a wide variety of described agile practices. For instance, the Agile Alliance lists 75 different practices in its Agile Glossary. This situation may lead to misunderstandings, as agile practices with similar names can be interpreted and used differently. *Objective:* This paper synthesize an integrated list of agile practices, both from primary and secondary sources. *Method:* We performed a tertiary study to identify existing overviews and lists of agile practices in the literature. We identified 876 studies, of which 37 were included. *Results:* The results of our paper show that certain agile practices are listed and used more often in existing studies. Our integrated list of agile practices comprises 38 entries structured in five categories. *Conclusion:* The high number of agile practices and thus, the wide variety increased steadily over the past decades due to the adaption of agile methods. Based on our findings, we present a comprehensive overview of agile practices. The research community benefits from our integrated list of agile practices as a potential basis for future research. Also, practitioners benefit from our findings, as the structured overview of agile practices provides the opportunity to select or adapt practices for their specific needs.

Keywords: Agile practices · Agile methods · Agile software development · Tertiary study

1 Introduction

The use of agile methods in software development has grown steadily over the past two decades [51]. More and more companies, regardless of their size or industrial sector, are using agile approaches. As a consequence, agile approaches are used in diverse settings. It follows that the use of agile methods and practices deviates from one another, which leads to several adaptions [38].

Various authors describe that agile methods such as Scrum or extreme programming (XP) are usually not fully adapted and used in companies (e.g., [12,52]). This statement follows Ken Schwaber, co-author of the Scrum Guide [45]. He assumed that 75% of all companies do not use Scrum as described in the Scrum Guide, but in an adapted approach [43]. According to Abrahmsson

© Springer Nature Switzerland AG 2022
A. Przybyłek et al. (Eds.): LASD 2022, LNBIP 438, pp. 19–37, 2022.
https://doi.org/10.1007/978-3-030-94238-0_2

[1] the adaptation of agile methods and practices is often argued with the complexity of the agile transition. Stray et al. point to organizational aspects when introducing and adapting agile roles, artifacts, and practices [48]. This results in a high number of agile practices with many variants used in practice and described in literature. The Scrum and XP guidelines [8,45] describe 12 different practices, each. Furthermore, the Agile Alliance lists 75 different practices in its Agile Glossary [3]. Due to the combined use of agile practices of different agile methods such as Scrum, and increasingly on Lean approaches like Kanban, steadily new variants of agile practices are developed and used.

This situation leads to the challenge of getting an overview of the agile practices used in diverse settings. In the past, secondary studies such as systematic mapping studies and systematic literature reviews were carried out in order to ascertain the current state of research regarding agile practices in different contexts. These contexts include, for example, the affiliation of agile practices to methods and processes [52], the use in different project-related contexts [12] or in global software development [21,22]. Due to their different research contexts and focus, the listed agile practices in these studies differ from one another. However, we did not find an integrated list of agile practices, which aims to provide a comprehensive overview of well-known agile practices described in recent literature and/or used in practice. This leads us to our two research questions:

RQ 1: *Which agile practices are described and/or listed in the literature?*
RQ 2: *How can we synthesize the listed agile practices related to their characteristics/purpose?*

This paper is structured as follows: First, we describe the background and related work of the study in Sect. 2. We explain the selected research approach in Sect. 3. An overview of the agile practices found in the literature is given in Sect. 4. We present our approach for synthesizing the extracted agile practices from the literature and as the result our integrated list of agile practices in Sect. 5. Before the paper closes with a conclusion in Sect. 7, we discuss the limitations of our study in Sect. 6.

2   Background and Related Work

Today, agile methods are well-known approaches in software development [51]. The idea of iterative and incremental approaches goes back to the 1950s [32]. In the past decades, agile methods are often understood as a reaction on plan-driven approaches like the waterfall model. For instance, this is argued due to their aim of fast time response on changes during the project period and their iterative structure [52]. According to Abrahamsson [2] agile methods are incremental, adaptable and cooperative approaches.

Another aspect concerning agile methods is the value-based work and the strong focus on social aspects like collaboration and interaction. The agile manifesto defines a set of four value-pairs and twelve principles [9]. In addition, further values and principles are defined in guidelines for agile methods like the

Scrum Guide for Scrum [45]. Also, other elements of agile methods like artifacts, roles and practices are described in these guidelines. Agile methods like Scrum or XP were created with the purpose to provide specific approaches for an agile transition and usage in software development. We know from the literature [29] and practice [51] that the adaption of agile practices (e.g., the combination of several agile practices from different methods) is the normal case.

In order to find the related work of our study, we searched for surveys and systematic mapping studies or literature reviews (SLR) dealing with agile practices and, if available, provide a list of agile practices.

Several authors deal with agile practices in different contexts. Diebold and Dahlem present a systematic map of agile practices in practice [12]. The authors focus on empirical studies dealing with the use of agile practice in software development projects. Also they present an overall usage of agile practices in software development projects. The used list of agile practices consists of 18 entries.

Jalali and Wohlin investigate the use of agile practices in the field of global software engineering [21,22]. Their studies focus on the use of 26 different agile practices in the several distribution types. Also, Camara et al. dealing with a similar topic in their systematic literature review on agile global software development [11]. They identified 48 different agile practices in use in that context.

The authors [11,12,21,22] also found, that agile practice were adapted and thus, customized agile methods were applied. Other studies only addressed subproblems. For instance, Albuquerque et al. deal with agile requirements engineering [4]. The authors considered 14 different agile practices in their mapping study. Sandstø and Reme-Ness investigating in their systematic literature review the relation of agile practices and their impact on project success [44]. The authors identified 12 agile practices and describe their impact on specific conditions for project success, such as communication or motivation of the team members.

However, to the best of our knowledge we did not find any study aiming to synthesize the variety of agile practices and provide an integrated overview of agile practices. Thus, we decided to conduct a tertiary study, which takes the findings from the recent literature into account. We present our research approach in the next section.

3 Research Method

According to Petersen et al. [42] systematic mapping studies are used to ascertain the current state of research in a field of interest in Software Engineering. The motivation of this study is to provide an overview of agile practices used and described in the literature and, based on this, to create a synthesized list of agile practices. From our point of view, the approach of a systematic mapping study is suitable for this purpose. Nonetheless, we have also used methods of the SLR guidelines of Kitchenham and Charters for conducting systematic literature reviews [24]. This combined approach (for conducting systematic literature reviews and systematic mapping studies) has already been chosen by several authors in the past (e.g., [12,26]). To increase the traceability and transparency of our systematic mapping study, this approach appears to be useful.

As recommended by Kitchenham and Charters [24], we developed and used a protocol to document our study. The protocol contains the relevant information of the study including the research goal and questions, search strategy, study selection procedure and data extraction. We describe our approach in the following subsections based on the protocol.

3.1 Search Strategy

We selected Scopus for applying our literature search. We decided to use Scopus as the library lists various publishers (such as SpringerLink, ACM, or Wiley). Besides, other authors have used Scopus for conducting systematic literature reviews and systematic mapping studies (e.g., [23,48]).

In a first step for developing the search string, we derived keywords and grouped them based on our first research questions. Next, we connected the keyword groups with a Boolean operator and defined specific keywords for the related keyword group: <Agile practice> AND <Agile software development>

Using our initial search string, we carried out test runs in Scopus and Google Scholar. During the test runs, we skimmed the results (title, keywords, abstract) and optimized the search string based on the findings, for example, whether keywords were missing. After several iterations, we defined our final search string, which we used for the search in Scopus:

(("agile practice*") AND ("agile" OR "agile software development" OR "agile method" OR "agile methods" OR "agile methodologies" OR "agile methodology" OR "lean software development"))

The final search run was performed in June 2021 with an activated year range filter set to "since 2010". We argue the choice of a selected time range filter as our study aims to create an integrated list of agile practices based on the recent literature, including the actual state of usage of agile practices. The result set contained 876 potentially relevant studies. We used the Scopus interface to export the meta data of the studies and imported them to our data extraction file, which we created with Microsoft Excel.

3.2 Study Selection

In order to be able to perform the study selection it is recommended by Kitchenham and Charters [24] to define inclusion and exclusion criteria. We defined three inclusion and eight exclusion criteria (see Table 1). The inclusion criteria IC1 was implicitly obtained by the activated search filter on year range setting when conducting the search in Scopus. Besides the structural exclusion criteria EC1 to EC4, we defined five content related exclusion criteria (EC5 to EC9).

We used the structural exclusion criteria EC1 to EC4 for an initial selection of the primary studies. During this check we excluded nine studies: Five, because of gray literature (EC1) and four, because the studies were not written in English (EC3).

Table 1. Study selection criteria

Category	Criterion
Inclusion	**IC1:** Studies published between 2010 and 2021
	IC2: Studies written in English
	IC3: Studies published in the field of agile software development
Exclusion	**EC1:** Gray literature (e.g., technical or experience reports)
	EC2: Contributions with less than three pages
	EC3: Studies not written in English
	EC4: Studies not peer-reviewed
	EC5: Studies not dealing with a list of specific agile practices
	EC6: Studies focus on educational contexts (e.g., agile methods in higher educational)
	EC7: Studies dealing with agile methods without a connection to software development
	EC8: Studies dealing with software development and related topics without a connection on agile software development and agile practices in particular

Based on the result set of 867 studies we performed a four stage study selection procedure[1] (see Fig. 1). In the first step, we screened title and keywords of the respective study and excluded 525 studies. While reading the abstract in the second step, we excluded 144 studies. In the third step, reading the introduction and conclusion, we excluded 55 studies. During the fourth step, reading the whole content of the paper, we excluded 106 studies. The high number of removed studies in this step are due to the fact that any borderline cases left in the previous steps. The final result set contains 37 studies, which we used for data extraction.

Most of the studies (757) were excluded because they are not dealing with a list of specific agile practices (EC5). Also, we excluded 49 studies, because they are focusing on educational contexts (EC6). For instance, the adaption of agile methods in higher education. Further 16 studies were excluded due to their missing connection to software development (EC7). Five studies were not dealing with agile methods in software development (EC8). Only three studies were duplicates.

---

[1] The protocol of our selection procedure is available at: https://sync.academiccloud.de/index.php/s/1nNipuDD655EJKF.

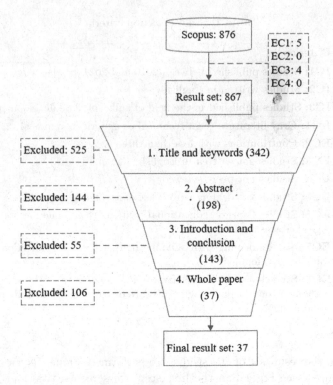

Fig. 1. Results of the study selection process

3.3 Data Extraction

We read each paper of our result set of 37 studies completely in order to be able to extract the relevant information from the studies. We documented the data extraction in a Microsoft Excel file. The file contains general information like author/s or title of the study and specific data such as the research focus and method or the agile practices described in the study (see Table 2).

Table 2. Structure of the data extraction sheet

Attribute	Information
Author	General information
Title	General information
Year	General information
DOI	General information
Document type	Conference paper or journal article
Research focus	Is the study focusing on practical aspects (like projects) or theoretical contributions (like descriptive models)
Research method	The research approach used in the paper (e.g., quantitative survey, case study, ...)
Agile practices	The list of the agile practices described, named or used in the study

The general information (author/s, title, year, DOI and document type) were extracted automatically based on the Scopus export file. The author checked the content of each attribute manually. In some cases the document type used to be corrected manually. The specific data (research focus, method and agile practices) were extracted manually for each paper. We extracted the agile practices in the form of lists, because in all studies several agile practices were named or used.

4 Results of the Literature Review

4.1 Overview of the Studies

Before we discuss the results of the study and answer the research questions in the following subsection and Sect. 5, we give a structural overview of the studies.

The document type information had to be adjusted manually for the respective studies, as Scopus does not export this information correctly in some cases. The studies are published as conference papers (27) and articles in journals (12). Figure 2 visualizes the distribution of the number of studies per year of publication. While only eight studies on this topic were published in the first five years of observation from 2010 to 2015, 29 studies have been published since 2016. Of these 29 studies, 24 studies have also been published since 2018, with only the first six months of 2021 being considered. Although a decrease can be determined in 2020 with only four publications, we have noticed an increased interest in the topic of agile practices.

There are several research methods used in the included studies. Eight studies use secondary research methods like systematic literature reviews (5) and systematic maps (3). The majority of the reported studies result from surveys (15). Also mixed approaches (8) and case studies (6) are often used by the authors.

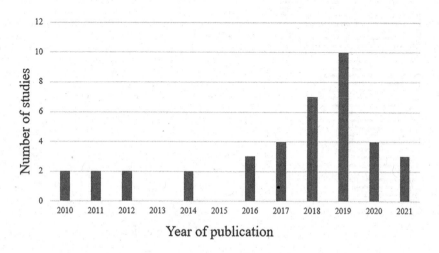

Fig. 2. Overview of the studies per publication year

4.2 The Current State of Agile Practices

Based on the discussion in this subsection we answer our first research question, *RQ 1: Which agile practices are described and/or listed in the literature?*

First and foremost, our extracted data show a high variety and number of agile practices in use. In total, the 37 studies list 944 agile practices. The count of listed agile practices in the included studies range from 4 [41] to 93 agile practices [6]. Almost half of the studies (17) list between 20 and 40 agile practices (see Fig. 3).

The agile practices listed in the studies are related to several characteristics. For example, various practices with a technical characteristic are used (such as refactoring or continuous integration). Also we found agile practices with an organizational characteristic like the office structure or energized work. However, it is not surprising that we found also collaborative focused practices such as daily stand up, planning, review or retrospective meetings. Interestingly, several studies describe/use/list these agile practices related to agile methods, especially Scrum and XP.

The high variety of agile practices used in the literature is related to the research method and focus of the respective studies. The majority of the studies point to practical phenomena under study. Only one paper describes an overview of agile practices and methods [52]. We also analyzed the research focus. Here we found, that most of the studies (30) dealing with the usage of agile practices. Four studies each deal with the topics of adapting and adopting agile practices.

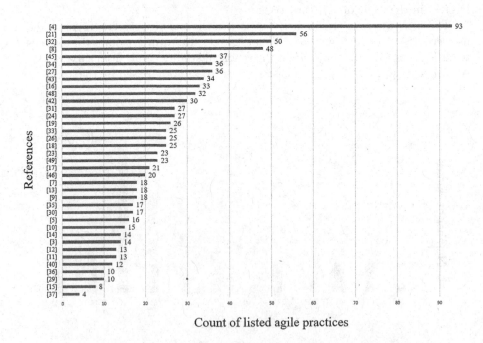

Fig. 3. Count of listed agile practices per study

Although we identified a high variety of agile practices, we found several redundancies (same agile practice listed at least two times in different studies) of the listed agile practices in the included studies. Also, we identified that similar agile practices are listed, described or used under different names. Our handling with the redundancies in order to create a synthesized list of agile practices is described in the next Sect. 5.

5 The Integrated List of Agile Practices

5.1 Synthesizing Agile Practices

We answering our second research question in this subsection: *RQ 2: How can we synthesize the listed agile practices related to their characteristics/purpose?*

We used the extracted data from the 37 studies as the basis for the procedure of synthesizing the lists of agile practices. For the synthesis, we created a new Microsoft Excel sheet and listed the agile practices of the 37 studies per column. We have also transferred the extracted information from the respective studies such as the title, author/s and year to the new Microsoft Excel sheet to ensure that the relevant information from the respective study to the list of agile practice is documented[2]. As mentioned in Sect. 4, we identified various redundancies and found that the level of detail of the listed practices is different. This situation leads us to the following procedure:

First Step: Identify and Remove the Redundancies. We removed any agile practice redundancies, we could find. An agile practice was marked as redundant when it is listed in at least two different studies. We also removed agile practices, if they did differ in name, but had essentially the same meaning. An example for this is the *Daily meeting*, which is named and described as *Standup Meeting* [21,22,52], *Daily discussion* [12] and *Stand Up* [30]. Based on our findings we identified that the practices in some studies are on a more detailed level (e.g. according to Arcos-Medina [6]). The list of agile practices without any redundancies is the basis for the following steps.

Second Step: Synthesize Agile Practices on an Abstract Level. We screened the result list from step one in order to analyze the differences concerning the level of detail of the agile practices. We found, that the level of detail of the listed agile practices is heterogeneous. As a result, we identified that the majority of agile practices is from a more detailed level. Thus, we decided to cluster the agile practices possible to a more abstract. The decision to cluster agile practices on an abstract level of detail was made, when we identified specific practices with the same purpose. Also, we mapped agile techniques (such as estimation techniques)

---

[2] The protocol of our synthesizing procedure is available at: https://sync.academiccloud.de/index.php/s/0YpKzzP56QBgmxU.

to the agile practice on a more abstract level. This led to a more homogeneous level of detail across all agile practices on our list and provides clarity.

For instance, we mapped testing practices from a more detailed level described in various studies (e.g., Test driven development, acceptance tests, automated testing or unit testing from Jalai and Wohlin [22]) to the agile practice *Agile Testing* in our list. We give another example with the agile practice *Planning Game*. Here, we mapped specific estimation techniques such as *Planning Poker* (e.g., from Williams [52]) and practices listed as *Planning Game* (e.g., from Caires [10]).

Figure 4 shows the number of the mapped (redundant, similar in terms of different names or level of detail) practices per synthesized agile practices in all included studies.

The most mappings were conducted related to the agile practices *Agile Testing*, *Tracking progress* and *Continuous integration and builds*. We identified more than 50 redundant or similar listed practices of these three agile practices, each. The high count of mapped practices to the synthesized agile practice *Agile Testing* is due to the several testing practices (e.g., Acceptance Test, Test Driven Development and Unit Testing), methods and approaches listed in the included studies.

Third Step: Managing Borderline Cases. We identified borderline cases during the step-by-step check of the redundancies (see step one) and the synthesizing on an abstract level (see step two). Some studies have listed practices that we did not classify as agile practices. For instance, Küpper et al. [31] list roles of agile methods such as Scrum Master or Product Owner. Also, agile methods such as SAFe [28] or Kanban [27] are listed in several studies. In addition, methods and practices such as coaching [11] are described in the studies, which have non-related characteristics. We have marked these practices as borderline cases and checked them individually in this third step. During this check, we identified and documented a mapping to a few practices in our list (e.g., co-located team). In most cases, however, we have not added the borderline cases to our list of agile practices and not assigned them to practices that have already been listed.

5.2   Introducing the Integrated List of Agile Practices

Before we introduce the integrated list of agile practices, we describe its structure and explain how we categorized the synthesized agile practices.

As explained in Sects. 2 and 4, the characteristics and purposes of agile practices differ from one another. In order to increase the clarity of our list of agile practices, we decided to categorize the agile practices. The categorization is based on the characteristics of the respective agile practices. In order to identify possible categories, we analyzed our list of agile practices entry per entry. We verified the agile practices characteristics mainly based on the guidelines from

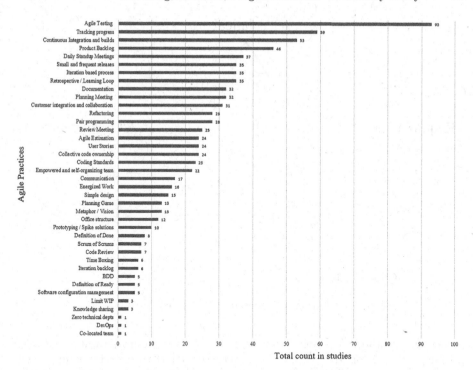

Fig. 4. Overview of the total count of mapped agile practice per synthesized practice

the well-known approaches Scrum [45] and XP [8]. Also, we used the glossary of agile practices from the Agile Alliance [3]. However, some agile practices may relate to more than one category. This lay in the specific implementation of the respective agile practice. For example, a definition of done relates to a requirements characteristic, but also may be associated with a collaborative aspect as it is usually defined by the team. In order to follow our purpose to provide an integrate list of agile practices, we set the main characteristic described in the literature in focus. To minimize the risk of bias, we decided to conduct the categorization in three iterations. The first iteration of the categorization was conducted by the first author. In the second iteration two other researchers from the group did the categorization by themselves. In the following, we compared our results and discussed the very few mismatches we identified. In the final third iteration, we went through our categorization with four experts from the agile community and discussed the categorization for each agile practice. Below, we describe the five categories and provide examples. The distribution of the listed agile practices to the categories is presented in Fig. 5.

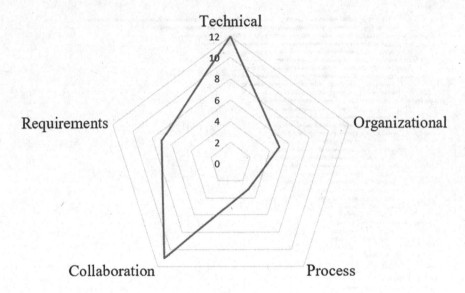

Fig. 5. Distribution of clustered agile practices per category

As agile methods focusing on social facets like communication, it is not surprising, that we found several agile practices related to the characteristic of **collaboration**. In this category we assigned all agile practices concerning this characteristic. For example, agile practices within the team is collaborate closely together like in retrospective meetings. Furthermore, we found agile practices, which supports the collaboration. An example for this is the co-located team practice. In total, we added eleven agile practices to this category.

We also found several agile practices with **technical** characteristics in our list. As technical associated agile practices are described for XP [8], we assumed to find those in the literature. Examples for agile practices mapped to this category are coding standards, continuous integration and collective code ownership. Totally, 12 agile practices were mapped to the technical category.

Some agile practices concerning to an **organizational** characteristic. In this category, we clustered team-oriented agile practices like self-organization as well as other types of practices such as the office structure. Five agile practices are added to this category.

Another facet of characteristics is related to a more **processual** background. This characteristic comes with agile practices as iteration based process. We added three practices this category.

Finally, we created the **requirements** category. In this category, we clustered all agile practices, which are related to any kind of requirements facets. These are, for example, using and maintaining a backlog as well as more detailed practices like the definition of ready or user stories. We added six agile practices to this category.

The result of the synthesizing and categorizing process is the integrated list of agile practices. The list comprises 38 agile practices structured in five categories. We present the integrated list of agile practices in Table 3.

Table 3. The integrated list of agile practices

Category	Agile practice (References)
Technical	Agile testing [6, 7, 10–12, 16, 18–22, 25, 27, 28, 30, 31, 33, 35–41, 46, 47, 49, 50, 52, 53]
	Code review [6, 11, 28, 31, 38, 49]
	Coding standards [6, 7, 10, 11, 19–22, 27, 28, 30, 31, 33–39, 46, 49, 50]
	Collective code ownership [6, 7, 10, 11, 16, 20, 25, 27, 28, 30, 34–40, 46, 47, 49, 52]
	Continuous integration [6, 7, 10–13, 16–22, 25, 27, 28, 30, 31, 33–40, 44, 46, 47, 49, 50, 52, 53]
	DevOps [28]
	Prototyping and spike solutions [4, 28, 31, 35, 36, 38, 46, 47, 49, 53]
	Refactoring [6, 7, 10–12, 16, 19–22, 25, 27, 30, 31, 33–39, 41, 46, 47, 49, 50, 52, 53]
	Simple design [6, 7, 10, 11, 19, 20, 25, 31, 34–36, 39, 46, 47, 50]
	Small and frequent releases [6, 7, 11, 12, 14–17, 19, 25, 27, 30, 35–37, 40, 44, 46, 47, 50, 52, 53]
	Software configuration management [6, 25, 30, 36, 47]
	Zero technical depts [6]
Collaboration	Agile estimation [4, 11, 13, 15, 16, 19, 20, 25, 28, 33–38, 47, 49]
	Customer integration [6, 10–12, 18, 20–22, 27, 28, 30, 31, 34–36, 38, 39, 44, 46, 49, 50, 53]
	Co-located team [31]
	Communication [4, 6, 11, 12, 22, 30, 35, 36, 39, 50, 53]
	Daily standup meetings [6, 7, 10–22, 25, 27, 28, 30, 31, 34–39, 41, 44, 46, 47, 49, 50, 52, 53]
	Pair programming [6, 7, 10, 11, 16, 19–22, 25, 27, 28, 30, 31, 33–35, 37–40, 44, 46, 47, 49, 50, 52, 53]
	Planning game [7, 10, 11, 21, 22, 25, 30, 37, 39, 46, 52]
	Release planning [38, 49, 53]
	Retrospective/Learning loop [4, 6, 7, 10–22, 25, 27, 28, 30, 31, 33–40, 44, 46, 49, 50, 52]
	Review meeting [4, 6, 10–14, 16, 17, 19–22, 30, 31, 33, 36–38, 46, 49, 50, 52]
	Scrum of scrums [11, 13, 16, 20, 25, 38, 49]
Process	Iteration based process [6, 10, 11, 13, 15, 18–22, 25, 28, 30, 31, 34–37, 39, 40, 44, 46, 47, 50, 52, 53]
	Limit WIP [19, 38, 49]
	Tracking progress [6, 7, 11–13, 15–17, 19–22, 25, 27, 28, 30, 31, 34–39, 44, 46, 47, 49, 50, 52]
Requirements	Behaviour driven development [16, 25, 27, 33, 37, 47]
	Definition of done [14, 15, 19, 25, 31, 36, 38, 49]
	Definition of ready [6, 25, 28, 31, 36, 49]
	Documentation [11, 13, 17, 19, 21, 30, 31, 36, 38, 44, 47, 49, 53]
	Metaphor/Vision [6, 11, 12, 17, 19, 20, 22, 30, 31, 39, 46, 50]
	User stories [6, 11, 13, 19–22, 25, 27, 30, 31, 36, 38, 46, 47, 49, 52, 53]
	Using and maintaining a backlog [4, 6, 7, 10–12, 14–17, 19–22, 25, 31, 34–38, 44, 46, 47, 49, 50, 52, 53]
Organizational	Empowered and self-organizing team [6, 11, 12, 17, 19, 25, 30, 31, 37, 39, 40, 44, 46, 47, 52, 53]
	Energized work [6, 10, 11, 19, 20, 25, 30, 31, 34, 36, 46, 47, 50, 52, 53]
	Knowledge sharing [12, 30]
	Office structure [10, 21, 25, 27, 30, 34, 36, 37, 46, 47, 50, 52]
	Time boxing [6, 12, 36, 39, 47]

6 Limitations

Although we performed our study based on the guidelines by Petersen [42] and according to Kitchenham and Charters [24], some limitations apply. A major challenge in systematic literature research is ensuring the completeness of the result set. To minimize the risk of omitting potentially relevant studies, we performed our test search runs in Scopus and Google Scholar. The search results showed high redundancies. Furthermore, several studies has proven the opportunity to work with Scopus as a single database for secondary studies (e.g., [5,23,48]). However, there is a possibility that we did not find all relevant studies due to the search being carried out in one database.

In addition, a limitation occurs due to the limited quality assurance of other researchers. The first author carried out the literature research, selection and data extraction by himself without systematic and iterative quality assurance measures by a second author. Therefore the potential risk arises that possible errors have been made while performing the literature search, e.g., optimizing the search string or selecting the studies due to bias. Similar limitations exist concerning the synthesizing procedure of the agile practices while creating the synthesized list of agile practices. We minimized these risks by performing cross-checks of our results by experts from the agile community and researchers from another research group.

Another limitation relates to the selection of studies. We have defined various inclusion criteria, which have implicitly limited the result set. This concerns, for example, the limitation relating to the publication year. We have only considered results that were published since 2010. Even if our study shows that high redundancies in the naming of agile practices were already identified in the 37 included studies, it is conceivable that potentially relevant studies have already been published before. Furthermore, we have defined various exclusion criteria in order to be able to carry out and document the selection systematically and comprehensibly. It is also conceivable that we have excluded studies (e.g., due to non-English language) that are potentially relevant to the exclusion criteria.

7 Conclusion and Future Work

This tertiary study was conducted with the purpose to create an integrated list of agile practices based on the literature to provide a comprehensive overview of agile practices. We analyzed 37 primary and secondary studies on detail in order to get an understanding of which agile practices are listed and/or used in the current state of research. We identified a high variety of agile practices related to the level of detail, which concerns due to the specific context of the respective studies. Furthermore, we found that various agile practices are listed redundantly in the included papers.

In order to provide an integrated list of agile practices we decided to synthesize the agile practices extracted from the studies of our result set. The synthesize process consists of three steps. First, we removed the redundancies of the listed agile practices. The result of this first step was the basis for the upcoming procedure. Second, we analyzed the level of detail of the listed agile practices. We found that several agile practices are of a high level of detail while others are more abstract. To increase the clarity and simplicity we decided to cluster the agile practices to a more abstract level of detail wherever possible. Finally, we managed the borderline cases in the third step of our synthesizing procedure.

After the synthesizing of the agile practices we structured our list of agile practices. The basis structure are five categories, which we identified by analyzing the 38 agile practices on detail. We implemented quality assurance measures for the categorization of the agile practices with the support of other researchers and practitioners from the agile community. The result of the two approaches is the integrated list of agile practices, which consists of 38 entries.

The findings of our study contributes to both, the research and practitioners community. For other researchers the integrated list of agile practices provides a comprehensive overview of agile practices used based on recent findings presented in the literature. The list of agile practices also contribute to a better understanding of the high variety of agile practices in practice, as almost of the included studies focus on practical phenomena under study. Thus, other researchers, which are dealing with agile practices may compare their findings with our integrated list of agile practices.

We will use the integrated list of agile practices as a basis for our future work. In the next step, we aim to create a documentation of each agile practice. This documentation will provide more detailed information of the specific agile practices related to the purpose, their specific relation to agile method/s, a description and conceivable constraints. We also want to analyze to what extent the agile practices are related to one another to identify useful combinations of agile practices or even constraints.

References

1. Abrahamsson, P., Warsta, J., Siponen, M.T., Ronkainen, J.: New directions on agile methods: a comparative analysis. In: ICSE 2003, pp. 244–254. Institute of Electrical and Electronics Engineers, Los Alamitos (2003). https://doi.org/10.1109/ICSE.2003.1201204
2. Abrahamsson, P., Salo, O., Ronkainen, J., Warsta, J.: Agile software development methods: review and analysis (478), 7–94 (2002)
3. Agile Alliance: Agile glossary and terminology (2015). https://www.agilealliance.org/agile101/agile-glossary/
4. Albuquerque, D., et al.: Defining agile requirements change management: a mapping study. In: Proceedings of the ACM Symposium on Applied Computing, pp. 1421–1424 (2020). https://doi.org/10.1145/3341105.3374095
5. Alsaqaf, W., Daneva, M., Wieringa, R.: Quality requirements in large-scale distributed agile projects – a systematic literature review. In: Grünbacher, P., Perini, A. (eds.) REFSQ 2017. LNCS, vol. 10153, pp. 219–234. Springer, Cham (2017). https://doi.org/10.1007/978-3-319-54045-0_17

6. Arcos-Medina, G., Mauricio, D.: Identifying factors influencing on agile practices for software development. J. Inf. Organ. Sci. **44**(1), 1–31 (2020). https://doi.org/10.31341/jios.44.1.1
7. Bastarrica, M., Espinoza, G., Marín, J.: Implementing agile practices: the experience of TSoL. In: International Symposium on Empirical Software Engineering and Measurement (2018). https://doi.org/10.1145/3239235.3268918
8. Beck, K.: Extreme Programming Explained: Embrace Change, 5th print edn. Addison-Wesley, Boston (2000)
9. Beck, K., et al.: Agile manifesto (2019). https://agilemanifesto.org/
10. Caires, V., Rios, N., Holvitie, J., Leppänen, V., De Mendonça Neto, M., Spínola, R.: Investigating the effects of agile practices and processes on technical debt-the viewpoint of the Brazilian software industry. In: Proceedings of the International Conference on Software Engineering and Knowledge Engineering, SEKE. vol. 2018-July, pp. 506–511 (2018). https://doi.org/10.18293/SEKE2018-131
11. Camara, R., Alves, A., Monte, I., Marinho, M.: Agile global software development: a systematic literature review. In: Proceedings of the 34th Brazilian Symposium on Software Engineering, pp. 31–40 (2020). https://doi.org/10.1145/3422392.3422411
12. Diebold, P., Dahlem, M.: Agile practices in practice: a mapping study. In: Proceedings of the 18th International Conference on Evaluation and Assessment in Software Engineering (2014). https://doi.org/10.1145/2601248.2601254
13. Diebold, P., Mayer, U.: On the usage and benefits of agile methods & practices: a case study at Bosch chassis systems control. In: Proceedings of the 18th International Conference on Agile Software Development, vol. 283, pp. 243–250 (2017). https://doi.org/10.1007/978-3-319-57633-6_16
14. Diebold, P., Theobald, S., Wahl, J., Rausch, Y.: Stepwise transition to agile: from three agile practices to Kanban adaptation. J. Softw. Evol. Process **31**(5) (2019). https://doi.org/10.1002/smr.2167
15. Diebold, P., Zehler, T., Richter, D.: How do agile practices support automotive spice compliance? In: Proceedings of the 2017 International Conference on Software and System Process, vol. Part F128767, pp. 80–84 (2017). https://doi.org/10.1145/3084100.3084108
16. Diel, E., Bergmann, M., Marczak, S., Luciano, E.: What is agile, which practices are used, and which skills are necessary according to Brazilian professionals: findings of an initial survey. In: Proceedings of the 6th Brazilian Workshop on Agile Methods, pp. 18–24 (2017). https://doi.org/10.1109/WBMA.2015.10
17. Gabriel, S., Niewoehner, N., Asmar, L., Kühn, A., Dumitrescu, R.: Integration of agile practices in the product development process of intelligent technical systems. In: Procedia CIRP, vol. 100, pp. 427–432 (2021). https://doi.org/10.1016/j.procir.2021.05.099
18. Gren, L., Knauss, A., Stettina, C.: Non-technical individual skills are weakly connected to the maturity of agile practices. Inf. Softw. Technol. **99**, 11–20 (2018). https://doi.org/10.1016/j.infsof.2018.02.006
19. Heredia, A., Garcia-Guzman, J., Amescua-Seco, A., Velasco-Diego, M.: Agile practices adapted to mass-market application development. J. Softw. Evol. Process **26**(9), 818–828 (2014). https://doi.org/10.1002/smr.1671
20. Jain, R., Suman, U.: Effectiveness of agile practices in global software development. Int. J. Grid Distrib. Comput. **9**(10), 231–248 (2016). https://doi.org/10.14257/ijgdc.2016.9.10.21
21. Jalali, S., Wohlin, C.: Global software engineering and agile practices: a systematic review. J. Softw. Evol. Process **24**(6), 643–659 (2012). https://doi.org/10.1002/smr.561

22. Jalali, S., Wohlin, C.: Agile practices in global software engineering: a systematic map. In: 5th IEEE International Conference on Global Software Engineering, pp. 45–54. IEEE, Piscataway (2010). https://doi.org/10.1109/ICGSE.2010.14

23. Jarzębowicz, A., Weichbroth, P.: A systematic literature review on implementing non-functional requirements in agile software development: issues and facilitating practices. In: Przybyłek, A., Miler, J., Poth, A., Riel, A. (eds.) LASD 2021. LNBIP, vol. 408, pp. 91–110. Springer, Cham (2021). https://doi.org/10.1007/978-3-030-67084-9_6

24. Kitchenham, B., Charters S.: Guidelines for performing systematic literature reviews in software engineering (2007)

25. Klotins, E., et al.: Use of agile practices in start-up companies. E-Inform. Softw. Eng. J. **15**(1), 47–64 (2021). https://doi.org/10.37190/E-INF210104

26. Koskinen, M., Mikkonen, T., Abrahamsson, P.: Containers in software development: a systematic mapping study. In: Franch, X., Männistö, T., Martínez-Fernández, S. (eds.) PROFES 2019. LNCS, vol. 11915, pp. 176–191. Springer, Cham (2019). https://doi.org/10.1007/978-3-030-35333-9_13

27. Kropp, M., Meier, A., Biddle, R.: Agile practices, collaboration and experience. In: Abrahamsson, P., Jedlitschka, A., Nguyen Duc, A., Felderer, M., Amasaki, S., Mikkonen, T. (eds.) PROFES 2016. LNCS, vol. 10027, pp. 416–431. Springer, Cham (2016). https://doi.org/10.1007/978-3-319-49094-6_28

28. Kuhrmann, M., et al.: Hybrid software development approaches in practice: a European perspective. IEEE Softw. **36**(4), 20–31 (2019). https://doi.org/10.1109/MS.2018.110161245

29. Kuhrmann, M., et al.: Hybrid software and system development in practice: waterfall, scrum, and beyond. In: Bendraou, R., Raffo, D., LiGuo, H., Maggi, F.M. (eds.) Proceedings of the 2017 International Conference on Software and System Process, pp. 30–39. ACM, New York (2017). https://doi.org/10.1145/3084100.3084104

30. Kurapati, N., Manyam, V.S.C., Petersen, K.: Agile software development practice adoption survey. In: Wohlin, C. (ed.) XP 2012. LNBIP, vol. 111, pp. 16–30. Springer, Heidelberg (2012). https://doi.org/10.1007/978-3-642-30350-0_2

31. Küpper, S., Pfahl, D., Jürisoo, K., Diebold, P., Münch, J., Kuhrmann, M.: How has SPI changed in times of agile development? Results from a multi-method study. J. Softw. Evol. Process **31**(11) (2019). https://doi.org/10.1002/smr.2182

32. Larman, C., Basili, V.R.: Iterative and incremental developments. A brief history. Computer **36**(6), 47–56 (2003). https://doi.org/10.1109/MC.2003.1204375

33. Lautert, T., Neto, A.G.S.S., Kozievitch, N.P.: A survey on agile practices and challenges of a global software development team. In: Meirelles, P., Nelson, M.A., Rocha, C. (eds.) WBMA 2019. CCIS, vol. 1106, pp. 128–143. Springer, Cham (2019). https://doi.org/10.1007/978-3-030-36701-5_11

34. Licorish, S., et al.: Adoption and suitability of software development methods and practices. In: Proceedings of the 23rd Asia-Pacific Software Engineering Conference, vol. 0, pp. 369–372 (2016). https://doi.org/10.1109/APSEC.2016.062

35. Mamoghli, S., Cassivi, L.: Agile ERP implementation: the case of a SME. In: Proceedings of the 21st International Conference on Enterprise Information Systems, vol. 2, pp. 188–196 (2019). https://doi.org/10.5220/0007700501880196

36. Myklebust, T., Lyngby, N., Stålhane, T.: Agile practices when developing safety systems. In: Proceedings of the 14th Probabilistic Safety Assessment and Management Conference (2018)

37. Neto, F., De Oliveira Rodrigues, B., De Souza França, R., Ziviani, F., Parreiras, F.: Impact of agile practices adoption on organizational learning: a survey in Brazil. In: Proceedings of the 31st International Conference on Software Engineering and Knowledge Engineering, vol. 2019-July, pp. 583–588 (2019). https://doi.org/10.18293/SEKE2019-059

38. Noll, J., Beecham, S.: How agile is hybrid agile? An analysis of the HELENA data. In: Franch, X., Männistö, T., Martínez-Fernández, S. (eds.) PROFES 2019. LNCS, vol. 11915, pp. 341–349. Springer, Cham (2019). https://doi.org/10.1007/978-3-030-35333-9_25

39. Nurdiani, I., Börstler, J., Fricker, S., Petersen, K.: Usage, retention, and abandonment of agile practices: a survey and interviews results. E-Inform. Softw. Eng. J. **13**, 7–35 (2019). https://doi.org/10.5277/e-Inf190101

40. Paez, N., Fontdevila, D., Gainey, F., Oliveros, A.: Technical and organizational agile practices: a Latin-American survey. In: Proceedings of the 19th International Conference on Agile Software Development, vol. 314, pp. 146–159 (2018). https://doi.org/10.1007/978-3-319-91602-6_10

41. Pantiuchina, J., Mondini, M., Khanna, D., Wang, X., Abrahamsson, P.: Are software startups applying agile practices? The state of the practice from a large survey. In: Proceedings of the 18th International Conference on Agile Software Development, vol. 283, pp. 167–183 (2017). https://doi.org/10.1007/978-3-319-57633-6_11

42. Petersen, K., Feldt, R., Mujtaba, S., Mattsson, M.: Systematic mapping studies in software engineering. In: 12th International Conference on Evaluation and Assessment in Software Engineering, EASE 2008 (2008). https://doi.org/10.14236/ewic/ease2008.8

43. Salo, O., Abrahamsson, P.: Agile methods in European embedded software development organisations: a survey on the actual use and usefulness of extreme programming and scrum. IET Softw. **2**, 58–64 (2008)

44. Sandstø, R., Reme-Ness, C.: Agile practices and impacts on project success. J. Eng. Proj. Prod. Manage. **11**(3), 255–262 (2021). https://doi.org/10.2478/jeppm-2021-0024

45. Schwaber, K., Sutherland, J.: The scrum guide (2020). https://www.scrumguides.org/scrum-guide.html

46. Sletholt, M., Hannay, J., Pfahl, D., Benestad, H., Langtangen, H.: A literature review of agile practices and their effects in scientific software development. In: Proceedings of the 33rd International Conference on Software Engineering, pp. 1–9 (2011). https://doi.org/10.1145/1985782.1985784

47. Souza, R., Silva, F., Rocha, L., Machado, I.: Investigating agile practices in software startups. In: Proceedings of the 33rd Brazilian Symposium on Software Engineering, pp. 317–321 (2019). https://doi.org/10.1145/3350768.3350786

48. Stray, V., Memon, B., Paruch, L.: A systematic literature review on agile coaching and the role of the agile coach. In: Morisio, M., Torchiano, M., Jedlitschka, A. (eds.) PROFES 2020. LNCS, vol. 12562, pp. 3–19. Springer, Cham (2020). https://doi.org/10.1007/978-3-030-64148-1_1

49. Sánchez-Gordón, M., Colomo-Palacios, R., Sánchez, A., Sanchez-Gordon, S.: Integrating approaches in software development: a case analysis in a small software company. In: Yilmaz, M., Niemann, J., Clarke, P., Messnarz, R. (eds.) EuroSPI 2020. CCIS, vol. 1251, pp. 95–106. Springer, Cham (2020). https://doi.org/10.1007/978-3-030-56441-4_7

50. Tolfo, C., Wazlawick, R., Ferreira, M., Forcellini, F.: Agile practices and the promotion of entrepreneurial skills in software development. J. Softw. Evol. Process **30**(9) (2018). https://doi.org/10.1002/smr.1945

51. VersionOne, CollabNet: 15th annual state of agile survey report (2021). https:// www.stateofagile.com/
52. Williams, L.: Agile software development methodologies and practices. In: Zelkowitz, M. (ed.) Advances in Computers, vol. 80, pp. 1–44. Academic Press, London (2010). https://doi.org/10.1016/S0065-2458(10)80001-4
53. Yang, C., Liang, P., Avgeriou, P.: Integrating agile practices into architectural assumption management: an industrial survey. In: Proceedings of the 23rd Evaluation and Assessment on Software Engineering Conference, pp. 156–165 (2019). https://doi.org/10.1145/3319008.3319027

Agile Teams Working from Home During the Covid-19 Pandemic: A Literature Review on New Advantages and Challenges

Necmettin Ozkan[1,2(✉)], Oya Erdil[2], and Mehmet Şahin Gök[2]

[1] Kuveyt Türk Participation Bank, Kocaeli, Turkey
necmettin.ozkan@kuveytturk.com.tr
[2] Department of Business, Gebze Technical University, Kocaeli, Turkey
{erdil,sahingok}@gtu.edu.tr

Abstract. Whilst co-location is the common and preferred kind and key standard for self-organizing agile teams, this option is not always possible for some organizations that have to lead to the distribution of teams and/or individuals in one or another form, especially because of Sars-Cov-2 pandemic (Covid-19) today. The pandemic has forced a shift to virtual working for many organizations, which makes it necessary to investigate its possible effects on the self-organizing agile teams. In this manner, this study aims to investigate emergent challenges and advantages arising from working at home for self-organizing agile teams where every team member works from home with the impact of the Covid-19 pandemic by systemically reviewing the literature. Finally, all the findings, derived from the literature, were discussed from coordination, collaboration and communication, agile practices, agility, emotions and feelings, leadership, productivity, and quality aspects. The results demonstrate that along with some specific challenges for the agile teams during the pandemic, there are several advantages of working at home for them.

Keywords: Agile · Scrum · Software development · Sars-Cov-2 pandemic · Covid-19 · Advantages · Disadvantages · Challenges · WFH · Working from home

1 Introduction

Agile software development (ASD) has generated interest due to the increasing demands from varying kinds of organizations [1]. It highlights the importance of a people-oriented approach to software development [2]. Flourished by the proper people-oriented approaches, well-functioning teams that are advised to work collocated are acknowledged as a key success factor for ASD [3]. Co-location allows frequent in-person contacts, builds trust quickly, simplifies problem solving, encourages instant communication, and enables fast-paced decision-making [4].

From the standpoint of locational distances, whilst co-location is the common and key standard for self-organizing agile teams [5, 6], this option is not always possible for

© Springer Nature Switzerland AG 2022
A. Przybyłek et al. (Eds.): LASD 2022, LNBIP 438, pp. 38–60, 2022.
https://doi.org/10.1007/978-3-030-94238-0_3

some organizations that have to lead to the distribution of teams and/or individuals in one or another form. At this point, the distribution comes in three main veins: geographically distributed teams, dispersed individuals in a particular team, and hybrid teams [6]. In hybrid teams, a part of team members works from office and the rest of them from home. Mostly seen in the off-shoring and global software development forms, geographically distributed teams are common for many years [8]. While the teams are split into different geographic locations, individuals in the sub-teams are usually co-located. The geographically distributed software development is mainly in relation to the global software development where software development projects are implemented with international cooperation [7]. The individually dispersed teams differently address the case where each individual in the team is located in different places so each individual is on his own [6]. While geographically distributed teams are fully distributed in multiple geographic locations, times or organizations, in the case of individually dispersed individuals, a particular team's individuals are distributed across multiple locations, such as homes in the pandemic. Geographically distributed, hybrid and individually dispersed teams differ in terms of challenges they have. Since the basic work unit in agile software organizations is the team rather than the individual [36], preserving the nature of the team from distance (e.g. homes) confronts us as a new challenge for the individually dispersed teams.

The case of individually dispersed teams has become common nowadays for many organizations, especially because of Sars-Cov-2 pandemic (Covid-19) and the shift to virtual working from homes. This working model has brought several challenges and complexity for agile teams [9] who have a heavy focus on in person interactions [10]. Moreover, Comella-Dorda et al. [12] claim that agile teams, earlier confirmed to be effective with remote working, can be inefficient when working fully remotely. Therefore, it becomes necessary to investigate this new form's possible effects on the self-organizing agile teams to give them insights in particular for this pandemic period and in general for the future. From this unique model of working, important lessons can be learned about both software development and agile software development. While some challenges related to co-located and distributed remote teams have been explored in prior literature, the context of individually dispersed agile teams has a unique nature exhibiting new challenges [7, 13] and little is known about challenges resulting from and experienced by the self-organizing teams working from home [14].

In this manner, this study aims to investigate the emergent key concerns arising from individually dispersed self-organizing agile teams working from home within the context of Covid-19 pandemic by using Systematic Literature Review (SLR). In this regard, we identified one of the Research Questions 1 (RQ1) as below. Apart from identifying the challenges, it would be interesting whether working from home enhances some of agile teams' abilities. For this purpose, this aspect is looked at in the RQ2.

RQ1: What new challenges have agile team members working from home faced during the pandemic?
RQ2: What kind of new advantages do agile team members working from home have during the pandemic?

The remaining of this paper is organized as follows: Sect. 2 summarizes the applied research method in this study. Section 3 delivers related works. Section 4 presents the results based on the applied method. Section 5 discusses the results and Sect. 6 states the limitations of the study and directions for future works.

2 Research Method

The aim of this study is to review the status of current challenges and advantages for the self-organizing agile teams working from home, in particular by concentrating on studies providing any kind of comparisons between the pre- and pandemic era. This study has been undertaken based on the SLR guideline proposed by Kitchenham et al. [15], with some deviations from its original protocol. As one of the deviations, we did not purposely apply any quality assessment to the papers identified since the topic is relatively new and the literature naturally has a scarce of resources. In this case, publications with a high-quality level and those with a relatively low level of quality were included and evaluated together. We have decided on this way in order to make the scope as wide as possible for this subject that has a lack of resources, at the expense of compromising the quality of our study in terms of the included papers.

Having a lack of resources on this subject also shaped our selection of the libraries to conduct the review. The initial searches were done in Scopus, IEEE, and ACM Digital Library with the search strings elaborated below. Then, it is realized that the results obtained from them are not sufficient to go further as seen in Table 1 at #4, 5 and 6 yielding 5, 0 and 0 related results respectively. One of the reasons for this may be that the literature on this subject is not very extensive yet. Then, we considered including Google Scholar that covers more resources such as master theses that can be helpful for our study, but, not transformed into a peer-reviewed publication yet. Then, we decided to use Google Scholar as the main library for further searches since it already indexes well-known digital libraries and more and, thus, provides the most extensive source for such a new topic. Even so, a cross-checking was conducted with the five results from Scopus as it is another extensive source of academic papers to cross-check our search results coverage in Google Scholar. It was seen that all results are covered by Google Scholar searches. When it comes to the year range and publication types, all the searches included the peer-reviewed and supervised resources for the years of 2020 and afterwards.

In designing the search strings, we aimed to reach a comprehensive and also reasonable list to investigate the result set by using not a single but multiple search string. Regarding the structural body of the search strings, we identified and merged two substrings representing the two parts in our scope. Our scope includes the keywords specific to our target domain (software development) and those representing the pandemic side of the strings.

To identify the appropriate and effective keywords for both sides of the strings, the search process was operated iteratively. In the first iteration, to determine the appropriate keywords, a preliminary search was conducted in Google Scholar with the word including "agility" (#1 in Table 1). 46 results were examined both in terms of the effectiveness of the search key and relatedness of the results. We realized that most of the studies including the "agility" word in their titles belong to other domains (such as health, logistics, strategic agility, and marketing agility) and we found that all of them are out of our scope by applying our standard paper selection method described in our study. Then, we decided to exclude the "agility" keyword from our further searches to narrow the results down to the relevant scope. For the part representing the Agile domain, "("agile teams" OR "agile team")" in full text search and "(scrum OR agile OR XP OR Kanban)" in title search in Google Scholar were formed. The side representing the pandemic part was formed as "(covid OR sars OR pandemic OR corona OR coronavirus OR lockdown OR outbreak)" after some pilot iterative searches are done in Google Scholar. Regarding the working from home, the "home" keyword was a good candidate to include in this string yet this adding brought many irrelevant results, which renders the manual review almost unreasonable.

Regarding the search locations, we anticipated and were largely satisfied with the effectiveness of searching in the titles after realizing that almost all results returning from #2 search in Google Scholar include the keywords we identified in their titles; that is the corresponding authors locate the relevant terms (agile or the specific agile method name and the pandemic specific word(s) in their paper titles). Moreover, we realized that all results from the Scopus search were covered by our former search in Google Scholar, #3. After all, Table 1 summarizes the reviews conducted with the aforementioned keywords.

Based on the scope and context of our study, for the selection of the papers, the following propositions of inclusion criteria (IC) and exclusion criteria (EC) were specified and applied to the search process.

IC1: Papers investigating effects of the pandemic on the agile software development.
IC2: Papers on working from home rather than the conventional global software development or hybrid teams.
IC3: Peer-reviewed and supervised academic works including conference, workshop, proceedings, journal papers, thesis, etc.
EC1: Papers not available in English.
EC2: Papers published in non-peer-reviewed or non-supervised academic sources such as web pages and books.
EC3: Papers not accessible by the authors.
EC4: Papers investigating effects of being agile to cope with issues specific to the pandemic.
EC5: Papers investigating effects of the pandemic on the software development in general without any explicit relation to the agile software development.

After defining the keywords, libraries, IC, and EC, the full searches were conducted by the first author between 13.09 and 16.09.2021 to identify the relevant studies by applying the detailed inclusion and exclusion criteria to the papers. In this process, total number of 1004 of works were obtained from the search results as seen in Table 1. After removing the duplicate records, the list included 964 distinct records. All papers were examined through their titles and, where necessary, abstracts in order to identify whether they are in our scope. If even the abstracts were not sufficient to decide to include or exclude the papers, then, a scanning through the full texts of the papers was done for those that were further included or excluded. 883 papers were investigated only through their titles, 37 of the them through their titles and abstracts and 44 of them through their titles, abstracts and full texts.

Excluded 9 studies are within the scope of our study, but they were ignored, as they are not peer-reviewed (yet) coming from Google Scholar, in relevant EC2. The exclusion was applied for 2 papers regarding EC3 because the papers' full texts were not accessible by the authors. We applied EC1 to specify the papers not available in English either by filtering via the relevant features of libraries allowing eliminating non-English studies forehand or via the manual investigations. 12 papers were manually excluded as they have an abstract in English but have a non-English full text. EC4 and EC5 are about the content details of the papers, then, they were applied during the meta-data or the full text investigation stages, yielding 925 papers' exclusion. After all, 16 distinct studies were identified as relevant and listed in Table 2 in the order of identification time. In the further examinations of all identified studies, the relevant contents were extracted from the studies and grouped under some main customized items by the first author based on their contents. This grouping was elaborated further in this study.

Table 1. Search details

#	Library	Place	Search string	Number of results	Number of relevant results
1	*Google Scholar	Title	(agility) AND (covid OR sars OR pandemic OR corona OR coronavirus OR outbreak OR lockdown)	46	0
2	Google Scholar	Full text	("agile teams" OR "agile team") AND (covid OR sars OR pandemic OR corona OR coronavirus OR outbreak OR lockdown)	791	14
3	*Google Scholar	Title	(scrum OR agile OR XP OR Kanban) AND (covid OR sars OR pandemic OR corona OR coronavirus OR outbreak OR lockdown)	91	14
4	Scopus	Meta-data	(agile AND software AND (covid OR sars OR pandemic OR corona OR coronavirus OR lockdown OR outbreak))	55	5
5	IEEE Xplore	Meta-data		16	0
6	ACM	Meta-data		5	0
Total				1004 (964 in distinct)	33 (16 in distinct)

*Google Scholar does not provide searching in metadata except specific to title

3   Related Works

Several studies and SLRs are available for the software development during the pandemic. For instance, Nolan et al. [16] covered the learning from working at home during the pandemic in their SLR. Several other studies such as Rehberg, et al. [17] discuss the advantages of applying agile approaches to better deal with issues in the pandemic. As mentioned before, these two types of scope were ignored in our study; our study rather focuses on the effects of the pandemic on agile teams rather than the effects of the pandemic on the software development in general or on agile capabilities to deal with pandemic specific issues.

When it comes to our scope, there are several studies identified as relevant as listed in Table 2; yet none of them is an SLR study like ours. Since these studies have already been included in our study with details, it was not preferred to mention them in detail in this section. Our list includes only the academic literature, however, we encountered some grey literature as related works, such as [12] and [13]. In the study [12], the authors provide their ideas about how to ensure that agile teams are effective where Covid-19 has forced them to work remotely. Study [13] gives personal ideas about the challenges of agile software development from home along with the practical examples and what will probably happen to agile software development teams when the crisis is over.

The included studies and excluded grey literature analyze the pandemic through challenges, new practices, tools, and possible solutions in the agile teams' context. Our study differs from the existing literature in some aspects. Firstly, it reviews and combines other studies' findings and as far as we know, it is the first in this regard. Secondly, it also differentiates and compares working from home and normal work, which has not been clearly expressed in other studies.

4   Results

As seen in Table 2, five of the studies are published in a conference proceeding. Four papers out of these five papers were presented in one of the leading Agile conferences, LASD (International Conference on Lean and Agile Software Development). A considerable number of the remaining papers, nine of them, are master theses, indicating a positive reflection of academia to the subject. The remaining two papers are journal articles. When we look at the geographical distribution, we see that Northern and Central Europe surface. In terms of the time distribution, it is seen that the times near the end of the university semesters are dominant.

Table 2. Results from the literature review

Paper code	Reference	Type	Method	Date (of Publication)	Country conducted
P1	[18]	Conference	Survey with 250+ people	January 2021	Pakistan
P2	[19]	Journal	Survey with 171 people	June 2021	Germany

(*continued*)

Table 2. (*continued*)

Paper code	Reference	Type	Method	Date (of Publication)	Country conducted
P3	[20]	Conference	Panel	September 2020	–
P4	[21]	Master thesis	Survey with 17 people + 2 semi-structured interviews	June 2020	Sweden
P5	[22]	Journal	Action research	July 2020	Brazil
P6	[23]	Master thesis	Interview with 8 people	May 2021	Finland
P7	[24]	Master thesis	Survey with 96 people + 7 semi-structured interviews	June 2021	Sweden
P8	[25]	Master thesis	Interview with 13 participants	May 2021	Sweden
P9	[9]	Conference paper	Case study - one team	January 2021	Ireland
P10	[26]	Master thesis	Multinational company case study with interview of 10 people	June 2020	Switzerland, France, Romania
P11	[27]	Master thesis	Survey with 114 people	June 2021	Canada, Estonia, India, Ireland, United States of America
P12	[28]	Master Thesis	Survey with 67 people + A census study with 105 employees	February 2021	Finland
P13	[29]	Master thesis	Interview with 9 people	May 2021	Iceland
P14	[30]	Master thesis	Interview with 19 people	July 2021	Belgium
P15	[7]	Conference	Case studies	January 2021	Germany
P16	[31]	Conference	Survey with 120 people	January 2021	Poland

Topics of challenges and advantages of the agile teams during the pandemic that were extracted from the identified studies were classified by the first author based on the aspects as seen in Table 3. Coordination, Collaboration, and Communication aspects among the distributed individuals were obvious enough to point out in the contents of the papers. Productivity and Quality items have also taken their place as one of the compelling topics of the pandemic period. In some papers, it was also discussed how agile practices were affected and performed during the pandemic period. Apart from the practices, some agile values and principles about transparency, flexibility, and self-organization were included by some identified works. Even though the Leadership, Coherence, and Feeling of the team members are relevant to agile values and principles, we handled them separately since they have a considerably high number of items. At the end of all these, as a result, changes in Agility degree in the organizations have also been the subject of research.

Along with these dimension items, the table presents the information about how many times each item was addressed by which study. Accordingly, it is seen that the most intensively discussed dimension is about Coordination, Collaboration, and Communication (it accounts for more than one-third of all items). It is noted that in this dimension, there are challenges and a considerable number of advantages as well. The second place is about the findings on the effects of working from home on Agile Practices. The table shows that working from home produces the most disadvantage at Leadership and Coherence aspects. The item with a relatively high advantage is about the increase in Agility. Apart from the dimensions, the study P8 numerically contributes at most to the all list.

Table 3. Number of advantages and challenges per each paper

Aspects	Effect	P1	P2	P3	P4	P5	P6	P7	P8	P9	P10	P11	P12	P13	P14	P15	P16	Total	Total by aspect
Coordination, collaboration and communication	Negative	2		2	2	3	1	11	9	3	2	2	1	3	3	2		46	70
	Positive			2				2	8		1	1	2	2	2	3	1	24	
Agile practice	Negative			1		1	2	2	3	3				1	1	1		15	25
	Positive							2						3	1	2	2	10	
Feeling	Negative	1		1		1		5	3	2		2	2	2	1			20	24
	Positive								1				1		1		1	4	
Productivity	Negative	5	1	1	1			1				2		1	1			13	22
	Positive				2			1				1		3		1	1	9	
Leadership	Negative			1			1	1	5				1		1	1		11	12
	Positive								1									1	
Agility	Negative	1																1	9
	Positive		2					1	1		1		1			2		8	
Coherence	Negative					1	2					2	2		1	1		9	9
	Positive																	0	

(*continued*)

Table 3. (*continued*)

Aspects	Effect	P1	P2	P3	P4	P5	P6	P7	P8	P9	P10	P11	P12	P13	P14	P15	P16	Total	Total by aspect
Quality	Negative																	0	1
	Positive															1		1	
Total	Negative	9	1	6	3	5	5	22	20	8	4	6	7	7	7	5		115	-
	Positive		2	2	2			6	11		2	2	4	8	4	8	6	57	-
	Grand total	9	3	8	5	5	5	28	31	8	6	8	11	15	11	13	6	172	-

Tables 4 and 5 illustrate the disadvantage and advantage of the content items extracted from the papers, mapped for each paper and grouped by each identified aspect. In this table, under each content item, it is seen which studies include the content items and by how many studies each item was included. The top item about challenges shows that in spite of the technological advancements, lack of face-to-face communication is a clear challenge that conflicts directly with one of the agile principles; "the most efficient and effective method of conveying information to and within a development team is face-to-face conversation". In a similar vein, integration, coordination and involvement of stakeholders, forming effective new teams and onboarding staff become more difficult in remote working from homes because of more difficult, less or slower communication capabilities the teams have. This leads to decrease of productivity especially because of fewer interactions with others. Among other items, building work-life balance surfaces as one of the most mentioned issues of the agile teams.

Table 4. Map of disadvantage of items per each paper

Negative content item	Frequency	Citing paper(s)
Coordination, collaboration and communication		
Lack of face-to-face communications to experience the social aspect	9	P1, P3, P5, P7, P9, P10, P12, P13, P15
More difficult, less and slower communication	6	P6, P7, P8, P10, P13, P14
Integration, coordination, and involvement of stakeholders are more difficult	5	P1, P8, P9, P13, P15
Lack of constant communication	3	P4, P7, P8
Misunderstandings in communications	3	P5, P7, P8
Plethora of interruption	3	P7, P8, P9
Less spontaneous informal communication among team members	2	P7, P11
Making voice heard	2	P7, P8

(*continued*)

Table 4. (*continued*)

Negative content item	Frequency	Citing paper(s)
A need for communicating more with fewer abilities, increased number of meetings and less effective meetings	2	P8, P14
Dealing with problems on their own instead of doing together	1	P8
Unable to cheer up each other when mentally down	1	P11
Suffering from interpersonal friction	1	P3
Trouble with expressing themselves	1	P4
Establishment of tools to support working	1	P5
Lack of visibility	1	P8
A distance created with the transversal roles such as the Product Owner or Scrum Master	1	P14
Easier to deviate from unwritten rules	1	P7
A reluctance to bring up sensitive conversations digitally	1	P7
A fear of leaving digital traces when writing down certain things	1	P7
A decrease in knowing the extent of the team members' working	1	P7
Productivity		
Productivity decreased because of fewer interactions with others, low working hours of developers or no work pressure on them	6	P1, P2, P4, P7, P10, P12
Teams suffered from interpersonal friction are exacerbated	1	P3
Motivation and efficiency affected negatively	1	P10
Delay in the project delivery time	1	P1
Not applied sprint meetings	1	P1
Stress and emotional and mental instability affecting productivity	1	P1
Work pressure and home life leading to a conflict and resulting in less productive teams	1	P1

(*continued*)

Table 4. (*continued*)

Negative content item	Frequency	Citing paper(s)
Decreased productivity [with no specified reason]	1	P13
Agile practice		
Agile work practices getting harder to perform due to the virtuality of meetings and interactions	2	P3, P7
Hardship in knowledge management	2	P5, P7
Challenge of establishing a new way of working with digital tools	2	P8, P15
Cyclical Agile nature of the team moved to pure execution and mechanical version of Scrum	2	P6, P9
Higher reliance on documentation, tools, processes, and more structured work	1	P6
Scrum meetings taking much unnecessary time	1	P8
No longer "touch" hardware products	1	P8
Difficult to stay within tighter time-box	1	P9
For sprint planning, engagement remaining for a shorter period of time	1	P9
Increased number of meetings	1	P14
Meetings can continue longer without being decided beforehand	1	P13
Feeling		
Damaged work-life balance	5	P3, P9, P11, P12, P14
Loneliness and feeling forgotten	3	P8, P12, P13
Decreased motivation	2	P7, P8
Decrease in team morale	2	P7, P13
Fatigue	2	P7, P9
Decreased ergonomics and comfort	1	P5
Easiness of disturbance	1	P8
Not using skills to full extend	1	P11
Less ambition and work satisfaction	1	P1
Decrease in breaks	1	P7
Changes on feelings and personalities like being more introverted at long term	1	P7

(*continued*)

Table 4. (*continued*)

Negative content item	Frequency	Citing paper(s)
Agility		
Less effective agility	1	P1
Leadership		
Forming effective new teams and onboarding staff	5	P3, P6, P8, P12, P15
Having trouble with keeping track of people and how they feel	3	P7, P8, P14
The leadership affected since the workload increased	1	P8
Mental breakdowns	1	P8
Increased workload since the team's wellbeing getting worse	1	P8
Coherence		
Integrating new employees	3	P6, P7, P14
Affinity, togetherness	2	P12, P15
Team spirit	1	P11
Less communication resulted in more conflicts and less trust	1	P11
Feeling of disconnected	1	P12
More difficulties in creating personal relationships	1	P7

In terms of advantages, increased efficiency of meetings, fewer interruptions and increased productivity and flexibility are prominent.

Table 5. Map of advantage items to each paper

Positive content item	Number of frequency	Citing paper(s)
Coordination, collaboration and communication		
Fewer interruptions and more status updates with the present status in the communication tools	5	P3, P7, P8, P10, P15
Saved time from commuting	3	P7, P8, P12,
Meetings start on time and run more efficiently and more effectively	3	P3, P13, P14
Increased frequency of communication	2	P11, P16

(*continued*)

Table 5. (*continued*)

Positive content item	Number of frequency	Citing paper(s)
More factual and precise, objective and efficient communication and collaboration	2	P13, P15
Easier communication	1	P8
Increased and faster interaction with customers	1	P8
Ability to speak naturally in front of a big group of people	1	P8
Became good at respecting who is talking	1	P8
Follow-up communication; written communication within teams is stored and visible	1	P8
The documentation clearer and more structured	1	P8
Employees preferring virtual communication and cooperation	1	P12
Able to do several things at the same time for less interesting meetings	1	P14
Teams forced to adopt more state-of-the-art communication practices	1	P15
Productivity		
Increased productivity [with no specified reason]	4	P7, P13, P15, P16
Productivity improved due to less distractions from coworkers	2	P4, P13
Improved speed of achieving work goals	1	P11
Productivity improved due to the reduced amount of tension the employees feel	1	P4
A longer workday from home	1	P13
Agile Practice		
Saved time for Scrum meetings	3	P13, P14, P16
Scrum meetings getting more goal-oriented, factual, and more efficient	3	P7, P13, P15
Agile approach becoming more transparent	2	P7, P15
Increased accountability	1	P16
Easier time planning for sprints	1	P13
Feeling		
A better "we" feeling by connecting different geographical locations	1	P8
Improved work-life balance	1	P12

(*continued*)

Table 5. (*continued*)

Positive content item	Number of frequency	Citing paper(s)
Trust and flexibility in the company	1	P14
Increased accountability	1	P16
Agility		
Increase in flexibility	4	P2, P7, P10, P12
Increase in perceived agility	2	P2, P8
Better self-organization	1	P15
Increased transparency	1	P15
Leadership		
Leaders better at realizing if someone has something to do	1	P8
Quality		
More automation	1	P16

5 Discussion

Unlike co-located or distributed teams, being distributed on an individual basis rather than on a team basis opens door to new challenges. Since the basic work unit in agile software organizations is the team rather than the individual [36], preserving the nature of the team during working from distance (e.g. homes) confronts us as a new challenge for dispersed teams. In addition to these challenges, it has been seen that the items on the right of the agile manifesto, whose contribution to agility has not been investigated sufficiently by the agile communities until this catastrophic change brought by the pandemic, can also support agility when the circumstances demand it. In history, such catastrophic changes are few, even fewer in the information technology era, and can be considered as the first instance in the age of agile software development. From a wider perspective, such changes provide lessons not only for the pandemic but also for the post-pandemic time. In this sense, in the following, the implications for this review study are presented.

5.1 Implications for Agile Practitioners

Among the challenges of working remotely from home, we have seen that the communication dimension has a considerable place during the pandemic as it was before the pandemic. Communication, which plays a key role in many issues, is prominent especially in the context of Agile. Korkala [32] highlights the project failures in agile teams because of the poor communication that can be also the root cause of other problems within the teams. Within this scope, individuals' ability to express themselves, understand each other correctly, coach people, communicate without loss of emotions and feelings, conflict resolutions, and a desire for having intensive human contact can be counted. It is expected that the first challenge faced by teams accustomed to close working with high interactions is about communication and its related aspects.

Even though many tools support the interactions efficiently, they are still not as effective as a face-to-face conversation [20]. Non-verbal communication carries a lot more information like facial expressions, gestures, posture, proximity, tone of voice, pitch, etc. in comparison to verbal communication [33]. However, a big part of non-verbal communication is lost in the virtual teams' processes [34], like happened across the (members of) teams. During the working from home, without adequate capabilities that the traditional face-to-face teams have, contact is prone to be harder, kept at a minimum and more formal. Along with these shortcomings, working from home may also open the door to other problems such as a quality decrease in software products. As Agile requires intensive coordination, collaboration, and a coordination-based approach extending to the broad parties including clients and end-users, the regular and continuous involvement of them in the cycles in the development activities can have problems. The lack of communication within team members may also lead to misunderstandings that deteriorate the team's coherence. Because of the lack of sensing, the social fabric of the team may be in danger, making communication more difficult, less and slower.

Agile teams prefer constant and spontaneous communication and make voices heard to facilitate an agile and transparent way for their information to flow across and inside the teams. These abilities decrease during the pandemic since to convey the information in the (even increased number of) meetings or online during the pandemic seems ineffective to provide these abilities. As a side effect of these decreased abilities, agile teams lose the feel of togetherness, and start to behave introvertedly and individually. There are several instances of that such as, dealing with problems on their own, being unable to cheer up each other, suffering from interpersonal friction, having trouble with expressing themselves, having a distance occurred with the transversal roles, deviations from unwritten rules, and decreases in knowing the extent of the team members' working.

During the pandemic, after dealing with the challenges of the establishment of digital tools to support working and finding state-of-the-art communication practices, agile teams need less effort to communicate. For instance, they can save time from commuting to come together, ignore irrelevant subjects easily, and present their status in the communication tools. This easiness in communication brings increased frequency and equality of communication and collaboration. Online meetings can start on time and run more efficiently and more effectively and support more factual and precise, objective and efficient communication and collaboration of group members and customers. With digitalization, the documentation becomes clearer and more structured.

Some issues for coordination, collaboration, and communication have both positive and negative sides. For instance, the form of interruptions only changes in the manner of interrupting during the pandemic; having interruptions physically at the office turns into digital interruptions during the pandemic. While digital tools and documentation are effective for having a corporate memory, they are not preferred for discussing sensitive issues by some agile teams because of the fear of leaving digital traces.

In a similar vein, the productivity aspect has positive and negative effects during the pandemic. Productivity decreases because of ignored and not applied agile practices, fewer interactions, less direct contact of people, less motivation, more interpersonal friction and more stress and emotional and mental instability emerged in home-life during the pandemic. Meanwhile, we see positive reflections of improvements in communication dimensions, including fewer distractions and commuting effort, and improved speed of information, on productivity. The number of studies stating that productivity increases during the pandemic without providing a clear reason is also noteworthy.

Agile work practices get harder to perform during the pandemic due to the virtuality of meetings and interactions. It is possible to say that relatively more abstract phenomena like knowledge management, engagement, and the spirit of agility are also negatively affected by the pandemic. Agile teams are prone to pose a pure mechanical execution under the constraints of the pandemic, laying more on the doing rather than being (agile), on documentation, tools, processes, and more structured work. The state of being ineffective under this condition is tried to compensated with having more meeting durations, taking much unnecessary time, and posing difficulties to stay within time-boxes.

On the other hand, Agile practices benefit from the pandemic conditions in terms of especially efficiency and effectiveness aspects. Agile teams save time from the (unnecessary parts of) rituals and focus on the main issues in the meetings by getting more goal-oriented, factual, efficient, and transparent. In this case, it is possible to say that Agile practices are under a conflicting influence during the pandemic.

Study [12] suggests modifying Scrum ceremonies as appropriate rather than sticking to a guide. They also stress the need for a different approach of processes [due to the decrease in ability in tacit knowledge] to produce a so-called single source of truth as the memory of the teams and organizations. In parallel to this suggestion, the teams should come with some out-of-box set-up for Scrum to meet the challenges of implementing Scrum specific activities during working from home. The teams also are expected to recalibrate their agile processes in their remote environments. Adaptation of Agile work practices, which is encountered as one of the challenges during the pandemic period, can be considered in this context. Although some studies state that implementations of these practices still exist as usual [31], there are cases of changes in the way these practices are performed by the agile teams [12]. These deviations may lead to inconsistent work practices observed in the agile teams.

A similar recalibration is required to strike a work-life balance for the individuals, especially after the intense involvement of life dynamics into every possible moment of working hours during the pandemic. In general, well-being and emotions of agile teams working at home have been negatively affected by the conditions of working from home, especially in terms of work-life balance with the new blurred boundaries of the business and life, feeling loneliness, decreased motivation and morale and more fatigue. Qualitatively speaking, all these effects regarding the Feeling aspect are strong enough to have severe negative impacts on teams in the long run. For the later stages of the pandemic or any form of working from home, the long-term impacts of these deep-seated effects on the Feelings of the teams should be thoroughly investigated. Besides, during working from home, with the possibilities of digitalization, agile teams in different geographical locations experience a better feeling of connectivity. In general, there are some studies assert that the teams can have an improved work-life balance and increased accountability.

For the Agility aspect, there are conflicting results of the studies. The majority of the results state positive impacts on agility as a result of increased flexibility, self-organization, and transparency. There are more negative effects than positive effects regarding leadership during the pandemic as it requires intensive communication with people, especially with newcomers. Like negative effects on the individuals in the agile teams, we see a similar case for the coherence within the individuals and their relationships. This situation can be attributed to the weakening of invisible ties across the individuals during working from home. Like the Feeling aspect of the individuals, the issues about the Coherence aspect can have unexpected and severe damages on the teams in the long run.

The more usage of digitalization, documentation, tools, and processes, play more crucial roles during the pandemic. In our work results, it is clearly seen that digitalization, documentation, and tools provide many benefits and directly affect the flexibility and agility of the teams. These artifacts stand on the right side, which is the less preferred side of the Agile Manifesto, can open a door for us to reconsider discovering more balanced ways with the right side. Even though the Agile Manifesto suggests to value individuals and interactions over processes and tools, we have seen how processes and especially tools support agility to be sustainable and interactions in a more efficient, faster, convenient, and, in other words, agile way. As stated by the study [7] "business people and developers [can] work together daily throughout the project" with the support of the digitalization tools.

It was stated by some studies that digitalization, compared to physical boards, enhances visual capabilities, and facilitates feedback channels and clarifications, resulting in more factual and precise, objective and efficient communication and collaboration, increased transparency and involvements of partners. Making meetings more goal-oriented, factual, and more efficient in this way raises doubt on the correctness of the following principle of the manifesto; "the most *efficient* and effective method of conveying information to and within a development team is face-to-face conversation". In the same vein, more documentation is needed in remote working to foster organizational memory. The fact that the pandemic has emphasized the need of having a proper enterprise memory, which is also valid in the form of close working, can be considered as a belated awareness of the Agile committee.

Within the online environment, the "frequent" meetings resulting from rituals of Scrum can be more casual and easier for the teams. As a reflection of this enhanced capability, it can become easier to establish closer contact with business units while the frequent meetings could be more difficult in an office environment hardly supporting these capabilities. Moreover, the extra exhaustion resulting from being in the office, combined with the high efforts for the frequent meetings of Scrum, appears as an additional challenge.

There may appear a loss of energy and motivation during working from home resulting in a decrease in the team's coherence. Easy and asynchronous communication causes more interruptions during working at home. Asynchronous and easily initiated digital communication in the pandemic may lead teams to more multitasking and distractions and less opportunity for focus. Especially in review and retrospective meetings of Scrum, which require intense human contacts [38], the online environments in this regard can reduce the impact on people compared to physical environments. However, the business units can involve more in the meetings with the support of the convenience of digital platforms.

A decrease in the "real" contact and connection capabilities within teams and team members during the pandemic may put a distance within people and, thus, may threaten trust in remote work. In this regard, a possible decrease in the capabilities of improvements, leadership, team cohesion and feeling of isolation, loneliness, low motivation, and disconnectedness are relevant. In the case of virtually working individuals, Sen [37] states that in communication, when body language, subtle tones, and facial gestures are not added to the spoken word, misinterpretations and misunderstandings and individual interpretations may create situations where each team member unknowingly "does his/her own thing" rather than following the team's agenda. That study adds the lack of relationship and trust, isolation, loneliness, and the feeling of disconnectedness that may erode energy and lessen commitment to the team. It is important to underline that it is possible for teams experiencing isolation, loneliness, and disconnectedness because of specialist culture, and cross-functionality after a while in the pandemic. Similarly, for the teams with high autonomy but low maturity or living in their early stages, control and balance issues may take part in organizations' management agenda.

Mancl and Fraser [20] foresee that many people appreciate working at home. Our study also exhibits several advantages and also several challenges of working at home. In particular, for the challenges, there can also be some other issues for the teams that have not raised in pandemic yet. In addition, the expectation that the pandemic will be temporary may have kept some organizations away from some long-term actions. After all, all these identified and further challenges may imply that self-organizing teams in Agile should re-invent some code of life that can be naturally very complex for the formation of remote working in the pandemic.

The results relating to the Coordination, Collaboration and Communication, Feeling, Productivity, Leadership, Coherence, and Quality aspects might also help non-agile teams with their working from home, since many aspects are transferable also to traditional processes. Putting Productivity and Quality aside since these two are more about the generic results, rest of these common themes emerged in agile teams experienced as deeper issues compared with the classical software development teams. The unique characteristic of agile teams in software development requires to deal with these encountered challenges to maintain a sustainable agile culture, as they need these capabilities more than the traditional teams. Additionally, in contexts where there is a problem about team cohesion within agile team members and/or agile teams, having estrangement from the central authority and different perceptions of authority by the teams may be a more possible and crucial problem compared to classical teams, because of the agile teams' self-organizing characteristics. In self-organizing agile teams, rather than applying a centralized decision structure, the structure of decentralized decision is applied where team members make independent decisions. It may make interactive decision-making process through dispersed team members problematic that may cause different perceptions of authority by the teams.

Geographically distributed and individually dispersed teams share common issues around virtually working. Like geographically distributed teams, individually dispersed teams operate in virtual environments leading to concerning virtual communication and collaboration [7], lack of face-to-face direct, synchronous and non-verbal communication, difficulties in building and maintaining trust, different perceptions of authority, lack of mechanisms for creating shared understanding, misunderstandings, inconsistent work practices, reduced cooperation and coordination, and control, knowledge management and leadership challenges that need to be overcome [35, 37]. Like in individually dispersed teams, the absence of togetherness and team cohesion, accompanied by common view of goals, and feeling of isolation, loneliness, low motivation and disconnectedness are also issues of the geographically distributed teams [35, 37]. Differently, study [35] reports the specialist culture problem for geographically distributed teams that has not been encountered in the studies for individually dispersed teams, yet.

5.2 Implications for Researchers

The research community is paying great attention to issues related to self-organizing teams in software development [35]. As a result, we have seen that considerable effort has been paid to identify the problems faced by co-located agile teams. There are also secondary studies that combine primary studies on this subject. It is possible to say that the subject is beyond the identification of the problems, rather at the stage of handling the issues of the teams working co-located. A similar result can be obtained for the teams that work in a classically distributed way. The relative saturation of the publications in these two fields is remarkable.

Although it is known that some cases exist for traditional teams, we have come across rare cases of agile teams working as individually dispersed teams before the pandemic, which is not surprising because of the agile teams' inclination to and need for working in co-location. When we look at the pandemic period, we can say that some earlier studies have just started to emerge. Specifically speaking, considering the year 2020 and 2021, publications at the LASD (International Conference on Lean and Agile Software Development) conference, which is specific to the field of Agile and the venue including the most papers in this scope, are remarkable in the number of the academic publications on this subject.

Co-location for agile teams allows frequent in-person contact, encourages instant communication, quickly builds trust, simplifies problem solving, and enables fast-paced decision-making [12]. Therefore, by considering the benefits gained from (co-located) agile teams, working from home in the pandemic that should come with a considerable shift in multiple facets needs further studies. Alternatively, the need for studies that will guide practitioners about the hybrid model, which includes the advantages of both working types, is increasing.

Although it is possible to say that the belief that the pandemic will not last long is prevalent, examining the effect of such a catastrophic change on agile teams will provide useful insights. It is a suggestion to academy to focus more on agile teams during the pandemic period. In this regard, our scope of the literature review was extended with so called grey literature, a non-peer-reviewed but supervised academic theses. Considering the relatively long durations of the publishing processes, it would be appropriate to say that this preference to expand the sources studied to find a sufficient number of papers strengthens our study conducted at this particular time. In addition, the fact that all of the studies from this particular branch are empirical studies has reduced our worry about their reliability.

6   Conclusion, Limitations and Future Work

This paper presents a systematic literature review to evaluate the effects of the Covid-19 pandemic on the agile software development teams. Two research questions were proposed: what new challenges the team members have faced and which advantages have occurred. Our study focuses on a timely new topic relevant for today and provides further insights into the post-pandemic time. It focuses on an important topic which is likely to play a greater role in the future after the pandemic. This topic has practical relevance since it affects most of the teams that had to change their way of working during the pandemic. Team members' distribution was already relevant and not sufficiently researched ahead of the pandemic, and also in the post-pandemic time, many teams are likely to keep a more flexible and remote way of working.

The study reveals that working from home during the pandemic poses some challenges and advantages. The challenges stress the importance of face-to-face communication that is vital especially for the agile teams. The newly learned advantages imply that we can lead to revising the understanding and value of the underestimated classical artifacts such as (digital) tools to communicate not effectively but efficiently and processes to connect dispersed members.

Our study contains all the hereditary limits and threats to the validity of a review study. Thus, the procedures used in our study have limitations in several ways. Only a single researcher extracted the data from the studies and this poses a threat to reliability. Also, we may have missed some relevant studies, as we did not include all possible variations of keywords since it is not practically possible to cover them all. In addition, we did not include all possible libraries. In particular, we may have missed the studies published in not-peer-reviewed sources. To mitigate the risk of this issue, we have used not an equivalent but multiple search string to cover a more comprehensive area. In addition, we have searched in the most appropriate databases such as Scopus and Google Scholar, in terms of their coverages.

For the quality of the selected papers, due to the relatively low number of relevant studies, we did not want to set a threshold value as it reduces the number of studies any further. Therefore, it may become an issue when including studies that were not very systematic. For instance, even though the data in some particular studies are insufficient, we included them. However, we have seen that the studies of low quality with insufficient data have a minor part of the whole. Some papers such as P1, P5, P6, and P9 seem to focus on negative aspects and P16 seem to focus on advantages. However, we are not sure if the involved people were asked neutrally about their work in these studies. Therefore, the studies may include a bias in this regard and this bias inherently transfers to our work.

. We have not seen a study among the existing works that makes a review on this subject. This study aims to fill this gap, for now. We are planning to repeat this study in the future to reach more better results. As a possible avenue for further studies, we plan to conduct a quantitative study to investigate the difference between on-site and working from home challenges. Working from home during the pandemic is not equals to dispersedly remote working during "normal times". Similar research can be conducted for dispersedly remote working during normal times and hybrid working (partially on-site and partially dispersedly working). The challenges specific to the pandemic imply that organizations should address issues and accordingly provide more flexible work environments for working at home, and that can be a subject for further studies in this area. Some adequate agile responses to such extreme crises can be located from technology startups, providing another further study for researchers to transfer those abilities to conventional organizations.

References

1. Madsen, D.Ø.: The evolutionary trajectory of the Agile concept viewed from a management fashion perspective. Soc. Sci. **9**(5), 69 (2020)
2. Fowler, M., Highsmith, J.: The agile manifesto. Softw. Dev. **9**(8), 28–35 (2001)
3. Gren, L., Torkar, R., Feldt, R.: Group development and group maturity when building agile teams: a qualitative and quantitative investigation at eight large companies. J. Syst. Softw. **124**, 104–119 (2017)
4. Brosseau, D., Ebrahim, S., Handscomb, C., Thaker, S.: The journey to an agile organization. McKinsey.com, May 2019
5. Moe, N.B., Dingsøyr, T., Dybå, T.: A teamwork model for understanding an agile team: a case study of a Scrum project. Inf. Softw. Technol. **52**(5), 480–491 (2010)
6. Sharp, H., Barroca, L., Deshpande, A., Gregory, P., Taylor, K.: Remote working in an Agile team (2016)
7. Neumann, M., Bogdanov, Y., Lier, M., Baumann, L.: The Sars-Cov-2 pandemic and agile methodologies in software development: a multiple case study in Germany. In: Przybyłek, A., Miler, J., Poth, A., Riel, A. (eds.) LASD 2021. LNBIP, vol. 408, pp. 40–58. Springer, Cham (2021). https://doi.org/10.1007/978-3-030-67084-9_3
8. Vallon, R., Dräger, C., Zapletal, A., Grechénig T.: Adapting to changes in a project's DNA: a descriptive case study on the effects of transforming agile single-site to distributed software development. In: Agile Conference, pp. 52–60 (2014)
9. Griffin, L.: Implementing lean principles in scrum to adapt to remote work in a Covid-19 impacted software team. In: Przybyłek, A., Miler, J., Poth, A., Riel, A. (eds.) LASD 2021. LNBIP, vol. 408, pp. 177–184. Springer, Cham (2021). https://doi.org/10.1007/978-3-030-67084-9_11
10. Herbsleb, J.D.: An empirical study of speed and communication in globally distributed software development. IEEE Trans. Software Eng. **29**(6), 481–494 (2003). https://doi.org/10.1109/TSE.2003.1205177
11. Przybyłek, A., Albecka, M., Springer, O., Kowalski, W.: Game-based Sprint retrospectives: multiple action research. Empir. Softw. Eng. **27**(1), 1–56 (2021). https://doi.org/10.1007/s10664-021-10043-z
12. Comella-Dorda, S., Garg, L., Thareja, S., Vasquez-McCall, B.: Revisiting agile teams after an abrupt shift to remote (2020). https://www.mckinsey.com/southern-us/~/media/McKinsey/Business%20Functions/Organization/Our%20Insights/Revisiting%20agile%20teams%20after%20an%20abrupt%20shift%20to%20remote/Revisiting-agile-teams-after-an-abrupt-shift-to-remote.pdf
13. Kude, T.: Agile software development teams during and after Covid-19 (2020). https://knowledge.essec.edu/en/innovation/agile-software-development-during-after-COVID19.html

14. Cucolas, A.A., Russo, D.: The impact of working from home on the success of scrum projects: a multi-method study, Computing Research Repository (CoRR), July 2021 (2021)
15. Kitchenham, B., Brereton, O.P., Budgen, D.: Systematic literature reviews in software engineering–a systematic literature review. Inf. Softw. Technol **51**, 7–15 (2009)
16. Nolan, A., et al.: To work from home (WFH) or not to work from home? Lessons learned by software engineers during the COVID-19 pandemic. In: Yilmaz, M., Clarke, P., Messnarz, R., Reiner, M. (eds.) EuroSPI 2021. CCIS, vol. 1442, pp. 14–33. Springer, Cham (2021). https://doi.org/10.1007/978-3-030-85521-5_2
17. Rehberg, B., Danoesastro, M., Kaul, S., Stutts, L.: How to remain remotely agile through COVID-19. Boston Consulting Group (2020)
18. Butt, S.A., Misra, S., Anjum, M.W., Hassan, S.A.: Agile project development issues during COVID-19. In: Przybyłek, A., Miler, J., Poth, A., Riel, A. (eds.) LASD 2021. LNBIP, vol. 408, pp. 59–70. Springer, Cham (2021). https://doi.org/10.1007/978-3-030-67084-9_4
19. Schmidtner, M., Doering, C., Timinger, H.: Agile working during COVID-19 pandemic. IEEE Eng. Manage. Rev. **49**(2), 18–32 (2021)
20. Mancl, D., Fraser, S.D.: COVID-19's influence on the future of agile. In: Paasivaara, M., Kruchten, P. (eds.) Agile Processes in Software Engineering and Extreme Programming – Workshops, XP 2020. LNBIP, vol. 396, pp. 309–316. Springer, Cham (2020). https://doi.org/10.1007/978-3-030-58858-8_32
21. Christoffersson, E., Djup, P.: How Covid-19 and working from home have affected agile software development. Master thesis (2021)
22. da Camara, R., Marinho, M., Sampaio, S., Cadete, S.: How do agile software startups deal with uncertainties by Covid-19 pandemic? Int. J. Softw. Eng. Appl. (IJSEA) **11**, 4 (2020)
23. Salnikov, N.: How software development methodologies affect dynamic capabilities under extreme contexts: a COVID-19 study on agile and waterfall methodologies. Master thesis (2021)
24. Ågren, P., Knoph, E.: COVID-19's impact on agile software development. Master thesis (2021)
25. Karlsson, A., Skötte, P.: Impact of Covid-19 on agile teams in small and medium-sized software companies. Master thesis (2021)
26. Badiale, M.E.: The dynamics of communication in global virtual software development teams: a case study in the agile context during the Covid-19 pandemic. Master thesis (2020)
27. Jose, J.: The effect of pandemic related restrictions on agile team productivity in software industry. Master thesis (2021)
28. Saarenoksa, M.: The impact of flexible working on productivity and job satisfaction: case future of work in agile R&D. Master thesis (2021)
29. Valgeirsdóttir, H.: The scrum master's responsibilities in distributed work. Master thesis (2021)
30. Palumbo, G.: The impacts of the Covid-19 crisis on teams working with agile methods in the IT sector. Master thesis (2021)
31. Marek, K., Wińska, E., Dąbrowski, W.: The state of agile software development teams during the Covid-19 pandemic. In: Przybyłek, A., Miler, J., Poth, A., Riel, A. (eds.) LASD 2021. LNBIP, vol. 408, pp. 24–39. Springer, Cham (2021). https://doi.org/10.1007/978-3-030-67084-9_2
32. Korkala, M.: Waste identification as the means for improving communication in globally distributed agile software development. J. Syst. Softw. **95**(C), 122–140 (2014). https://doi.org/10.1016/j.jss.2014.03.080
33. Mehrabian, A.: Nonverbal communication. In: Nebraska Symposium on Motivation. University of Nebraska Press (1971)
34. Ivetic, P.: Holding the house of cards together: possible pitfalls with self-organizing teams in organizations. Econophys. Sociophys. Multidisc. Sci. J. (ESMSJ), 51–57 (2017)

35. Kaur, H., Haddad, H.M.: Distributed agile development: a survey of challenges and solutions. In: Proceedings of the International Conference on Software Engineering Research and Practice (SERP) (2015)
36. Moe, N.B., Dingsøyr, T., Dybå, T.: Overcoming barriers to self-management in software teams. IEEE Softw. **26**(6), 20–26 (2009)
37. Sen, S.: Globally dispersed project teams: interaction space management. Doctoral dissertation, Massachusetts Institute of Technology (2001)

How a 4-Day Work Week and Remote Work Affect Agile Software Development Teams

Julia Topp[1]([✉]), Jan Hendrik Hille[1], Michael Neumann[1]([✉]),
and David Mötefindt[2]

[1] Hochschule Hannover - University of Applied Sciences and Arts,
Ricklinger Stadtweg 120, 30459 Hannover, Germany
{julia.topp,jan-hendrik.hille}@stud.hs-hannover.de,
michael.neumann@hs-hannover.de
[2] Agile Move, Ackerstr. 16, 30851 Langenhagen, Germany
info@agile-move.de

Abstract. *Context:* Agile software development (ASD) sets social aspects like communication and collaboration in focus. Thus, one may assume that the specific work organization of companies impacts the work of ASD teams. A major change in work organization is the switch to a 4-day work week, which some companies investigated in experiments. Also, recent studies show that ASD teams are affected by the switch to remote work since the Covid 19 pandemic outbreak in 2020. *Objective:* Our study presents empirical findings on the effects on ASD teams operating remote in a 4-day work week organization. *Method:* We performed a qualitative single case study and conducted seven semi-structured interviews, observed 14 agile practices and screened eight project documents and protocols of agile practices. *Results:* We found, that the teams adapted the agile method in use due to the change to a 4-day work week environment and the switch to remote work. The productivity of the two ASD teams did not decrease. Although the stress level of the ASD team member increased due to the 4-day work week, we found that the job satisfaction of the individual ASD team members is affected positively. Finally, we point to affects on social facets of the ASD teams. *Conclusion:* The research community benefits from our results as the current state of research dealing with the effects of a 4-day work week on ASD teams is limited. Also, our findings provide several practical implications for ASD teams working remote in a 4-day work week.

Keywords: Agile methods · Agile software development · Remote work · 4-day work week · Alternative work schedule · Covid 19

1 Introduction

In the last two decades, agile approaches became state-of-the-art in the area of software development [27]. The agile manifesto was developed 20 years ago in

© Springer Nature Switzerland AG 2022
A. Przybyłek et al. (Eds.): LASD 2022, LNBIP 438, pp. 61–77, 2022.
https://doi.org/10.1007/978-3-030-94238-0_4

order to provide a common understanding of values and principles [5]. Agile methods are characterized by an intensified involvement of stakeholders and many interactions among the team members [1]. This focus on collaboration and communication is manifested by agile practices [29], which are described in the guidelines of well-known agile methods like Scrum [25] or Extreme Programming [4].

Alternative work schedules and the 4-day work week in particular is a topic of interest in research and practice, which goes back to the 1970s [13]. Though the concept of a 4-day work week is not established in practice, several companies [7] and public administrations [28] implemented experiments and pilots to test the effects of a compressed work week. Several studies present empirical findings concerning the effects of a compressed work week (e.g., [8,10]). For instance, Facer and Wadsworth [12] investigate the effects of a compressed work week schedule on facets like the employee satisfaction and the work-life balance. They emphasize that the productivity of the employees is positively influenced. Further, they did not find a significant change concerning job satisfaction or work-life balance. One can assume, that a switch to a compressed 4-day work week may affects the work of agile software development teams due to the high relevance of social aspects of agile methods, as described above.

Another facet related to alternative work forms and work organization types can be observed by the effects of the Covid 19 pandemic and the switch to remote work [19]. As remote work seems to be a suitable solution to keep companies in business and their employees safe, many companies worldwide sent their employees to work from home. Several studies describe the switch to remote work as a challenge for agile software development teams, as it affects teams collaboration, communication, productivity (e.g., [6,21,24]) and performance (e.g., [16,18,20]). The switch to remote work also lead to a adaption of agile practices and roles in use [9]. For instance, the methodological implementation of agile practices like estimation techniques or retrospective and review meetings are affected by the virtualization of the collaboration [18,20]. Schmidtner et al. [24] emphasize the effects on future work in agile software development. They point to the expectation of agile software development team members and experts that the remote work and use of tools will increase.

In this study, related questions concerning a 4-day work week and the switch to remote work are addressed to teams of a global company using agile methods in their software development departments. A pilot of a 4-day work week was introduced at the beginning of 2021. Our key objective of the study is the investigation and analysis of the effects on agile software development teams working in a 4-day work week and a remote working environment. Thus, we defined the following research questions:

RQ 1: Does the 4-day work week affect the use of agile methods? If so, how do teams adapt to the new circumstances?

RQ 2: Do the 4-day work week and remote work affect the productivity of agile software development teams?

RQ 3: Do the 4-day work week and remote work affect the job satisfaction and stress level of agile software development team members?

RQ 4: How does the 4-day work week combined with remote work due to the Covid 19 pandemic affect the social culture of agile software development teams?

This paper is structured as follows: In Sect. 2, we provide an overview of the related work. We explain the selected research design in Sect. 3. We present the results of the paper at hand in Sect. 4 and present our findings based on the research questions in the Subsects. 4.1, 4.2, 4.3 and 4.4. The discussion of our results and practical implications are presented in Sect. 5. We describe the Threads to Validity in Sect. 6 before the paper closes with a summary in Sect. 7.

2 Related Work

In order to identify related work, we searched for studies and surveys, which are dealing with topics close to our context. In this section, we present an overview of the related work. We start with the recent studies dealing with the effects of the remote work during Covid 19 and close the section with the related work on 4-day work week.

The effects of the switch to remote work before the Covid 19 pandemic on agile software development teams have been barely investigated in recent years. However, against the backdrop of the Covid 19 pandemic, the topic gained in importance. As a result, several studies have been published dealing with the influences of the switch to remote work during the pandemic, the accompanying changes in agile software development team work organization, and the challenges of the new circumstances [19].

Various studies dealing with the influence on productivity and performance of agile software development teams during Covid 19. However, the results presented in the recent studies show differences. Butt et al. [6] investigated the positive and negative effects on agile software development teams during the pandemic in early 2021 by setting productivity in focus. The authors found that the productivity of agile software development teams decreased due to a minor coordination in the teams. Russo et al. [23] present in their study a correlation between the well-being and productivity. They point to the increased well-being of team members during the pandemic. In contrast, Ralph et al. [21], which are also dealing with the correlation of well-being and productivity, found that the productivity of agile software development teams decreased during the Covid 19 pandemic. The finding of a decreased productivity is also presented by Schmidtner et al. [24].

Neumann et al. [18] investigated the effects on the performance of agile software development teams during the Covid 19 pandemic. They found that the perceived performance of German agile software development teams did not decrease due to the switch to remote work. The authors emphasize the positive influence of an increased transparency of the development process and the agile artifacts in use. Another qualitative study presented by O Connor et al. [20] shows a positive effect on the performance of agile software development teams.

Furthermore, Marek et al. [16] do not find significant changes concerning the performance of agile software development teams in their survey results.

Various studies show, that agile software development teams are able to rapidly react to the new circumstances due to the switch to remote work. The adaptions mainly occurred by the virtualization of agile practices. DaCamara et al. [9] and Neumann et al. [18] found, that the specific method of used agile practices is affected. For example, they point to the use of tools like Retrium for retrospective meetings or the digitization of Kanban and Sprint Boards using Miro. Also specific techniques according to the effort estimation in planning meetings changed. Smite et al. [26] investigated the effects of remote work on the agile practice pair programming. The authors found that the use of pair programming decreased during Covid 19. They argue this with the increased effort of conducting the agile practice and a faster fatigue of the involved team members.

Another facet presented in several studies is the impact on social aspects, especially the communication and collaboration when using agile methods. Marek et al. [16] analyzed the impact of the switch to remote work on agile software development teams. The authors emphasize communication as an effect that has a positive impact on the work of agile software development teams through the stable productivity. In contrast, several authors describe a rather negative influence on communication and collaboration (e.g., [18,23]). Neumann et al. [18] referring to the challenge of intercollegiate communication and thus, a decreased social exchange between the team members. Also, DaCamara et al. [9] and O Connor et al. [20] describe similar negative effects on the social aspects of agile software development teams. Griffin [14] describes that the risk of distractions during remote work is increased.

To the best of our best knowledge, we found no peer reviewed studies in similar research context related to agile software development and the 4-day work week. Thus, we decided to search for literature dealing with the 4-day work week related to software development. Alfares [2] presents a model for scheduling a 4-day work week, which aims to optimize the work organization and decrease the cost (and number) of employees. Also, we found grey literature related to our study. For instance, two white papers describe that a 4-day work week increases employee productivity as well as work motivation and satisfaction [3,15]. This results especially from the flexibility between the professional activity and the private environment. Furthermore, several articles discussing a experiment, which was performed by Microsoft (e.g., [7,11]).

3   Research Approach

3.1   Research Design

We selected a case study approach and conducted the study based on the guidelines from Runeson and Höst [22]. We chose the exploratory research approach and argue our choice with the limited published research in the field. From our point of view, it is important to gain a deep understanding of how the agile software development teams react to the new situation working in a remote setting in a 4-day work week organization environment. Thus, we decided to select a qualitative research approach according to the guidelines from Yin [30], Runeson and Hoest [22].

Our research design is mainly organized in three steps. We present the research design in Fig. 1. First, we searched for existing literature in order to be able to identify the relevant influencing factors related to our topics 4-day work week and remote work during the Covid 19 pandemic. Based on these influencing factors we defined our research questions, which we present in the introduction. The research questions are the structural basis for our data collection methods. In a second step, we used the research questions to prepare the data collection, which we describe in detail in Subsect. 3.3. Based on the influencing factors and our research questions, we structured the data analysis (see Subsect. 3.4).

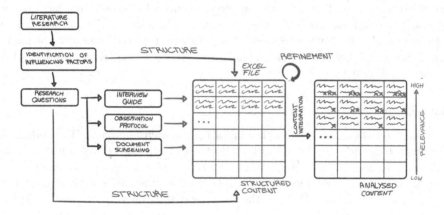

Fig. 1. Research design

3.2 Research Context

We conducted our study at the company Pritchett Inc. (anonymized). The Pritchett Inc. is an online marketing company and operates worldwide. Approximately 1000 employees working for the company.

As our study deals with agile software development, we focus on the software development departments of the company. Pritchett Inc. owns five software development departments in four countries (Germany, Poland, United Kingdom and United States of America). We performed the study in one software development department in Germany and conducted the data collection in two agile software development teams: Manny and Mitchell (both also anonymized).

Pritchett Inc. sent their employees worldwide to work from home caused by the Covid 19 pandemic in March 2020 and closed the offices for onsite work partially related to the Covid 19 situation in the country or region. The switch to remote work were new for most of the employees at the German software development departments, as it was totally common to work onsite in the offices. However, the switch to remote work was supported by several tools, which were already in use by the teams. The agile software development teams under study used Microsoft Teams and Slack, also before the switch to remote work, because stakeholder and product owners are working from other departments, also from other countries. Actually, the company is organized by a work where ever, whenever you want principle. The employees can decide by themselves, if they want to work from home or be onsite in the office. This also applies to Pritchett Inc. departments in other cities or countries the employees want to go and work remotely.

In summer 2020, Pritchett Inc. started an experiment of a compressed work week. For the second half of 2020 the company switched to a 4.5-day work week. This experiment was adapted in January 2021, as Prittecht Inc. announced the switch to a 4-day work week, which means one off day per week by non-effects of the salary. For the support of this major organizational change, the company provided several guidelines to the employees concerning aspects on vacation or illness. The employees have the opportunity to define one off day per week. The off day can vary from week to week. Also, the Pritchett Inc. management made clear, that the 4-day work week still has the status of an experiment. Today, this status is still active.

3.3 Data Collection

As described above, we selected a qualitative research approach. We conducted the data collection in three ways in both agile software development teams between March and May 2021: Semi-structured interviews with agile software development team members, observations of agile practices and team meetings and screening of documents from the software development teams and Prittchet Inc.

We conducted the semi-structured interviews in English based on a prepared interview guideline (see Appendix A). The interview guide consists of four phases: Information phase, warm-up and introduction phase, main phase and closing phase. In the information phase the interviewee get an introduction of the interviewer, a clarification of the objectives of the study based on prepared text phrases and organizational aspects, like asking the agreement of audio recording. The warm-up and introduction phase aims to collect specific information of the interviewee. For instance, what is the current role in the team. The main phase is organized based on the four research questions. In the closing phase we ask the interviewee for further questions or any aspects the person wants to add. The interview closes with thanks for participating.

In total, we conducted seven interviews. An overview of the interviewees concerning their roles, teams and experiences is presented in Table 1. We selected the interviewees based on two criteria. First, the interviewee should be working at Pritchett Inc. at least since 2019. Second, we wanted to interview at least two members of each team. Every interview was conducted by an interviewer and at least one other researcher, which protocols the interview. Also, we were able to record the audio of the interviews by the consent of the interviewees. Later, we created transcripts of each interview. We conducted all interviews with activated cameras on both sides: The interviewer and the interviewee. The interviews took an' average of around 40 min.

Table 1. Profiles of the interviewees

ID	Current role	Team	Years of experience in ASD
P01	Scrum Master	Both teams	12
P02	Lead Engineer	Mitchell	5
P03	Lead Engineer	Manny	13
P04	Software Engineer	Mitchell	1.5
P05	Software Engineer	Mitchell	4
P06	Software Developer	Mitchell	12
P07	Software Developer	Manny	11.5

The collected data through observation of agile practices and team meetings was documented in a standardized protocol (see Appendix B). We conducted 14 observations in total. An overview of the observations is given in Table 2. Every meeting was held virtually using Microsoft Teams. The observation was planned in collaboration with the Lead Engineers of the teams. Two researchers observed the agile practices meetings and documented their notes in the above mentioned protocol. After the observation the researchers cross-checked the collected data. The observed Sprint Plannings consists of the agile practices planning, retrospective and review meetings. The Sprint Planning 2 is used for the creation of work items related to the specific backlog items.

The third data source are several documents created by the agile software development teams and the Prittchet Inc. company. In total, we screened eight documents. Three of these documents are provided by Pritchett Inc.: Guideline for organization requirements related to the 4-day work week, guideline for requirements concerning the work wherever/whenever principle and an employee survey. The survey aims to gain an understanding of "drivers" (aspects) like the well-being, workload, management support or job satisfaction of the employees.

The survey data was filtered to the department under study. The team related documents we screened are: Two team radar protocols from retrospective meetings, team internal guidelines concerning meeting organization and remote work. Finally, we checked the performance analysis data from the teams, which are exported from the task management system Jira.

Table 2. Overview of the observations

ID	Meeting/Agile practice	Team	Nr. of participants
B01	Coffee break	Both teams	7
B02	Sprint planning	Mitchell	9
B03	Sprint planning 2	Mitchell	4
B04	Sprint planning	Manny	10
B05	Sprint planning 2	Manny	5
B06	Monthly department meeting	Both teams	20
B07	Daily stand up	Manny	3
B08	Daily stand up	Mitchell	5
B09	Coffee break	Both teams	5
B10	Sprint planning	Mitchell	10
B11	Sprint planning 2	Mitchell	5
B12	Sprint Planning	Manny	8
B13	Daily stand up	Manny	10
B14	Daily stand up	Mitchell	10

3.4   Data Analysis

As shown in Fig. 1, our data analysis was done in three steps. First, we created an Excel file and used the research questions and identified influencing factors from the literature as a structural basis. In a second step we transferred our collected data to the structured Excel file. Based on the structured data in the Excel file we coded our data into 25 codes and eight categories. This coding was initially done close to our collected data and refined by cross check iterations from the researchers. Third, we used the structured (coded and categorized) content to analyze, which information is more or less relevant for our study results. This was mainly done by content triangulation using a virtual whiteboard in Miro. We checked individually, which information can be found how often in the structured data content per data collection method and discussed our results in the researcher group. The more often information was identified, the relevance of the finding increases. Finally, the analyzed content provides us the possibility to evaluate the information ordered by their relevance according to the research questions.

4   Results

4.1   RQ 1: Effects on the Agile Method in Use

Due to the introduction of the 4-day work week, the agile method used has been adapted, because less time with a constant workload resulted in a tighter schedule. This adjustment was reflected in the statements made during the interviews. These revealed that the length of the sprints was reduced from two to one week

(P01–P07), as P01 described: *"We also did sprint time boxing and shortened our sprints from two weeks to one week."* As a consequence of the shortened sprint length, agile practices related to the sprint change (sprint n → sprint n+1) were adapted. The affected agile practices are the planning, review and retrospective meetings. All of these agile practices were shortened in time (P01, P05). Several interviewees mentioned, that all non-urgent meetings were marked as optional as an additional adaption (P01, P02, P04, P06). For instance, P02 said: *"In the past we had more spontaneous meetings that were not well prepared because we immediately go to a meeting room when a topic was coming up. Now when a topic is raising up we discuss if the meeting is needed."* Non-urgent meetings are all those meetings, that do not actively contribute to the productive progress of a project. In addition to the statements of the interviewees, the observations confirmed these results (B01–B14).

4.2 RQ 2: Effects on the Productivity

With regard to the productivity of the agile software development teams, the effects of remote work and the 4-day work week in relation to professional communication, effectiveness and stress were examined. We found that professional communication had become more efficient. All interviewees indicated that meetings are more coordinated and focused. Almost half of all interviewees declared that the number of meetings were decreasing and were taking less time (P01, P04, P07). The Scrum Master (P01) explains: *"The number and the duration of meetings changed. So we also reduce the time for meetings as well where it was possible"* In addition, fewer private conversations and interruptions are taking place in meetings (P01–P04), as P03 describes: *"The meetings in remote work are much more focused. There is less small talk and not that many interruptions during the meeting for example that someone needs a break or comes late. It's easier to deal with meeting series"* The other interviewees noted that the number of meetings had not changed (P02, P05, P06). The different statements are probably affected due to the roles of the team members, as lead roles generally attend more meetings. Furthermore, discussions arising in meetings were overly technical (P01, P03, P04): *"Communication is way more efficient communication and on point. In the office there were more small talks an personal conversations at the beginning and in the end of a meeting. Now we have nearly only work-related discussions in the online meetings."* (P01) Nine out of 14 observed meetings showed that work-related communication was mostly not interrupted by private conversations (B03, B04, B06, B07, B08, B11, B12, B13, B14). Since the beginning of 2021, one project team has set meeting guidelines in their Confluence space. They not only contain a code of conduct but also rules for meeting organization, participation, and documentation. This provides a better structured communication in meetings. In both agile software development teams, staff absence days are tabulated in Confluence in relation to the 4-day week to ensure better coordination for meetings.

Similarly, we found that work had become more efficient since the switch to remote work. Six out of seven interviewees reported the same amount of work

(P01, P02, P06, P07) or more work (P03, P04) in the same amount of time since the introduction of remote work. One Engineer describes: "*Reducing one day per week, its obvious that this will produce overtime. But I have to mention that the company is still working 5 days a week, just the employees are working 4 days a week. So I just work further when I know I have my day off tomorrow.*"(P04) This was argued by the agile software development team members due to concentrated a focused manner while working from home, because there are no decreased disruptive factors such as loudness, small talks with colleagues or other interruptions (P01–P07 and B01, B03-B09, B11, B12–B14): "*Before we had a big office space where it was sometimes very loud and even if colleagues pass by we just have a short conversation what was kind of interrupting you.*" (P01). The working time on the four working days had basically increased (P01, P03–P06), as an engineer states (P06): "*Yes, [I work more overtime] because we have our goals in the sprint planning. And if we see that the time is running out, we do some overtime to get these tasks finished.*" However, this could be attributed more to the project-related time pressure in the individual projects than to the 4-day work week or remote work (P05–P07). The statements from the interviews were also reflected in retrospective meetings. We verified retrospective protocols and found that since the deployment switch of remote work the workload increased temporarily but not continuously. In addition, the velocity report and the log of the solved tickets show a positive increase in the velocity and solved tickets in the time of the changeover to remote work and the 4-day work week. This strengthens our findings about the increase of efficiency.

4.3   RQ 3: Effects on the Job Satisfaction and Stress Level

Effects on the Job Satisfaction: The 4-day work week and remote work have a positive effect on the work of the agile software development teams by increasing job satisfaction: "*Definitely [I like working from home]. I feel more productive. To go to office is more for socializing, team-building and workshops. Currently I think it's the best way how we could work in the future.*" (P02) The quieter working place and flexible work scheduling enable a more productive work environment (P01–P03, P05–P07). Likewise, the elimination of commuting (P03–P06) and a better work-life balance (P06, P05) lead all respondents to be satisfied with remote work (P01–P07). The observations and document review confirm this by noting a calm work atmosphere without any interruptions in 11 out of 14 observed meetings (B01, B03–B14), as well as an upward trend in the "Satisfaction" section of the team radar since the introduction of remote work.

In addition, the introduction of remote work leads to an increase in work motivation among the employees (P01-P05, P07). Only one respondent noted that his work motivation dependents on the project (P06), the engineer describes: "*It always depends for me on the project, not on the remote work. For 4-day-work week the motivation is higher, because at the moment it's a test phase so we need to be successful with that so we can continue. I think that's what motivates everyone.*" The section "Accomplishment" in the employee survey reflects the statements of the interviewees. Since the introduction of remote work, satisfaction with work performance has increased. Besides, the sufficient provision of work equipment also contributes to employee satisfaction (P01–P07), as P03 explains: "*We all have Notebooks from [Pritchett Inc.] and we are allowed to collect some hardware from the office.*" Due to defined guidelines in advance, the procurement of equipment for remote work is determined. These guidelines enable employees to obtain additional equipment at company's expense. This option was taken up by some respondents, for example, to get a better keyboard or a screen with a higher resolution (P02, P05). In addition to remote work, the 4-day week also leads to job satisfaction among employees because they feel happier, more balanced, and more satisfied (P01–P07). One lead engineer (P02) states: "*I think the biggest change is that everyone is really happy with it. You see it in terms that everybody is motivated. Everyone seems very satisfied. The 4 day week is a real life changer.*" Reasons for this are the individually usable day off once a week, which offers more relaxation (P02, P04), the more flexible work schedule (P01–P06) and the additional time with the family (P01, P03). The Section "Engagement" and "Workload" in the employee survey reinforced these statements, because firstly, the employee satisfaction has steadily increased since the introduction of remote work and secondly, a further increase is visible since the 4-day work week. Furthermore, employees do not perceive any negative impact on their workload, but rather draw positive effects from the introduction of remote work and the 4-day work week.

Effects on the Stress Level of Agile Software Development Team Members: Due to the 4-day work week, the work-related stress of the employees had increased (P02, P04, P06, P07): "*Sometimes it's a bit more stressful than before. On some days the organization of tasks is harder because certain people may not be in office at that day because of 4-day work week. So, we need to organize more, that results in a bit more stress.*" (P06) According to the interviewees, this is related to the compressed workdays (P03, P06, P07) and the frequent context changes (P03, P07). However, for agile software development team members, an additional day off as well as the elimination of commuting time seem to be more important benefits (P01–P05, P07), as Engineer P04 states: "*I would say because of one day more, its more flexibility and its relaxing my week more. I can plan this day as I want, so that's improving my private life.*" Although work stress had increased, this did not lead to more intercollegiate conflicts (P02–P04, P06, P07) in the teams. This statement is also confirmed by the aspect "Peer Relationship" in the employee survey, in which the relationship between colleagues was examined. Here, there are no changes compared to the time before remote work. Despite the increased work-related stress, remote work and the 4-day work week leads to less stress in private everyday life due to more flexible leisure time and the elimination of commuting (P01–P06): "*I am less stressed. Right now, I have no way to the office and back home. So, there I have no stress to get the train. I have a better work life balance right now and I am more flexible.*" (P05)

4.4 RQ 4: Effects on the Social Culture

The 4-day work week has an impact on the social culture in the agile software development teams due to the compressed working schedule. This results mainly in a low willingness to participate in meetings with social context (B01, B09). Interviewees perceive these meetings as an interruption of active participation in the team (P01, P02, P05–P07). Engineer P07 states: "*For these meetings, it's always the same people who are participating in these kinds of meetings. Often, I don't participate either because in Pair-Sessions we just keep working instead of taking part because we have no time for this.*" Some would replace them by the continued work as soon as there were time constraints (P01, P05, P07), the Scrum Master describes: "*The acceptance of the personal online events is very rare because you skip these meetings instant when there is much work pressure due to the tight schedule. But some colleagues are taking these meetings every time. Some never come.*" The observations of meetings with a social focus confirm the interviewees' statements (B01, B09). Another effect on the social culture in the teams is caused by the more professional working environment mentioned by the interviewees (P02, P03, P05, P06). Reasons for this change were a propagated focus on work issues (P03) and a stronger separation of work environment and lunch break due to remote work (P06). In addition to the statements from the interviewees, the observed meetings also show a focused and goal-oriented execution. Furthermore, an efficient time management with adherence to time frames and no interruptions were observed (B03, B04, B06–B08, B11–B14). Besides, a low proportion of social communication in comparison to the total communication during these meetings was observed (B02, B04, B05, B08–B10). Despite the effects already mentioned, some interviewees assessed the relationship with their team members as unchanged (P02, P05–P07) or only slightly worse (P01, P02, P04). This estimation was also confirmed by internal documentation concerning the team member satisfaction, where no negative change in the relationships between team members can be seen.

5 Discussion and Practical Implications

Based on the results of our study, we discuss the findings with the aim to provide practical implications.

First and foremost, our results show a higher level of the perceived work-related stress due to the tighter schedule. The facet of increased stress in agile software development teams is also shown by other studies (e.g., [17]). However, an increased stress level by the development team members may occur due to other aspects like the project situation or is only temporarily due to the new situation and decreases if new routines had been established. Also, this aspect may affected by the switch to remote work of the agile software development teams (e.g., [6]) even though the teams under study switched to remote work due to the Covid 19 pandemic in March 2020. We recommend questioning time boxes, such as meeting duration or sprint lengths, and experiment with shortening the time available in order to increase efficiency within the time boxes. Lean principles can be used to identify waste in all aspects of agile software development. This aspect should improve the performance especially due to the tighter time boxes of correlated agile practices like planning, review or retrospective meeting. We also assume that the tighter iteration time and more often performed the respective meetings lead to an increased optimization of work processes and organization. The focus of the actual prioritized requirements should also be increased, which seems to be helpful in the Covid 19 pandemic time as it provides the opportunity to react more quickly to changed circumstances. However, it should be taken into account that the work-related stress level of the team members may increase. Thus, we recommend coaching roles to focus on the social facets, especially the well-being and stress level of the team members to avoid negative effects.

Related to the introduction of a compressed work schedule we recommend a smooth switch to a 4-day work week. The switch to a 4.5-day work week for the first months seems to be a good approach, as it provides the opportunity for the agile software development teams to react to the new circumstances and test potential constraints of the work organization. The subsequent change to a 4-day work week seems to be easier for the teams as they are used to react to a compressed working schedule. Further, we point to several constraints concerning the 4-day work week. From our point of view, the maturity of the agile software development teams should be of importance as the team members have experience with relevant characteristics of agile methods especially the self-organization or Kaizen approach. Thus, they are able to react to new circumstances quickly and find solutions for related challenges. Teams without such an experience should be facilitated by supporting roles like agile coaches or scrum masters. It seems to be quite obvious that a compressed working schedule may not be useful for other business fields, e.g., the manufacturing industry, as the work processes are already optimized on a high level and the increase of efficiency should be quite low. We also point to other potential constraints like the organizational culture, which may effect the ability of the agile software development teams to experiment new approaches and optimize continuously one's own approach.

6 Threats to Validity

It is important to take several limitation into account when conducting case studies with a qualitative research method [22].

Construct Validity: In this study, we considered the 4-day work week and remote work together, as both work organization types were used simultaneously at the time of the research. The design of our interview guideline counteract this aspect, as we designed the questions specifically to the two work organization types (remote work and 4-day work week). The interviews took an average of around 40 min. This length can be tiring for the interviewees and may lead to shorter answers towards the end of the interview than at the beginning. To counteract this effect, we conducted all interviews during regular working hours and pointed out that a time buffer of at least 10 min should be planned for the next scheduled appointment. Another aspect is the risk of not identifying all of the relevant literature, as we used recent studies to identify the influencing factors. Thus, we searched for related literature in several digital libraries and refined our search rings in iterative search runs.

Internal Validity: Although a thorough analysis of recent literature was the basis for developing our interview guideline and observation protocol, some internal validity threats need to be taken into account. In order to avoid bias, we took several measures. First, the interview guideline consists of non-leading questions. Also, the interviews were designed as semi-structured. Thus, we were able to go in-depth in those directions the interviewee aims for. The interviewers did not personally know the interviewees. All interviews were conducted by at least two researchers. We also recorded every interview and created transcripts later. As a further measure, the researchers verified the transcripts from the recording, before we analyzed the data on detail.

Furthermore, we used several triangulation types to strengthen the validity of our results as recommended by Runeson and Hoest [22] and Yin [30]. We used different data collection types and sources. This triangulation helped us to optimize the consistency of our findings.

External Validity: It is worth to mention, that the external validity could be higher with integrating more cases considered in Prittchet Inc. and in other companies, industries or countries. Further, the phenomena under study should affect other departments (e.g., marketing or human resources). Thus, a further analysis of non agile software development teams may be interesting, as the switch to the 4-day work week and remote work affects the other departments.

7   Conclusion and Future Work

This study presents our findings on the effects of a 4-day work week and the remote work of agile software development teams. In this section we summarize the results and provide ideas for future work.

In summary, the 4-day work week and remote work have various positive influences on the agile software development teams under study. First, the introduction of the two work organization models leads to an increased job satisfaction and productivity. However, we also found that the stress level of the team members increased.

Second, the shortened work week and the resulting tighter schedule primarily affect the social exchange within the agile software development teams. In addition, the 4-day work week leads to adaptions of the agile method in use. Both, the sprint length and several agile practices such as planning, review and retrospective meetings were adapted in particular concerning their length due to the compressed working time of the team members. Due to the compressing of the working time and the adaption of agile practices, the communication and execution of the agile practices is straight forward and become more formal.

We confirm effects of the remote work presented by recent studies, such as the reduced social interaction among the team members.

The 4-day work week and remote work seem to represent a flexible working model for the future to enable a better work-life balance and generally increase the job satisfaction and motivation of employees. To counteract the observed negative effects of the reduction of social communication, we recommend to implement regular workshops and events organized in onsite settings.

In the context of this study, the 4-day work week and remote work were considered together, as both work organization models were used simultaneously at the time of our data collection. Future research could investigate which effects can be attributed to the 4-day work week or remote work in detail. This will gain a deeper understanding of these two work organization models and, where appropriate, provide new application scenarios and opportunities for organizing remote working agile software development teams. In addition, we recommend to transfer the research context to other settings to compare the two work organization models depending on aspects like the industry or company size.

Appendix A

The interview guideline is available at the academic cloud: Download Link

Appendix B

The observation protocol is available at the academic cloud: Download Link

References

1. Abrahamsson, P., Salo, O., Ronkainen, J., Warsta, J.: Agile software development methods: Rev. Anal. **478**, 7–94 (2002)
2. Alfares, H.K.: Flexible 4-day workweek scheduling with weekend work frequency constraints. Comput. Ind. Eng. **44**(3), 325–338 (2003). https://doi.org/10.1016/S0360-8352(02)00192-4
3. Andrews, J.: A 4-day working week? [white paper] (2016). https://bakerstuart.com/wp-content/uploads/2016/01/White-paper-Four-Day-working-week.pdf
4. Beck, K.: Extreme Programming Explained: Embrace Change. Addison-Wesley, Boston, 5. print edn. (2000)
5. Beck, K., et al.: Agile manifesto (2001). https://agilemanifesto.org/
6. Butt, S.A., Misra, S., Anjum, M.W., Hassan, S.A.: Agile project development issues during COVID-19. In: Przybyłek, A., Miler, J., Poth, A., Riel, A. (eds.) LASD 2021. LNBIP, vol. 408, pp. 59–70. Springer, Cham (2021). https://doi.org/10.1007/978-3-030-67084-9_4
7. Chappell, B.: 4-day workweek boosted workers' productivity by 40%, microsoft japan say (2019). https://www.npr.org/2019/11/04/776163853/microsoft-japan-says-4-day-workweek-boosted-workers-productivity-by-40
8. Chow, I.H., Chew, I.K.: The effect of alternative work schedules on employee performance. Int. J. Empoly. Stud. **14**, 105–130 (2006)

9. Da Camara, R., Marinho, M., Sampaio, S., Cadete, S.: How do agile software startups deal with uncertainties by Covid-19 pandemic? Int. J. Softw. Eng. Appl. **11**(4), 15–34 (2020). https://doi.org/10.5121/ijsea.2020.11402

10. Dunham, R.B., Pierce, J.L., Castaneda, M.B.: Alternative work schedules: two field quasi-experiments. Person. Psychol. **40**, 215–242 (1987). https://doi.org/10.1111/j.1744-6570.1987.tb00602.x

11. Eadicicco, L.: Microsoft experimented with a 4-day workweek, and productivity jumped by 40% (2019). https://www.businessinsider.com/microsoft-4-day-work-week-boosts-productivity-2019-11

12. Facer, R.L., Wadsworth, L.: Alternative work schedules and work-family balance: a research note. Rev. Public Person. Adm. **28**, 166–177 (2008). https://doi.org/10.1177/0734371X08315138

13. Goodale, J.G., Aagaard, A.K.: Factors relating to varying reactions to the 4-day workweek. J. Appl. Psychol. **60**, 33–38 (1975). https://doi.org/10.1037/h0076345

14. Griffin, L.: Implementing lean principles in scrum to adapt to remote work in a Covid-19 impacted software team. In: Przybyłek, A., Miler, J., Poth, A., Riel, A. (eds.) LASD 2021. LNBIP, vol. 408, pp. 177–184. Springer, Cham (2021). https://doi.org/10.1007/978-3-030-67084-9_11

15. Guardian, P., Barnes, C., of Technology, A.U., of Auckland, U., Watts, M.E.R.: The four-day week: guidelines for an outcome-based trial: raising productivity and engagement [white paper] (2019). http://hdl.voced.edu.au/10707/501849

16. Marek, K., Winska, E., Dabrowski, W.: The state of agile software development teams during the Covid-19 pandemic. In: Przybyek, A., Miler, J., Poth, A., Riel, A. (eds.) LASD 2021. LNBIP, vol. 408, pp. 24–39. Springer, Cham (2021). https://doi.org/10.1007/978-3-030-67084-9_2

17. Meier, A., Kropp, M., Anslow, C., Biddle, R.: Stress in agile software development: practices and outcomes. In: Proceedings of the 19th International Conference on Agile Processes in Software Engineering and Extreme Programming. (XP) p. 259 (2018)

18. Neumann, M., Bogdanov, Y., Lier, M., Baumann, L.: The Sars-Cov-2 pandemic and agile methodologies in software development: a multiple case study in Germany. In: Przybyłek, A., Miler, J., Poth, A., Riel, A. (eds.) LASD 2021. LNBIP, vol. 408, pp. 40–58. Springer, Cham (2021). https://doi.org/10.1007/978-3-030-67084-9_3

19. Nolan, A., White, R., Soomro, M., Dopamu, B.C., Yilmaz, M., Solan, D., Clarke, P.: To work from home (WFH) or not to work from home? lessons learned by software engineers during the covid-19 pandemic. In: Yilmaz, M., Clarke, P., Messnarz, R., Reiner, M. (eds.) Systems, Software and Services Process Improvement, pp. 14–33. Springer, Cham (2021). https://doi.org/10.1007/978-3-030-56441-4

20. O Connor, M., Conboy, K., Dennehy, D.: Covid-19 affected remote workers: a temporal analysis of information system development during the pandemic. J. Decis. Syst. (2021). https://doi.org/10.1080/12460125.2020.1861772

21. Ralph, P., et al.: Pandemic programming: How Covid-19 affects software developers and how their organizations can help. Emp. Softw. Eng. 1–35 (2020). https://doi.org/10.1007/s10664-020-09875-y

22. Runeson, P., Höst, M.: Guidelines for conducting and reporting case study research in software engineering. Emp. Softw Eng. **14**(2), 131–164 (2009). https://doi.org/10.1007/s10664-008-9102-8

23. Russo, D., Hanel, P., Altnickel, S., van Berkel, N.: Predictors of well-being and productivity among software professionals during the Covid-19 pandemic: a longitudinal study. Emp. Softw. Engi. **26**, 1382–3256 (2021)

24. Schmidtner, M., Doering, C., Timinger, H.: Agile working during Covid-19 pandemic. IEEE Eng. Manag. Rev. (2021). https://doi.org/10.1109/EMR.2021. 3069940
25. Schwaber, K., Sutherland, J.: The scrum guide (2020). https://www.scrumguides. org/scrum-guide.html
26. Smite, D., Mikalsen, M., Moe, N.B., Stray, V., Klotins, E.: From collaboration to solitude and back: remote pair programming during COVID-19. In: Gregory, P., Lassenius, C., Wang, X., Kruchten, P. (eds.) XP 2021. LNBIP, vol. 419, pp. 3–18. Springer, Cham (2021). https://doi.org/10.1007/978-3-030-78098-2_1
27. VersionOne, Collabnet: 15th annual state of agile survey report (2021). https:// www.stateofagile.com/
28. Wadsworth, L., Facer, R.L.: Work-family balance and alternative work schedules: exploring the impact of 4-day workweeks on state employees. Public Person. Manag. **45**, 382–404 (2016). https://doi.org/10.1177/0091026016678856
29. Williams, L.: Agile software development methodologies and practices. In: van Zelkowitz, M. (ed.) Advances in Computers, vol. 80, pp. 1–44. Academic Press, London (2010). https://doi.org/10.1016/S0065-2458(10)80001-4
30. Yin, R.K.: Case Study Research: Design and Methods, Applied Social Research Methods Series, 4th edn., vol. 5. Sage, Los Angeles (2009)

Impact of Turkish National Culture on Agile Software Development in Turkey

Aysegul Gelmis[1], Necmettin Ozkan[2(✉)], Ali J. Ahmad[3], and Mehmet Guray Guler[4]

[1] Turkcell Technology, İstanbul, Turkey
aysegul.gelmis@turkcell.com.tr
[2] Information Technologies Research and Development Center, Kuveyt Turk Participation Bank, Kocaeli, Turkey
necmettin.ozkan@kuveytturk.com.tr
[3] University of Warwick, Coventry, UK
ali.ahmad@warwick.ac.uk
[4] Yildiz Technical University, Istanbul, Turkey
mgguler@yildiz.edu.tr

Abstract. The effect of national culture in the software development especially in Agile Software Development industry has a considerable place since national culture affects and shapes organizations and individuals. Our study examines the impact of Turkish national culture on Agile software transformations and developments in Turkey, as the first instance in/for Turkey scope, to the best of our knowledge. We conducted semi-structured interviews with fourteen experts in prominent nine companies from three major industries including TechFin, Aviation, and Telecommunication. In the study, motivations of organizations for transforming Agile, challenges with transitioning to Agile, Agile culture specific to Turkey and preferences on Agile frameworks in Turkey were investigated. The results were discussed along with their implications for Agile in Turkey by considering Hofstede's model which is designed to investigate country-level cultural traits. Our results are largely parallel with the existing knowledge of Hofstede Insights specific to Turkish culture, yet we additionally present the impacts of this national culture of Turkey on the country's Agile Software Development. Consequently, it was observed that the national cultural background has a considerable effect on the Turkish Agile software development domain. We have witnessed some similar effects in the Eastern culture as well. By providing the country's cultural patterns through a localized lens, the study may contribute to those who may have a practical interest to Turkish in terms of which potential challenges they need to be prepared for once they move into the adoption of agile working in/with this country and more generally in/with the countries with which has similar cultures as in the Eastern civilizations. Our study also comes with global insights to the other countries in terms of understanding the use of agile methods and practices in companies located outside of the early adopters of agile methods.

Keywords: Agile software development · Agility · Scrum · Kanban · Culture · Nation · Hofstede 6D model

A. Przybyłek et al. (Eds.): LASD 2022, LNBIP 438, pp. 78–95, 2022.
https://doi.org/10.1007/978-3-030-94238-0_5

1 Introduction

The social aspect of Agile Software Development (shortly Agile) is a critical factor to consider for successful Agile implementations [1]. Culture, as one of the prominent social human aspects, is a keystone in Agile since agility requires proper changes in individual, team, and corporate culture. For instance, a successful cultural transformation is regarded as a very revealing litmus test to differentiate "being agile" from "doing agile". However, the cultural background of Agile is generally a neglected aspect by researchers [2]. Among the cultural dimensions, national culture has a special place even though it is relatively difficult to shape compared to other scales (individual, team and corporate). National culture can have a significant effect on the organizational culture and determine many facets including preferred leadership styles, decision-making, perceptions of authorities, formalization level, communication and interaction manners, business etiquette and motivation [3].

Despite its significance, national culture perspective has limited space in the current academic literature; rather the focus is on the cultural impact of organization, team and project contexts on Agile implementations [2, 4]. The most apparent area where national culture variations are investigated is in global/offshore software development, especially in the contexts of intercontinental software development. For example, cultural transitions between Eastern and Western countries manifest and even appear as a challenge to be managed. Many of the companies report challenges rooted in the cultural differences when introducing Agile in projects involving offshore engineers [5].

National cultural studies are (and should) not limited to this scope only; every country, whether involved in offshore development or not, has its own culture, and its culture considerably shapes its Agile patterns. However, recently, the national culture studies do not go much beyond the global/offshore software development boundaries in the literature.

Turkey has its own culture, like others, that could pose either benefits or challenges to its growing software development industry using more and more Agile approaches nowadays [6]. It has also a unique national culture lying between East and West in terms of geographical, cultural, and sociological aspects. However, there is a lack of resources about the Turkey's cultural impacts on Agile in the country's software development industry. This gap calls for an important research topic to study. In our study we focus on the impact of the Turkey's national culture on Agile context by providing cross-sectoral interview data to understand whether there is a sector depended effect or not. Specifically, we identified the research objectives (ROs) as follows:

- RO1: Motivations of organizations for transforming Agile in Turkey
- RO2: Challenges with transitioning to Agile in Turkey
- RO3: Agile culture specific to Turkey
- RO4: Preference on Agile frameworks in Turkey

The rest of this paper is organized as follows: Sect. 2 delivers the background for Hofstede's model [7] (a model designed to investigate country-level cultural traits) we used for analyzing Turkish culture, along with its implications for Agile in general. The Sect. 3 presents the scope of previous research confronting national cultures with Agile context. Section 4 depicts the research methodology adopted. Section 5 delivers results and Sect. 6 evaluates results with the consideration of the model. Finally, Sect. 7 depicts conclusion, limitations, and future work.

2 Background

Even though its validity has been criticized in some research (e.g. as listed by [8]), regarding the culture at national level, 6-D (six dimensions) Model of Hofstede [7] provides one of the most comprehensive studies and mostly cited model in Information Systems research [2, 9]. Additionally, based on this model, by using primary research data from more than a hundred thousand questionnaires conducted in a multinational company's (IBM) subsidiaries in more than 60 countries, Hofstede Insights [10] exhibits deeper insights about the nation's cultural characteristics through the lens of 6-D Model. The dimensions are namely Power Distance, Individualism, Masculinity, Uncertainty Avoidance, Long Term Orientation, and Indulgence. The succeeding parts convey their descriptions, Turkey's scores, and implications of the scores from the website of Hofstede Insights [10].

Power Distance is defined as "the extent to which the less powerful members of institutions and organizations within a country expect and accept that power is distributed unequally". Turkey scores high (66) on this dimension, characterizing the Turkish style: "dependent, hierarchical, superiors often inaccessible and the ideal boss is a father figure. Power is centralized and managers rely on their bosses and on rules. Employees expect to be told what to do. Control is expected and attitude towards managers is formal. Communication is indirect and the information flow is selective."

Individualism is "the degree of interdependence a society maintains among its members. It has to do with whether people's self-image is defined in terms of "I" or "We". In Individualist societies people are supposed to look after themselves and their direct family only. In Collectivist societies, people belong to 'in groups' that take care of them in exchange for loyalty". Turkey has a score of 37 referring a collectivistic society. This means that "communication and feedback is indirect, and the harmony of the group has to be maintained, open conflicts are avoided. The relationship has a moral base, and this always has priority over task fulfillment."

Masculinity with high scores indicates, "The society will be driven by competition, achievement and success, with success being defined by the winner/best in field. A low score (Feminine) means that the dominant values in society are caring for others and quality of life…The fundamental issue here is what motivates people, wanting to be the best (Masculine) or liking what you do (Feminine)." Turkey has the score of 45 and is on the Feminine side. This indicates, "The softer aspects of culture such as leveling with others, consensus, sympathy for the underdog is valued and encouraged. Conflicts are avoided in private and work life and consensus at the end is important."

The dimension Uncertainty Avoidance expresses "the degree to which the members of a society feel uncomfortable with uncertainty and ambiguity: should we try to control the future or just let it happen?" Turkey scores 85, high Uncertainty Avoidance, on this dimension. It means, "There is a huge need for laws and rules. To minimize anxiety, people make use of a lot of rituals."

Long Term Orientation dimension describes, "How every society has to maintain some links with its own past while dealing with the challenges of the present and future, and societies, priorities these two existential goals differently. A culture scoring high takes a more pragmatic approach." With the intermediate score of 46, no dominant cultural preference can be inferred for Turkey in this dimension.

Indulgence dimension is defined as "the extent to which people try to control their desires and impulses, based on the way they were raised. With an intermediate score of 49 for Turkey, no dominant cultural characteristic to this dimension cannot be determined.

When explored Turkish culture along with other world culture examples in Hofstede Insights [10], Turkey exhibits a similar picture with Eastern centuries such as China, India, Japan, South Korea in terms of high Power Distance and Collectivist characteristics as seen in Fig. 1. In the Western countries, these two dimensions are the opposite. The rest of the dimensions does not pose such a clear distinction between Turkey and Western or Eastern countries.

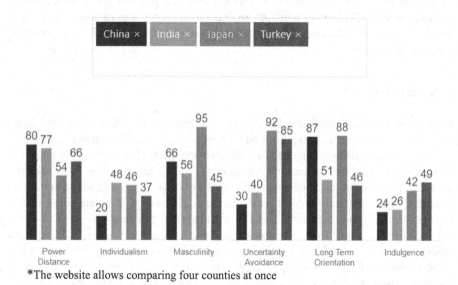

*The website allows comparing four counties at once

Fig. 1. Comparison of Hofstede insights dimensions of some Eeastern (Source: [10]). *The website allows comparing four counties at once

Regarding the impacts of these cultural dimensions on Agile, the literature has almost a clear consensus on the negative effect of high Power Distance, especially on empowerment, self-organization and collaborative management capabilities of the teams. Although, low Uncertainty Avoidance supports agility with embracing change in general and agility allows low Uncertainty Avoidance, Agile principles and frameworks such as Scrum (a "process framework") includes discipline, "regular intervals", fixed durations, determined roles, and planning rituals as the signs of high Uncertainty Avoidance. However, these aspects refer to the discipline side of Agile, rather than agility side of it. Therefore, we may consider low Uncertainty Avoidance largely supports agility.

While high Individualism has positive effects on Agile with direct communication, collectivist societies are, on the other hand, good at having team spirit and harmony that agility requires, which makes to identify if the Agile values favor individualistic or collective traits more difficult. This case at least requires a balance between these two edges for the proper agility.

Group interaction, face-to-face communication, collaboration, flexibility and looking for consensus, as feminine values on one side, having clear and tangible goals, being determined and result oriented, as masculine attributes on the other side, advance agility, which makes to draw a clear conclusion on the relationship between Agile and Masculinity hard. Agile calls for Long Term Orientation with customer collaboration rather than negotiating single contract, product development (supported by product roadmaps, product-based teams rather than temporary project-based teams), long-term relationships, "sustainable development" and "a constant pace indefinitely". On the other hand, delivery of working software frequently, early and continuously, with a preference to the shorter time scale imply Short Term Orientation. People in restraint societies hold the perception of out of own control where freedom of speech is not a common practice, which is against to agile values, while indulgent societies feel personal life control that supports agility.

3 Related Work

The national cultures and cultural differences have been studied in-depth by several social scientists [5], including investigations on influences by a particular cultural background to some aspects of software engineering. For instance, study [20] explores the impact of power distance's cultural aspects on requirement engineering activities by conducting interviews with software engineer practitioners from Saudi Arabia and Australia and using Hofstede's cultural model. Specific to the Agile context, there are some studies such as study [5] reporting results about cultural barriers impeding agile ways of working in distributed teams from an empirical study of a Swedish company working with offshore engineers from an outsourcing vendor in India. Such challenges are not limited to the countries of Western and Eastern cultures; Moe et al. [11] stated that during an onboarding process, the most important success factor is finding Portuguese developers that matched the culture of the existing Norwegian Agile teams.

The study [4], including the model we used in our research, focuses on analyzing and understanding the relationships between Agile and national culture values with respect to the Eastern and Western worlds (through Chinese, Indian and Finnish samples). It provides recommendations to help people understand what is needed to consider if they want to use Agile with culturally diverse teams. Briefly, the study puts forward that Agile seems to favor low Power Distance, high Individualism, high Masculinity, and low Uncertainty Avoidance.

Ayed et al. [2] gathered data about practices, challenges and impediments encountered by software development teams from interviews of 19 practitioners and two Agile events in three countries (Belgium, Malaysia, and Singapore). The results of the analysis were discussed using the Hofstede Model for the national cultures comparison and relevant hypotheses were developed. Their study reports positive impacts of high

Power Distance on commitment and management buy-in and its negative impact on team empowerment, transparency, customer involvement and process improvement. They state negative impacts of high Uncertainty Avoidance on commitment to (new) practices, team multidisciplinary and its positive impacts on management buy-in. Long Term Orientation has positive impact on commitment to (new) practices, team multidisciplinary, process improvement and management buy-in. They also state positive impact of high Indulgence on team transparency and team motivation.

Qiao's study [12], develops hypotheses between collectivist Chinese culture and Agile practices with data collected by four expert interviews in China. The study found high Power Distance has a conflict with Agile implementation and low-Uncertainty Avoidance, Collectivism, Masculinity, and Long-term Orientation are beneficial for Agile implementation.

Ramesh et al. [13] examine the relationship of Eastern cultural phenomena with Agile methods using multisite case study from China, India, and South Korea instances. The study mainly approaches to the subject from individualistic-collectivistic spectrum describing how the Eastern collectivist culture responses in complementary and conflicting ways with Agile methods.

Regarding the multicultural software development concerns, Sutharshan and Maj [9] analyzed the Agile principles (defined by Agile Manifesto) for cross-cultural factors. They come up with Agile specific cultural attributes relevant to multicultural concerns connected to Hofstede's cultural dimensions. Furthermore, they categorize the culture and Agile specific attributes into different groups based on Hofstede's cultural dimensions. In this study, the authors present this matching based mainly on their own views.

In the research study, Veerla and Subrahmanyam [8] studied the impact of national culture dimensions proposed by the Hofstede's model on Agile team behavioral characteristics especially from autonomy, shared leadership, redundancy, learning and team orientation aspects. They conducted a literature review to know the relationship between the Agile team behavior characteristics and cultural dimensions demonstrated by India and a web survey from 33 people. They aimed to find out whether Indian employees demonstrate the necessary behavior which is required for the effective functioning of Agile team or not.

Agile methods have spread to almost all countries in the world including Turkey, even to from which its original cultural backgrounds differ. In this regard, study [16] states that Agile works best in democratic type of organizations represented by the cultural scripts of Nordic and Anglo-Saxon countries where Agile methods like Scrum were originated from. Values in the manifesto and Scrum represent underlying national values of the authors, who are from Anglo-Saxon culture, which poses low Power Distance, high Individualism, and low Uncertainty Avoidance [4]. Moreover, Palokangas [4] explicitly states, "The rest of the world is more about high Power Distance and collective cultures, making adoption of these values harder for them." Turkish culture is somewhere in the middle of the West and East, and this cultural background affects the selection of particular Agile frameworks. We can regard Turkish culture as mostly an Eastern culture. On the other hand, Agile and Scrum are originated from Western-centered places, which makes its healthful implementations harder (for Turkey), as aforementioned by the studies above. Meanwhile, as study [5] puts forward, there is an interest in understanding the use of agile methods and practices in companies outside the locations of early adopters of agile methods.

Particularly, Agile experiences in Turkey are slightly new and visible after 2010 for the Turkish software development industry [14]. Besides, there are limited research about the understanding of Agile development in Turkish software development industry. Study [21] aims to get an understanding into the cross-factor correlation of various software engineering practices versus practitioner demographics including their companies and projects. To achieve this objective, they used the data from Turkey with a survey from 202 participated software engineers' practitioners. They found that usage of waterfall is low among participants employed by small-sized companies whereas Agile/Lean development is relatively popular among this class of participants. However, Agile/Lean development is not popular in the military and defense sector; its usage is the least by the participants employed by those companies. Practitioners employed by smaller companies favor Agile more than waterfall-like development that is popular in large companies. Agile and Lean development is the most popular among participants developing software for engineering/manufacturing, IT and telecommunication and health sectors. Study [22] aims to have a high-level view on type of software engineering practices in the Turkish software industry by using the survey data [apparently the same one] covering 202 participated software engineering practitioners in Turkey. In their study, most followed software development methods are waterfall life cycle, incremental development, and Agile/Lean development with adoption rates of 53%, 38% and 34% respectively. Their analyses on responses for development related practices revealed that pair programming, which is a highly praised popular practice within Agile methods, is not performed as frequently in Turkey. Among the participants, 13% of them did not report documenting the software requirements at all, which took attention of the authors for a further investigation. Although the reason for this case is not fully known in the study, one of the possible reasons was mentioned as Agile methods, addition to the other possible reasons including low quality awareness, emergence or something else.

There are already some other studies on Agile using data from organizations in Turkey, however, none of them includes any explicit link from their results to Turkish culture. We have not found any study because of our narrative literature review to search possible related studies focusing on the national culture aspects of Agile in Turkey (Our search utilized keywords such as "agile turkey" in prominent databases including IEE Xplore, ACM, Web of Science, Scopus and Science Direct within their metadata). Therefore, as far as we know, our study is the first one focusing on the national culture aspects of Agile in Turkey.

4 Research Methodology

For this paper, semi-structured interview method suites best since it is a qualitative and exploratory method, because questions asked during the interviews allowed exploring the ROs and the flow of the conversations and the order of questions were flexible to get more deep insights and obtain reliable and valid data at the same time. The first author of this paper thus prepared open-ended "how", "why" questions and/or topics for the discussions followed-up during the interviews.

Fourteen interviews from three major industries including TechFin (Technology - Finance), Aviation, and Telecommunication and nine companies were conducted to collect data to analyze. All the participants were selected from people who are currently operating in the industry, experienced in Agile and performing different roles, experts, managers, consultants and academician. Five of the participants were from Telecommunication, four of them were from TechFin, three of them were from Aviation and two of them were from consultancy. Three of the interviewees had also academic background and they have published some academic research about Agile. In the TechFin industry, different types of banking including regular banking, Islamic banking and the banking for clearing, settlement and custody services were covered. In the Aviation industry, in addition to the flag-carrier company, a low-cost example was also covered. In the Telecommunication industry, three major players of the Turkey industry were selected. The average years of experience of the participants regarding Agile is 5.8. Generally, the participants have experience with Scrum and Kanban, but some of them use tailored or scaled frameworks. List of interviewees and the general information about them are presented in Table 1.

Table 1. List of interviewees

Interviewee ID	Sector	Role	Total agile experience year
INT-1	Consultancy	Consultant/expert/Academician	5
INT-2	TechFin	CTO	1,5
INT-3	Telecommunication	Agile coach	5
INT-4	Telecommunication	Agile coach	4
INT-5	Aviation	Manager	4,5
INT-6	Aviation	Scrum master/Senior analyst	7
INT-7	TechFin	Expert/Academician	7
INT-8	Consultancy	IT & Project governance Consultant/Agile Coach/Founder	7
INT-9	TechFin	Software engineer	1,5
INT-10	TechFin	IT Architect	6
INT-11	Aviation	Product owner	6
INT-12	Telecommunication	IT Director	15
INT-13	Telecommunication	Manager	9
INT-14	Telecommunication	Manager/Academician	4

The interviews were conducted by the first author of this paper. The guiding questions asked to initiate the conversations are as follows; how is Turkish software development industry affected by Agile? How do you decide using Agile, what were the motivations for transformation? What challenges have you faced during the transition? What do you think about the Agile penetration in Turkey? What kind of frameworks are more useful for Turkish software industry? In terms of culture, geography, economical aspects etc., how is your experience specified for Turkish industry? Do you think Agile is used effectively in Turkey?

Prior to the interviews, the research questions were reviewed with an expert for the reliability of the research, and the ROs and questions were shared with the participants for their initial investigation. At the beginning of the interviews, confirmations were received from the participants to make sure the questions were understood.

For the interviews, face-to-face communication was preferred. Because of the Covid-19 pandemic, the interviews were conducted via video communication tools. Only one of the interviewee preferred e-mailing. All interviews were conducted in Turkish language and recorded with the consent of the interviewees. The interviews were carried out in a quiet place to endure recording quality. The average duration of the interviews is 33 min. The records were transcribed by an external resource to Turkish and translated into English by the same person. In the texts, participant and company names were expressed as codes, not in their real names. The translated texts were checked by the first author of this paper and shared with the interviewees to check against possible errors. Then, necessary corrections were made.

Due to the manual operations and interpretations, subjective opinions could bias our data. To minimize the bias, all transcript content was reviewed by the first and second authors for the extracted data and a consensus between them was reached. In doing so, a line-by-line reading of the English text was made to identify the relevant statements. The identified statements were agreed by the first and second author in terms of the relevance to the ROs. These statements were then grouped into the main themes under the ROs. Then, the results were used for discussions in this paper by considering Hofstede's model and other studies' findings.

In this research, the questions were determined aligning with the key points we have witnessed in the literature. Furthermore, the participants were all relevant individuals who have a working experience with Agile. Hence, all these dynamics provide to keep the validity high. To reduce possible biases, it is ensured that the three roles of interviewing, transcription and examining the texts were separate to different people. In contrast, both transcription and examinations results were reviewed by the researcher who conducted the interviews. In addition, the reviews of the interviewees also reduced possible errors.

5 Results

5.1 Motivations for Transforming Agile (RO1)

There are common motivation factors apparent in the literature and indicated by the interviewees for Agile transformations in their companies as well such as efficiency, productivity, performance, human friendly working environment, transparency, enhancing trust, frequent delivery, collaboration, alignment, high motivation, producing value and minimum viable product and getting quick feedback. Furthermore, the researchers explored that one of the main motivations for many of the organizations is keeping up with the popular trends and fashions in the business world, the idea of "everyone is doing it, so we have to do so". Many of the interviewees underlined the business fashion motivation for the Turkey case. For instance, it is expressed as, *"Generally, the first view is that everyone became Agile, and I laid behind. What am I going to do?"* [INT-1]. [INT-12] mentioned, *"There are fashions in the business world. There are those who follow this fashion wind."* [INT-12] also counted cutting cost by eliminating middle level management as the motivation for some organizations.

In terms of getting benefits from Agile, it is expected that the benefits will emerge hopefully and quickly. [INT-1] states: *"We [Turkish people] expect that we should earn a lot of money as quickly as possible, we should earn the most and we love this. I think the same logic appears for the agility in Turkey. Let us make teams in organizations Agile. Suddenly, we will have perfect teams, profitability will increase, and we will earn money. It will not happen, of course."* As a statement expressed by some interviewees, this desire may also be the underlying reason for the "quick" transformations directly applying (a) certain method(s) instead of starting with rationale and the essence of the mindset. In addition, [INT-7] stressed some personal interests expected from the Agile transformation by stating that *"[Agile] penetration is high [in Turkey] but there is a lot of market and some PR (public relations) stuff here. We like PR too. There is also a personal benefit. Perhaps personal benefits may be ahead of corporate benefits. Because there is a serious community [in Agile] and when it supports you, you shine suddenly. You used to be a developer and [then suddenly] you become a master."*

According to INT-2 and INT-4, Agile is demanded by employees to acquire one of the popular trends and to establish more human-friendly working environments: *"It [Agile] is an opportunity for development and attraction for digital talents"* [INT-2]. *"In terms of employees, it [Agile] is a more human-friendly working environment"* [INT-4].

INT-1, INT-8, INT-9, and INT-13 mentioned the motivations of productivity and speed aspects. Conversely, INT-12 stated that there is an illusion in this regard because Agile does not mean being fast. Agile means "changing direction very fast" as illustrated in the quotes: *"But such big companies say, of course, let's be Agile. Why? Let us be quick too... We use Agile and fast in the same sense. Agile is a bit of the opposite. It means changing the direction very fast"* [INT-12]. As a result, a disagreement emerged among the interviewees on this matter.

5.2   Challenges of Transitioning to Agile (RO2)

It is explored that one of the main and common challenges with transitioning to Agile is shifting the mindset from command-and-control style to leadership style, which, as stated by [INT-1], requires *"a crucial challenge"*. However, participants highlighted that it is hard to accept this paradigm shift and this subject brings some difficulties in Turkey. [INT-2] especially states, *"This [management] level needs to transform and change yet the resistance shown by top-level managers is biggest challenge"*. [INT-12] expressed the need of the self-managing flourished by leaving some rooms for the decision-making to the teams by the management levels. Generally, managers could not accept their authority being questioned, do not give self-management opportunity to the teams' and still ask the details of the works such as story points or end date of the tasks. In this regard, as mentioned by [INT-1], *"We are trying to act hierarchically because all organizations are in hierarchical structures like there is a chain of command"*. Apart from the outside effects, the teams may have clusters, classifications, or a secret rank inside the teams [INT-1].

[INT-1] and [INT-7] expressed that the transformation should spread from bottom-up because it is important to be accepted by the employees. Another point is that the transformation should be managed by internal teams that serve the organization, stated as, *"We have decided to launch an Agile office that serves the organization without any external support and make Agile live in our own culture. I think it was the right decision so that we could make some work about Agile peculiar to Turkey, Turkish culture, and companies"* [INT-1]. Besides, [INT-3] expressed that just converting the teams was not enough, to transform effectively; organizations needed to change, transform, and even invest in the organization culture, strategy, and many things.

Open culture is another challenge for Turkish culture. For instance, it is stated by [INT-1] as *"We love illustrating the project as if it is successful and get used to hide the failure. … It is hard to talk about the faults or problems transparently…building trust environment and providing psychological safety are hard issues for Turkish culture and it affects sharing faults, lesson learned etc.… You can also think that other people will take my idea and realize it if I tell them"*. [INT-14] also added that some IT teams hesitate to share knowledge with the business teams to prevent revealing their weak sides.

5.3 Agile Culture in Turkey (RO3)

In terms of the relationship between Turkish culture and the practices of Agile, there are some implications about the cultural background of Turkey that might affect the understanding and practicing of Agile. Participants mentioned that Turkish culture is human and family-oriented, quick, adaptive, emotional, action-oriented. They prefer to do, to share, to chat together as a team. In addition, it was stated that Turkish people prefer individual interactions like in a conversation during drinking tea together, to follow adaptive plans, but not prefer to documentation, processes, and tools. [INT-12] affirmed, *"The Turkish people are not actually in the classical project management culture. In terms of planning etc., we say that our crisis management is better in our nature because we can constantly re-prioritize somethings. We have such flexibility. We are not a nation that likes to make such a long-term plan and stick to it. Cultural and socioeconomic background do not allow it too much"*.

Turkish culture is somewhere in the middle; the culture is very hierarchical, but on the other hand, it is also in a place requiring acting very quickly and to change the direction very fast [INT-12]. The Turkish hierarchy is not too strict and extreme, like Japanese or Indian culture. Because of these cultural aspects, participants stated that Turkish people are very suitable for Agile who like conversations, which supports the value on the left-hand side of the manifesto [INT-7], "teamwork, to do something together, to achieve, to produce output, to bond, to talk, to chat and to be together" [INT-13].

Agile generally advises flatter organizations in which all the members can express their opinions easily. However, hierarchy, adherence to titles and promotions and misunderstanding of leadership style were mentioned as the main issues for Turkish culture. For instance, [INT-2] stated, *"Agile leadership is an important issue because it will be very difficult to leave the hierarchy in management"*. Interviewees stated that agility does not put such meaning to the roles, but Turkish people are stuck in the titles. The culture has created this perception and people trying to find a safe place in the organization not to lose their position. Interviewees generally stated that in Turkish culture, organizations are still hierarchical, and most of the managers is worried about losing their authorities. They also stated that people want the titles to feel important. Moreover, [INT-11] expressed that in Turkish culture, people also care about the titles and positions because the flat structure does not allow a similar motivation. Then, they try to apply the existing agility with a hierarchical structure, [INT-3] and organizations try to find workarounds to keep titles inside or around the Agile teams in Turkey, as stated by [INT-5] and [INT-8].

Agile promotes learning from the failures and sharing feedbacks with all the participants clearly. However, it was mentioned or accepted by almost all participants; Turkish people could not give or receive feedback sufficiently, with direct communication and share their faults transparently. This hierarchal and leadership style lead to not sharing the failures or shortcomings, giving, and receiving feedbacks, making criticism, and revealing improvement points and to lack of trust.

[INT-4] stated that the underlying reason behind this feedback issue in the society could be the fear of losing jobs. Social security or economic conditions are not as good as the many other countries where Agile emerged. Naturally, people do not want to risk themselves. Unless this trusted environment is provided to them, they cannot be clear enough. In addition, [INT-4] mentioned that experimentation or failure culture is not common. People do not have such a space right now in Turkish culture but it will change in the future. Another point participants highlighted is that older generations are having trouble, but the new generation is moving away from Turkish culture in this regard; they are more direct, and they can say what they want easily effecting this hindrance inside the culture positively.

Regarding adherence to titles and positions and paradigm shift of managers to leaders, [INT-12] highlighted that this management and hierarchical perception will change in the future with Z generation. Since they are open, the culture they are exposed to is a bit more global and they will not actually accept those hierarchical structures easily. It was also mentioned that the flat structure is not easy to establish but once people get used to it, they do not want to turn back to the old hierarchical structures. Especially young generations will like it very much because of the given responsibilities.

The participants stated that there is still a need to improve the experience and understanding of the agile mindset. For instance, [INT-2] states, "I see...in the market that there are teams saying they are Agile but working like Waterfall". [INT-7] stated, "The places that sell the mindset are still very rare". In the same vein, [INT-2] expressed that "It [Agile] is used effectively in some examples that I have seen, but I observed that it is not used effectively in most of them...We [Turkish industry] still need to move on. If we think this in terms of the journey of maturity, we are still in between doing Agile and being Agile and, we are trying to pass to the being side" [INT-1]. [INT-3] stated that compared to Europe, Turkey has made a great advancement in terms of agility in this journey because the people in Turkey needed and need to solve more challenging issues and learn from them. Most of the participants expressed that it is better to convey the rationale and benefits of the implemented practices specially to penetrate the Agile methods and mindset successfully.

5.4 Preference on Agile Frameworks (RO4)

Almost all the participants use Scrum or Kanban as an Agile framework and very few of them use some tailored frameworks suited for company dynamics. [INT-2] expressed that it is more appropriate for each company to use a framework that blends its own culture with global Agile frameworks, bringing together the world best practices with organization's unique culture. Some of them stated that both Scrum and Kanban are suitable for Turkish culture. Some others highlighted that starting an Agile transformation by using Kanban instead of Scrum could be beneficial because the Kanban rules are very simple and easy to implement and it does not touch the titles or positions of the people, requiring low "patience point". For instance, sharing the similar idea with [INT-14], [INT-4] mentioned, *"Kanban might be better...but for companies with patience...because Kanban involves not touching roles"*. [INT-13] expressed that the collectivist attribute of Turkish people fits well with the Scrum's team sprint and its intense communications channels, and it is supported by them.

Even though we live in a global world, [INT-7] stressed that it may not be that easy to get out of the cultural identities that the frameworks bear, especially "rigid", "aggressive" and "materialized" characteristic of Scrum, expressed as *"the West have packed it [Agile] very well. They have catholicized [it] with Scrum... It [Scrum] has a rigid structure. For instance, if you exceed 15 min, you sin, and if you come to the meeting late, you throw money to confess...It [Scrum] will come here and destroy whatever. I will establish something here...and if we look at the marketing side, there is materialism, serious capitalism. This can work in the capital world, but it does not fit us...I think we should have a bit of patience, a little wait, and a respect for people. This is also in Lean and Kanban"*. However, [INT-8] thinks that because of the Turkey's perspective, Scrum framework meets the expectations, culture's needs, and the way of doing business because of its being rules specific, adequate, simple, and providing enough space to move freely. As a result, within the scope of appropriate frame preferences, different views by the interviewees have been put forward.

6 Discussion

In this research, some motivations of organizations for transforming to Agile were determined as business alignment, providing human-friendly and enjoyable working environment, managing with short iterations, increasing speed, transparency, efficiency, collaboration, and communication, reducing bureaucratic processes, time-to-market time, and establishing a flatter organizational structure. These motivation factors are also common in the literature. Interestingly, the transition to Agile with the motivation of business fashion, PR or attracting people are relatively new factors, partially mentioned by Madsen [15] recently. Agile is a buzzword and some late adaptor companies can understand Agile as a "business fashion". These companies are generally starting Agile because of its popularity. However, this may lead to a possible underestimating and misunderstanding of the agile mindset and principles. Moreover, this may become a deeper issue for the Turkish software development industry if Agile in the country will become a short-term, temporary trend yet already embedded in the organizations' processes, structures, and cultures. If the sustainability of Agile applications is desired, more work should be done to improve the understanding of agile mindset for Turkish software development industry.

When it comes to speed and productivity as the motivators, they are not addressed in the Agile Manifesto, but many of the practitioners accept these aspects as the motivation factors. There can be a misunderstanding about the frequent delivery and speed in the industry, which may cause wrong expectations from Agile. Agile does not mean being very fast or cost-effective rather means changing directions and adopting the new situations very fast.

It is explored that Agile is suitable for the Turkish culture with its some advantageous characteristics such as ability to constantly re-prioritize things and flexibility. Agile approaches suggest talking about the failures or problems transparently. One of the basic principles of it is to express the faults clearly, to give clear feedback. However, in Turkish culture, there are some challenges about open culture and bureaucracy; it is hard to talk about the faults or problems. This condition affects building the trust and open environment, providing psychological safety, and diminishing the effectiveness of Agile practices. It is also explored that in the next years, with involving of the Z generation and new ways of working, the effects of the cultural background of the country may considerably change.

Agile promotes flatter organizations in which each team member acting as a leader in the organization, but it is explored that in Turkish culture, organizations largely have a hierarchical top-down structure. Agile adaptation to this culture may be challenging. Turkish people are very committed to the roles in the organizations and care about the titles and organizational hierarchy. Moreover, the management level is still following the old-style way of management and many of them is worried about losing their authorities. This hierarchical organization and the culture also influence giving and receiving feedback. Thus, the organizational cultures should be further adapted to the new style of leadership in Agile.

It seems that there is a inconsistency in Turkey between the organizational preconditions for Agile and the prevalent bureaucracy and hierarchical power distance features of Turkish corporations. However, despite this problem, Agile still appears to be delivering results because its inherent flexibility to adjust to potentially any organizational context. Even so, there should be extra effort to building new flatter organizational structures that support agility. Additionally, there is a need to study the Agile perspective of Human Resource Management including titles and positions and paradigm shift of managers to leaders. Especially younger generations have a potential to change this perception about hierarchy and leadership style. In the future, Z generation may influence the perception about the management and hierarchy, because they are coming from open culture exposing similar cultural background and they will not acknowledge hierarchical structures easily.

Because of popularity, Agile is remaining on the many of the organizations' agenda in Turkey but the mindset is not understood fully. Considering the cultural background of Turkey, it is explored that one of the main challenges is shifting the mindset from management level to leadership level. As pointed out by some interviewees, there could be fear, resistance, or uncertainty at the early stages. Participants mentioned that explaining the details of the transformation process openly, becoming clearer, having effective change management, participation of high-level management, training, coaching, consultancy, more appropriate office designs and being strong and determined are the key points for overcoming the challenges in this regard. If the organizations understand the importance of transition and accept its benefits with the help of management support and collaboration, the transition could be easier and more effective. Agile transformations can be challenging for organizations in Turkey, especially when implemented by Scrum with its disrupting the current structure of the organizations. Thus, such hesitations by the adopters may be since Scrum comes with a radical, not evolutionary, but revolutionary approach and destroys especially what Turkish nation regard important, titles. Thus, some extra actions could be taken to reduce the impact of the transformation challenges emerging from Scrum during the transitions in addition to the other actions.

The findings in this study may be replicable in the Turkish context. Particularly for culturally homogeneous onshore teams when scaling to the global level, the findings are expected to be similar to the nations with similar cultural textures. In line with our findings, previous studies (such as study [2, 4] and [19]) also report that communication is not always as open as expected in Asian Agile teams. They are reluctant to discuss negative and hard issues, exposing problems, warning about non-feasible deadlines, providing transparency, proposing alternatives to perceived directives from superior employees and try to ensure themselves against to the cases unfortunately happen. They hugely suffer from the lack of team empowerment as a critical issue. According to a study conducted in India, Jain, and Varma [17] stated that Indian teams generally do not have empowerment to make decisions. Cultures with high Power Distance prefer having strict division of roles and responsibilities [4] like in Turkey. Ayed et al., (2017) report that Malaysian and Singapore Agile teams feel less freedom to decide about their ways of working (because of high Power Distance) and do not realize self-learning. Šmite et al. [5] state that India and neighboring countries reveals impeding behaviors in terms of Agile likely caused by the hierarchical culture of the organizations and related management behavior. Thus, it is not surprising that study [2, 4] and [12] report that Agile teams in the Asian countries suffer from high Power Distance and Uncertainty Avoidance as in Turkey. Similarly, as Asian countries, Turkey has high Power Distance, and Uncertainty Avoidance. Our results indicate that high Power Distance and Uncertainty Avoidance in Turkey result in negative impacts on factors such as team empowerment, feedback loops, securely failing, transparency, and process improvement.

Our study findings are largely in line with what Hofstede Insights [10] reports for Turkey; Turkish nation are dependent on superiors, hierarchical and centralized in terms of power. Superiors are tied to their position of authority. Control is in place and information flow is selective. As a collectivistic society, communication is indirect and the harmony of the teams and issue about others are cared about. Open conflicts are avoided, and feedbacks are indirect. They consider softer aspects, consensus, and sympathy. They need for laws and rules (provided by a higher authority) and feel anxious, especially about their future because of socio-economic matters.

In our research, we found that interviewees mentioned some feminine attributes in organizations including human-friendly working environments, face-to-face communication, flexibility, being quick, adaptive, and emotional. These features make Turkish people somehow action-oriented. As a collectivist national they like to do something, share and chat together and teamwork. Owing to lack of building trust, transparent and psychologically safe environment, they do not have an open, feedback and sharing culture. They pretend to be successful and hide their failures. In this regard, lack of social security and socioeconomic conditions can lead to maintain their "hardly-won" positions. As a result, even though workers demand their voice heard from bottom-up to top levels, more transparency and less bureaucratic work, they still practice command and control style leadership in hierarchical structures. The managers keep their authority and titles and ask the teams about the details of the works.

As a sigh of Short-Term Orientation, Turkish people tend to keep up with the popular trends, fashions and quick wins like productivity and speed for their organizations, even for their personal interests. This case is a relationship also realized by Barnett and Sung [18]. Because of this, they may regard converting only teams to Agile almost enough to transform effectively without a proper agile mindset. They are also not a nation that like making long-term plans and not stick to documentation, processes, and tools.

Our study is also consistent with the Annual Agility Reports by Agile Turkey (one of the non-profit organizations of Turkey) conducted in different years ranging from 2012 to 2021. According to the 14th Annual State of Agile Report [6], one of top challenges of starting or expanding Agile in the organizations are the difficulty of changing the organizational culture and resistance to change, which is a common issue especially in cultures with high Power Distance score. In the report, organizational resistance is the most common barrier for moving and scaling Agile. Besides, insufficient management support and sponsorship, inconsistent process and practices across teams are top challenges. In addition to that, teamwork, cross-functionality, and transparency are counted among the top improvement points in the reports, which are also issues mentioned frequently in our study.

7 Conclusion, Limitations and Further Research

In this research, we analyzed the impact of Turkish national culture on how the Agile practices are applied in Turkey through the lens of Hofstede's Model [7] and Hofstede's Insights [10]. The aim of this study is to understand the experience of Agile in Turkish software development industry with cultural, social, and economic effects. To achieve this objective, an exploratory and qualitative research design was used. Although our results are parallel with the existing knowledge, they also present partially different outputs.

The social aspect of Agile Software Development plays a critical role in Agile implementations [1, 23]. Since Agile basically offers a people-oriented approach, we initially assumed that the human and culture factor would have an impact on the Agile experiences in the/any country. The main motivation to conduct this study is the lack of sufficient research on the use of Agile in Turkey considering the national cultural aspects. In order to investigate whether there is a sector effect, interviewees were selected from different sectors. As a result of the study, it was observed that the national cultural background has a considerable effect on the Turkish Agile software development domain. We have witnessed the similar effects in the Eastern culture as well. While the Agile experiences were related to the business dynamics, our results disclosed that the sectoral differences did not create a major effect on the results.

This study has several contributions. It sheds light on the country's cultural patterns through a localized lens. Another one is to give ideas about the topic to countries with similar cultures. The study makes a significant contribution that may be of practical interest to Turkish and more generally Asian enterprises in terms of which potential challenges they need to be prepared for once they move into the adoption of agile working culture. Moreover, we hope that the study provides insights to other countries working with Turkey in terms of national culture and its reflection on the agility context. The study not only comes with contextualized and localized new insights but also provides global insights to the other countries in this regard and in terms of understanding the use of agile methods and practices in companies located outside the locations of early adopters of agile methods.

Like any other study, this research has several limitations. It is limited to three industries and nine companies in the Turkish software development industry to represent and look for common patterns. Thus, this research does not claim that its findings are universal, because its access to appropriate resources was limited to those participants that voluntarily had attended to interviews. Even so, with approaches that are more systematic and increasing number of inputs in the future, outcomes that are more objective can be guaranteed.

The outputs could also change because the characteristics could differ from industry to industry or from one organization to another. Like any study addressing culture-related aspects, we are unavoidably prone to stereotype the cultural traits through individuals' findings. Also, the sole reliance on the Hofstede' model provides some limitations to the study.

This research presents opportunities for further research. It might be worthwhile considering using the same set of questions in different firm contexts with a quantitative approach. Apart from and addition to a single national aspect, it can be possible to provide a larger view on the impact of intercultural challenges on the adoption of agile practices. Effects of entering Z generation to the work-life can be analyzed more deeply. Moreover, there are limited research about the management fashion issue. Therefore, this could be important to understand the future of Agile.

Although these preliminary findings in our research simplify such a complex domain such as by focusing mainly on the national culture, rather than individual or organizational culture or the projects' constraints, which calls for more validation, they provide a good entry point for researchers and practitioners. The study should motivate researchers for further research on Agile teams to discover any fine-tuning potential of Agile implementation considering a nation's cultural characteristics.

References

1. Patanakul, P., Rufo-McCarron, R.: Transitioning to agile software development: lessons learned from a government-contracted program. J. High Technol. Managem. Res. **29**(2), 181–192 (2018)
2. Ayed, H., Vanderose, B., Habra, N.: Agile cultural challenges in Europe and Asia: insights from practitioners. In: 2017 IEEE/ACM 39th International Conference on Software Engineering: Software Engineering in Practice Track (ICSE-SEIP), pp. 153–162, IEEE (2017)

3. Hofstede, G., Hofstede, G.J., Minkov, M.: Cultures and Organizations. McGraw-Hill Education, New York (2010)
4. Palokangas, J.: Agile around the world-how agile values are interpreted in national cultures? Master's thesis (2013)
5. Šmite, D., Gonzalez-Huerta, J., Moe, N.B.: "When in Rome, do as the Romans do": cultural barriers to being agile in distributed teams. In: Stray, V., Hoda, R., Paasivaara, M., Kruchten, P. (eds.) XP 2020. LNBIP, vol. 383, pp. 145–161. Springer, Cham (2020). https://doi.org/10.1007/978-3-030-49392-9_10
6. https://www.agileturkey.org/raporlar/
7. Hofstede, G.: Dimensionalizing cultures: the Hofstede model in context. Psychol. Cult. 2(1), (2011)
8. Veerla, V., Subrahmanyam, M.: Influence of cultural dimensions on Agile team behavioral characteristics. Master's thesis (2011)
9. Sutharshan, A., Maj, S.P.: Enhancing Agile methods for multi-cultural software project teams. Mod. Appl. Sci. 5(1), 12 (2011)
10. Hofstede Insights (2021). https://www.hofstede-insights.com/
11. Moe, N.B., Stray, V., Goplen, M.R.: Studying onboarding in distributed software teams: a case study and guidelines. In: Evaluation and Assessment in Software Engineering, Trondheim, Norway. ACM, New York (2020)
12. Qiao, X.: Analysing the impact of Chinese cultural factors on agile software development. Master's thesis (2018)
13. Ramesh, B., Cao, L., Kim, J., Mohan, K., James, T.L.: Conflicts and complements between eastern cultures and agile methods: an empirical investigation. Eur. J. Inf. Syst. 26(2), 206–235 (2017)
14. Altunel, H.: Journey to the agile methodologies. PMI TR 4, 16–18 (2015)
15. Madsen, D.O.: The evolutionary trajectory of the agile concept viewed from a management fashion perspective. Soc. Sci. 9(5) (2020)
16. Siakas, K.V., Siakas, E.: The agile professional culture: a source of agile quality. Softw. Process. Improv. Pract. 12(6), 597–610 (2007)
17. Jain, D., Varma, T.: The state of agile transformation in the Indian subcontinent. In: Agile 2019 Conference (2019)
18. Barnett, G.A., Sung, E.: Culture and the structure of the international hyperlink network. J. Comput.-Mediat. Commun. 11, 217–238 (2005)
19. Lee, S., Yong, H.S.: Distributed agile: project management in a global environment. Empir. Softw. Eng. 15, 204–217 (2010)
20. Alsanoosy, T., Spichkova, M., Harland, J.: The influence of power distance on requirements engineering activities. Procedia Comput. Sci. 159, 2394–2403 (2019)
21. Garousi, V., Coşkunçay, A., Demirörs, O., Yazici, A.: Cross-factor analysis of software engineering practices versus practitioner demographics: an exploratory study in Turkey. J. Syst. Softw. 111, 49–73 (2016)
22. Garousi, V., Coşkunçay, A., Betin-Can, A., Demirörs, O.: A survey of software engineering practices in Turkey. J. Syst. Softw. 108, 148–177 (2015)
23. Przybyłek, A., Albecka, M., Springer, O., Kowalski, W.: Game-based sprint retrospectives: multiple action research. Empir. Softw. Eng. 27(1), 1–56 (2021). https://doi.org/10.1007/s10664-021-10043-z

Develop Sustainable Software with a Lean ISO 14001 Setup Facilitated by the efiS® Framework

Alexander Poth[✉] [iD] and Elisabeth Nunweiler

Volkswagen AG, Berliner Ring 2, 38436 Wolfsburg, Germany
{alexander.poth,elisabeth.nunweiler}@volkswagen.de

Abstract. This article suggests the design and application of a systematic approach to establish the ISO 14001 in the context of software systems. It covers the
different phases of the software life-cycle with focus on sustainability. For each
phase, it proposes principles and methods for specific software product instantia-
tions of the ISO 14001. The presented approach is embeddedable into the efiS®
framework - the agile framework for lean enterprises - as Level of Done (LoD)
layer building block to scale the approach. The possibility of rigorous refinement of the enterprise sustainability goals to the specific software for products
and services helps to find adequate trade-offs during development and delivery.
Additionally, the approach can be used to establish a sustainability governance for
IT and software based products and services. Furthermore, an instantiation as an
example of the proposed approach on a hybrid-cloud service of the Volkswagen
Group IT is presented.

Keywords: Sustainability engineering · Quality management · Agile
framework · ISO 14001 Environmental Management System

1 Motivation and Context

To address global warming driven by humans, all goods like products and services have
to be aligned with the sustainability goals of the United Nations (UN) [1]. The alignment
optimizes the consumption footprints and contributes to worthy life on earth now and in
future for the generations to come. To support the UN sustainability goals and objectives,
many companies like the Volkswagen AG have environmental policies [2] and environmental policy statements [3] and missions [4]. An option to address responsibility about
ecological impact of products and service can be part of the governance model of the
companies and is often established with the Environmental Management System (EMS)
defined by the ISO 14001:2015 [5]. The purpose of ISO 14001 is to provide a framework
for the protection of the environment and to respond to its changing conditions. The success of the EMS depends on all levels and functions of an organization and addresses the
whole life-cycle of a product or service that the organization may control or influence.
This life-cycle may include the aspects of software and its development. Nowadays IT
services gaining more and more importance in product development and services, thus
the aspect cannot be neglected within the life cycle thinking. However, as a generic

© Springer Nature Switzerland AG 2022
A. Przybyłek et al. (Eds.): LASD 2022, LNBIP 438, pp. 96–115, 2022.
https://doi.org/10.1007/978-3-030-94238-0_6

EMS approach, the ISO 14001 defines a general set of requirements, but does not offer detailed information or support for domain or technology-specific instantiation – like for software. This paper will take a deeper look on the adaption of the requirements of ISO 14001 into the software development process and into the agile way of working in the field of IT development.

In Organizations within large enterprises, agile and lean working can be fostered by the efiS® framework. With a focus on the integration of processes, and the scaling of knowledge, the framework is designed to systematically address typical large enterprise challenges such as governance of regulation requirements. ISO 14001 standard includes requirements for EMS. The efiS® framework building block to instantiate systematic regulation and standard requirements is Level of Done (LoD). This work will investigate how to structure ISO 14001 requirements to include these requirements into a LoD and as such in the efiS® framework [37].

Overall, this work proposes an approach for a rigorous refinement from the UN sustainability and specific environmental enterprise goals via the effected business domains with their dedicated products and services down to software, which is part of their deliveries for customers and users. This refinement is made with an end-to-end view of the software life-cycle to address development and usage. To establish a holistic sustainability view, not only energy consumption of the running software is in scope. This view addresses resource allocations for hardware and engineers etc. around the product and services, too.

The research questions are (RQ1) *how to derive a lean ISO 14001 aligned EMS for IT products and services?* and (RQ2) *how to integrate EMS and further aspects of sustainability into autonomous agile teams?*

2   Literature Overview on Sustainable Software Systems

In [6], the discussion about CO2 in the context of computation is imitated by watching the electrical power consumption. In [7], the sustainability goals are mapped to software sustainability. The GREENSOFT model proposed in [8] a structuring into *Life Cycle of Software Products, Sustainability Criteria and Metrics, Procedure Models* and *Recommendations and Tools*. A sustainable software life-cycle thinking is proposed in [9] to ensure an end-to-end evaluation of sustainability aspects. To measure sustainability in software, the work of [10] suggest a set of sustainable software performance metrics. In [11], a set of *Green Performance Indicators* (GPI) is defined. In [12], GPI for high and low level are distinguished from the organizational level down via the applications resource consumption to the compute node. In [13], the power consumption correlation with the design is demonstrated. In [14], the link from the software to real world impact initiated by software during the usage is made – this will become more and more important with the growing IoT.

In [15], software sustainability is distinguished into social, economic and environmental sustainability – the last is defined as *Software Greenability* and refines the ISO 25010 [16] quality characteristics. The sustainable software quality framework of [17] distinguish *social, environmental, technical and economic sustainability* this is derived from the approach of [18] with the additional dimension *individual*. GreenRM is a reference model proposed by [19] for sustainable software development oriented on the SPICE (ISO 15504) Process Assessment Model (PAM) based on a set of practices. In [20], methods of conventional and sustainable software development phases are compared and sustainable benefits are derived.

For sustainable architecture design decisions, [21] suggests decision map mapping with focus on immediate, enabling and systemic impacts. In [22], the *Principle, Rational, Strategies and Measure* (PRSM) approach is suggested for mapping sustainability aspects.

Sustainable software is characterized in [23] by measures of *extensibility, interoperability, maintainability, portability, reusability, scalability and usability.* In [24] the interaction of aspects of software quality and sustainability are identified – mostly on an energy efficiency focus.

To establish more energy efficient hardware different initiatives exists over decades like the "green star" symbol. For data center infrastructures, [25, 25] propose energy-proportional computing to realize higher power efficiency in a larger range of load.

The topic sustainable software development is addressed outside academic research with practical guides and tutorials of different companies like Microsoft [27], VMware [28] or SAP [29] and personal initiatives like [30].

To summarize, software sustainability aligned with [31] *Green Software* is distinguished between *green IN software* and *green BY software.* The green IN can refined more into aspects like software engineering or governance. Inadequate handling of sustainability aspects leads to sustainability debts [32] in the software and the derived products and services. Many of the named new methods and techniques demonstrate how to support sustainability in the development of software. Nevertheless, the software engineering body of knowledge (SWEBOK) [33] is a widespread and prevailing, generic approach and will be focused in the following to align the sustainability aspects of this domain.

However, no systematic approach for an ISO 14001 aligned software system lifecycle management is identified during the literature analysis. This gap can be closed by combining existing approaches, patterns etc. or developing new artifacts to closing gaps.

3   The Design of the Level of Done (LoD) Layer ISO 14001

The development of the proposed approach is based on Design Science Research (DSR) [34] and Action Research (AR) [35], which is slowly gaining prominence in software engineering research [36], for a rigor and practice relevance. The three DSR cycles are handled as follows: the relevance cycle derived the requirements of the global demand for a more sustainable economy (Sect. 1), the design cycle is handled in Sect. 3 and 4, the rigor cycle is handled in Sect. 2 which influenced the design and the final outcome is a Self-Service Kit (SSK) [55] as knowledge sharing artifact for the Group IT. However, agile working with AR leads to iterations for improvements in the design cycle driven by the observations and feedbacks. The objective is to design an approach to integrate global e.g. UN and enterprise sustainability goals into the product or service specific sustainability framework. The efiS® framework [37] – an agile framework which addresses quality and compliance - can be used to facilitate and establish a lean governance and compliance setup on product or service level with LoD layers [38]. The LoD layers are useful to offer agile teams the relevant regulations and standard requirements of their product or service domain. Each standard or regulations is described in an individual LoD layer. This work develops the ISO 14001 LoD layer for a specific use case in the IT domain. An important aspect of the LoD approach is that "raw" information is delivered to the teams and this ensures that no additional interpretation makes it difficult to establish lean value streams. However, everything needed to stay compliant in the domain and product or service context is part of the LoD layer. By adequate fulfilling of all relevant LoD layers the product or service reaches compliance and can be delivered to customers. The amount of levels is defined by the amount of handovers needed to be ready to deliver. Primarily, the demanded handovers is defined by the organizational structure. Furthermore, handovers can be required by regulation or standards e.g. for independent checks. All relevant requirements of standards and regulations are assigned to the latest level possible – motivated by the agile and lean principle to make decisions as late as possible.

The investigated setting of the ISO 14001 aligned EMS refinement is defined by:

- The IT/software organization is part of an enterprise with an established ISO 14001 aligned EMS.
- The IT/software organization is supported by an enterprise purchase organization which established supply chain management procedures.
- The software development and operation is independent from the IT infrastructure (data center etc.) delivery and support. Software teams do not "organize" hardware etc. they "use" what is deployed.
- The IT/software organization is driven by customers' demands form e.g. business departments.

The requirements presented by the chapters of ISO 14001 are identified as compliance aspects for EMS that need to be mapped to the identified levels. The ISO 14001 standard requires three levels for our example with the customer- (user-)driven IT organization. The review of the requirements with all stakeholders leads to a handover of the refined and reviewed requirements to the IT organization. Leadership commitment (ISO 14001, Chapter 5.1) and internal audits (ISO 14001, Chapter 9.2) are needed for strategic and independent approval. All other external/independent reviews could be modeled as handover, however, not all outcomes have to be independently reviewed in this case. Therefore, the explicit formal modeling of an additional level is not useful (as long as each level models handovers). This makes it possible to have the option to realize all relevant ISO 14001 aspects in three LoD levels: customer level, IT/software development/deliver level, and approval level. The requirement to understand the context of the organization (ISO 14001, Chapter 4.1) is assigned to the first level for the handover. As the cyclic checks by the authorities (ISO 14001, Chapter 4.3) and the audit (ISO 14001, Chapter 9.2) are the approval reviews in the third level. However, management review (ISO 14001, Chapter 9.3) is not assigned as approval, because the core mindset is to adjust and improve the EMS. All other identified aspects are mapped to the second level for the IT development, operating and/or service delivery. Table 1 presents an LoD layer for the ISO 14001 that has been established according to the logic explained above. Each line of the table addresses a topic. Some pillars have to handle more topics than others. By the usage of the LoD layer ISO 14001 in the context of an agile setup like with the efiS® framework this enables autonomous teams to integrate sustainability directly into their value stream.

Table 1. Example of an efiS® framework LoD layer ISO 14001.

Customer level	IT/software development/delivery level	Approval level
Identify requirements and (derive) compliance obligations (4.2)	**Context** Understand the needs and expectations of interested parties. Identify requirements and (derive) compliance obligations (4.2) Determine the scope of the EMS with is boundaries and authorities (4.3) and document the determinations (4.4)	Authorities are committed to their (control) duties (4.3)
	Leadership Leadership and commitment is established for effectiveness of the EMS and its organizational and business process integration to ensure the intended outcomes and continuous improvement (5.1) Establish, implement and maintain the environmental policy aligned with the EMS scope. The policy is documented, communicated and available (5.2) The responsibilities and authorities for relevant roles are assigned and established to ensure that the EMS conforms to requirements and standards as well for EMS performance reporting (5.3)	
	Planning Planning includes the handling of requirements and obligations as well as risks and opportunities to prevent undesired effects and ensure the intended outcomes of the EMS. The needed EMS processes and the identified risks and opportunities are documented (6.1.1) Determine the environmental aspects of activities and their products/services which are controlled and influenced in a life-cycle perspective. Document the aspects with their determination criteria and communicate them (6.1.2) Determine the compliance obligations from the environmental aspects and document them (6.1.3) The organization plans actions to address significant environmental aspects, compliance obligations, for the risks and opportunities and the needed processes of the EMS (6.1.4) Environmental objective are established, maintained and documented for significant environmental aspects and associated compliance obligations with the risks and opportunities (6.2.1) Planning actions to achieve environmental objectives, were possible integrated into the organizational processes or value streams. Actions are defined by what, who, when and how achievement is measured (6.2.2)	

(continued)

Table 1. (*continued*)

Customer level	IT/software development/delivery level	Approval level
	Support The organization determines and provides the needed resources for the EMS (7.1) Necessary competences for environmental performance and fulfillment of the compliance obligations are determined. Were need trainings etc. are associated. Competency evidences are documented (7.2) The organization ensures that persons doing work under awareness of the environmental policy, the significant environmental aspects, their contribution to the EMS and the impact of non-compliance by non-conforming with the EMS (7.3) The organization establishes relevant internal and external communication about the EMS addressing what, when, whom and how to communicate and document it (7.4.1) The organization internal (7.4.2) and external (7.4.3) communication about relevant EMS information is established The documentation is aligned with the ISO 14001 demands (as mentioned in this LoD layer explicit) and the internal necessary for an effective EMS (7.5.1) The document creation and update includes appropriate identification and description, format, media and review/approval information (7.5.2) Documented information for the EMS and the ISO 14001 is controlled for suitable use, adequately protected and version controlled within a document life-cycle. This includes external origins documents, too (7.5.3)	
	Operation Establish, implement, control and maintain processes to meet the EMS requirements and the planned actions (see 6) with established operating criteria and its controls. Identify unintended chances/side-effects and mitigate them. The EMS shall control/influence outsourced processes were possible. With a life cycle perspective: - ensure that environmental requirements are addressed in each product or service life cycle - supply chain (e.g. contractors, procurement) related relevant environmental requirements are determined and communicated - consider to provide information about relevant environmental impact of transportation, use, end-of-life treatment and final disposal Maintain documentation about carried out the processes as planned (8.1) Prepare for emergency response by prepare responds plans to mitigate environmental impacts, act according on demand, take actions to prevent or mitigate the consequences of potential environmental impacts. Periodical test the planned actions, where practicable. Periodically update the planes especially with learning. Inform and train relevant parties and related workforce. Maintain documentation about carried out the processes as planned (8.2)	

(*continued*)

Table 1. (*continued*)

Customer level	IT/software development/delivery level	Approval level
	Performance evaluation The organization determines needs for monitoring and measures; their methods to ensure valid results; indicators and criteria to evaluate the environmental performance. Determine when and how often the analysis and evaluation took place. If needed, take action and maintain the understanding of its compliance state. The organization shall calibrate or verify the evaluation equipment. The organization evaluate its EMS performance and effectiveness. The organization communicates relevant environmental performance information internally and externally as defined in the communication process or required by obligations. Maintain evidence documentation about the performance evaluation (9.1) The management reviews the EMS in planned intervals, to ensure suitability, adequacy and effectiveness The review considers: status of actions from previous reviews, changes in the setup and environment of the EMS, the environmental objectives, the environmental performance especially non-conformance aspects, resource adequateness, and improvement potentials. Retain documentation about the reviews and their results with focus on conclusions about suitability, adequateness and effectivity of the EMS; improvement decisions; needed actions to fit objectives; opportunities to improve the EMS; and implications to the strategy of the organization (9.3)	Internal audits are established, implemented and maintained which includes the frequency, methods, responsibilities and reporting of the audits. Audits are defined by scope and conducted by objective and impartiality auditors. The Results reported to the relevant management. Retain documentation about the audits and their results (9.2)
	Improvement Determine improvement opportunities for the EMS and implement them (10.1) React on non-conformities by taking corrective actions; deal with consequences and mitigate environmental impacts. Evaluate actions to avoid nonconformity in the future (determine root-cause and identify other similar potential occurrences). Implement needed corrective actions and review their effectiveness. If necessary, make changes to the EMS. Retain documentation about evidences about the nature of the non-compliance and the subsequent actions and its results (10.2) To enhance the environmental performance the organization continuously improves the EMS about suitability, adequateness and effectiveness (10.3)	

4   Leveraging Sustainable Software Systems and Services

To instantiate the LoD layer ISO 14001 in the context of software engineering possible content has to be identified. This chapter derives this software engineering related content. In organizations, the products and services typically can be aligned with an existing sustainability narrative [48] of the enterprise and aligned with the UN sustainability goals. The IT domain specific refinement of these goals can be oriented and structured on quality standards like the ISO 25010 or the SWEBOK [33]. Sustainability of software can be reduced to an end to end resource efficiency during the product and service life-cycle. Resources are the allocated human resources for the development, maintenance and operation of the software and the consumed energy of hardware and infrastructure to run the software deployments' workload. This leads in the deductive view to the consumption of deployed resources (like the engineers and hardware/infrastructure) life-cycle as a kind of related foot-print to the direct resource allocation time. For the allocated engineers it is the way they work (like online or on-site with related travel aspects etc.) and for the infrastructures their "foot-print"-part (facility construction supplement etc.) for the software workload deployment consumption. However, not all aspects are managed by the software life-cycle. It is not always possible to deploy in the greenest facility (data center [39]) available – and if, this will swamp out other software deployments to less green facilities. To act responsibly as long as not all resources are completely green, it is a replacement issue which can only be globally optimized by tuning software to the smallest foot-print possible during its life-cycle. Depending on the deployment facilities, a more or less big supplement factor to the runtime consumed energy is added to address the real physical conditions.

The proposed approach addresses all four sustainability dimensions [17]:

(i)   Social sustainability is addresses by the adequate engineering allocation.
(ii) Technical sustainability is addressed with an efficiency focused and maintenance friendly software architecture and design. This addresses the sustainability benefits of long time usage of a software from the
(iii) environmental sustainability and
(iv) economical sustainability view, too.

For software interacting with users, they are part of the UX design which contributes primarily to the economical sustainability – happy users come back and make revenue.

Simplification: Sustainability of software can be reduced to an end-to-end resource efficiency during its life-cycle. Resources are the allocated human resources for the development and operations of the software and the consumed energy to run the software deployments. The long usage of IT systems and software typically is a business goal. This business goal supports the goal to have a long life-cycle to amortize the high investments of the initial development. Life-cycle "stretching" directly supports sustainability, too. Figure 1 shows that hardware and software sustainability optimize the same resources and can be managed mostly independent without negative side-effects as long as both are optimizing the same sustainability goals about resource efficiency – primarily energy and "engineers". Sustainability debts are a specific sub-category of the well-known technical debts [40] of software and IT systems. Debts are making the future life-cycle more difficult and expensive – debts making a product or service older from a life-cycle perspective.

Fig. 1. Strategic sustainability refinement of IT comes to correlated optimizations.

To ensure that IT sustainability is holistically addressed around the definition of a structured software life-cycle, the SWEBOK can be used by mapping the aspects and their contributions or support together. In the following ten knowledge areas of SWEBOK within the field of software engineering are identified for the mapping of sustainability aspects and supports. As a generic collection this mapping can be used in a wide range of software engineering driven product and service setups. Table 2 presents the related building blocks for IT sustainability.

To summarize Table 2, the presented detailed analysis can be used to offer some technology and IT expert principles and patterns to deliver aligned with the strategic sustainability refinement of Fig. 1. In Fig. 2, these derived generic principles for software engineering are presented. The figure shows the software engineering relevant aspects, oriented on the life-cycle from raw material (IT infrastructure and its facilities), development, production, transportation and disposal. Transportation of data is important, the typical movement of IT infrastructure into the data center and its disposal can be neglect in mostly all cases.

For software engineers, the build time definitions are pivotal. The entire ecological footprint of any deployment significantly depends on included libraries and packages (reuse). The intelligent design of data structures for the specific use-case defines how many data has to be moved and transformed. The implemented algorithms are crucial for runtime and data movements during the workload handling. To react smoothly to workload changes, the dynamic scaling of the deployment is needed. To serve the users reliably, an intelligent resilience approach has to be built in. During runtime, the basic decision is to select the facility with the most efficient overall-package because often the change to other cooling, IT infrastructure or energy providers is not possible from the enterprise devops team view. Sometimes life-cycle aspects of some infrastructure components are manageable e.g. the leasing time selection. Mostly the optimization within the constraints is possible by e.g. selection of the right CPU type for the workload or active data management e.g. with clean-up policies and procedures to reduce the data foot-prints. The human behavior also impacts the sustainability of the software: e.g., there are legions of IT consultants flying in every week to build and run software. Find ways to reduce this secondary negative foot-print. Also, handovers coming typically with an overhead of inefficiency. To have a sustainable engineering develop adequate skilled teams around the software's life-cycle.

Table 2. The IT sustainability aspects oriented on SWEBOK.

SWEBOK	IT sustainability aspect/building block	Supports
SW requirements	*Emergent properties*: allocate sustainability goals at least for technical property of the software *Requirements negotiation*: negotiate the value and if needed the related investment into technical sustainability goals with the business stakeholders	Environmental, economic, technical
SW design	*Design principles*: establish software sustainability principles as first-class principles *Error and exception handling*: important for an efficient runtime support during the life-cycle *Fault tolerance*: avoid fault tolerance with additional resource allocation like (hot-)standby deployments; establish other techniques for fault tolerance like active pools of serving instance (e.g. clusters for serverless functions) *Security*: design the software for easy and fast security updates and fixing *UI design*: think in an holistic user experience to foster easy to use during the entire life-cycle *Quality attributes*: establish software sustainability attributes as first class attributes	Environmental, technical, social, economical
SW construction	*Minimize complexity*: select and build simple algorithms and data structures; keep communication simple *Constructing for verification*: reduces the effort and amount for safeguarding releases and deployments *Construction technologies*: select technologies which are fostering efficiency and a long life-cycle of the software like API, platforms and middleware components *Language*: select an adequate language for an efficient implementation *Construction for re-use*: to enlarge the life-cycle of at least components establish a re-use strategy were possible and adequate	Environmental, economic, technical

(*continued*)

Table 2. (*continued*)

SWEBOK	IT sustainability aspect/building block	Supports
SW testing	*Test technique*: establish test automation to validate all test objectives and goals over the life-cycle with an efficient procedure; avoid not needed test-runs; consider to run a test environment only if it is needed for testing (deployment foot-print);	Environmental, technical
SW maintenance	*Evolution of SW*: to enlarge the life-cycle of the software keep it updated and "fresh" from the technical and user perspective *Proactive and reactive maintenance*: optimize changes (content, frequency) on the software with focus on resource efficiency *Limited understanding*: establish a life-cycle devops team were possible and keep software simple and intuitive to avoid resource intensive "re-engineering" *Testing*: establish an efficient testing procedure to minimize test environment uptime and optimize the amount of test-runs needed to safeguard the software *Maintainability*: keep sustainability debts small *Outsourcing*: ensure that the supply chain applies at least the same high sustainability standards and objective that in-house *Unique or supporting activities*: design for reducing support efforts were possible *Retirement/migration*: realize second life and reuse of at least components were possible	Environmental, economic, technical
SW configuration management	*Building and release management:* find an adequate balance of build and release efforts to value and risks of late large releases	Environmental, economical
SW engineering	*Life-cycle*: focus on life-cycle sustainability instead of local optimizations *Behavioral and structural modeling*: make sustainability aspects of the software to a first class citizen during modeling *Group dynamics*: use group dynamics to push sustainability goals were possible *Cost-effectiveness analysis*: consider sustainability debts in the cost analysis; keep life-cycle cost in scope *Good enough principle*: keep focus on value and efficiency to avoid over-engineering *Trade-offs*: keep software sustainability in every trade-off analysis	Environmental

(*continued*)

Table 2. (*continued*)

SWEBOK	IT sustainability aspect/building block	Supports
SW quality	*SW quality requirements*: ensure that software sustainability is part of the elicitation of quality requirements (keep in mind, sustainability is not explicit part of the ISO 25010 software quality characteristics like functional suitability, performance efficiency, portability or usability) *Verification and validation*: ensure that sustainability requirements and goals are validated like all other requirements	Environmental, technical
Eng. foundations	*Reliability*: find ways to be reliable without the default-pattern with additional "hot-standby" deployments	Environmental
Comp. foundation	*Algorithms and complexity:* prefer RAM rather than CPU usage during algorithm design were possible *Data structure:* keep data structures small, but prefer RAM rather than CPU usage during data structure design were possible when focusing on run-time aspects Systems engineering: avoid movement and transformation of data were possible *CPU:* energy consumption correlates with amount of instructions; were possible focus is power efficiency per instruction which is depending on the processor model and its architecture [41–43] (rough approx. 10-20W/core TPD [44, 44]) *Memory:* energy consumption is "static"; approx. 2W/GB [46] *I/O*: in general energy consumption correlates with the amount I/O data – e.g. disk I/O often is routed via networks *DB*: in general energy consumption correlates with the amount transferred data, but differs from types of DB *Networking:* energy consumption correlates with the amount of data (bytes) and the distance (km); compress data were possible and route with less "hubs"	Environmental, technical

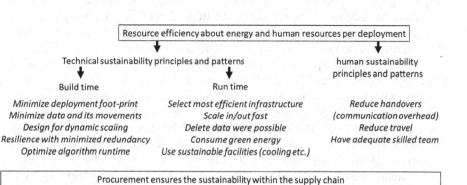

Fig. 2. Generic principles and patterns for a sustainable SW engineering life-cycle.

5 Instantiation, Evaluation and Improvement

In practice the outcome of Sect. 3 – the LoD layer ISO 14001 – and the outcome of Sect. 4 – the sustainable software engineering approach – have to be combined to demonstrate the effect on the specific product or service setup. In the following chapter, this combination is exemplified by a case study that also shows how to integrate EMS and further aspects of sustainability into autonomous agile teams.

To instantiate the LoD layer ISO 14001 in the context of a specific product or service, the build and delivery team has to find adequate selections of the proposed principles and patterns. These selections have to be instantiated to the specific product or service with its workload demanded by the users. During iterations in the agile way of working, the EMS with its related sustainability aspects and its instantiation will be optimized to better fit the demands. To give an idea how this works in practice, an example on from the Volkswagen Group IT Testing as a Service (TaaS) [47] is presented. The intention of TaaS is to reduce the large amount of Test-Runtime execution (T-Rex) environments. In the past, mostly all product and service teams deployed and maintained their T-Rex environments. This often allocates 24 * 7 resources of IT infrastructure. Furthermore, the right sizing was difficult for the teams which often lead to over-provisioning and unnecessary waste of resources. TaaS offers T-Rex on demand right-sized for the specific test workload. This business model by design leads to a more sustainable software development, but this is no excuse to not continuously optimize the service to improve its foot-print and efficiency for a more sustainable service delivery. Some core architecture requirements and building blocks like the hybrid-cloud capability and cluster based will have impact to the sustainability options.

The Volkswagen AG has instantiated and deployed in the context of the Vision *goTOzero* and be *A leading Automotive Software Company* [48] a set of prioritized UN SDGs—more specifically the goals 7, 8, 9, 11, 12 and 13—and the derived focus areas *decarbonization, circular economy, responsibility in supply chains and business, workforce transformation*. Based on these strategic sustainability goals, the primary focus on IT sustainability should be to reduce the CO_2 foot-print of its services, however also optimize the other focused SDGs where ever possible, too. These are the compliance obligations for the TaaS EMS instantiation. This is the "input" for the LoD layer ISO 14001 and the selection of the proposed SWEBOK mapped "sustainability potentials".

The refinement of the LoD layer ISO 14001 for the TaaS delivery team setup includes the application of the Product Quality Risk (PQR) approach [49] to identify potential sustainability risks with the pre-mortem based on the PESTLE (political, economic, social, technology, legal and environmental) mindset which includes environmental aspects, too. The PQR approach is based on Design Thinking. To ideate about the risks holistically, the aspects of PESTLE are reflected. The efiS® framework empowerment pillar with the building blocks aTWQ [50] and TTM [38] facilitates to develop the needed skill set and team maturity to ensure that the team setup is adequate for a sustainable service delivery, which seizes opportunities and mitigates risks adequately by keeping a focus on continuous improvement and support the planned actions within their day-by-day operations and development tasks.

For TaaS, the resource efficiency goal influences at built time following architecture and design decisions based on the following principles which are part of the planning of new features and capabilities during the cyclic refinement sessions:

– Use micro-services for workload specific fine-grained scaling

    o Package service in containers to optimize utilization of hardware instances

        • Is a base for choosing RAM-optimized instance for deployments

    p Keep container sizes small to run more deployments on hardware instance

        • Consider all container layers starting on e.g. Alpine Linux

    q Focus on direct data streaming without unnecessary proxies/hubs

        • Avoid overheads like e.g. istio as long as possible

– Avoid large and long-distance data movements

    o Co-locate micro-services on nodes and availability zone were possible

        • Work with for example with node affinities by keeping resilience
        • Reduce redundancy based on (hot) standby infrastructure

    p Avoid storage of data were possible and delete them as soon as possible

        • Stay state-less were possible
        • Apply policies e.g. on object storage to delete data rigor

    q Avoid transfer of data with local caching at least in the cluster

        • Establish caching strategies addressing typical user workloads

– Keep services simple

    o Optimize the usage of libraries

        • Technology selection e.g. Quarkus framework

    p Optimize runtime setting

        • optimize the runtime and their settings e.g. JVM GC

    q Focus on simple and clean code implementations

- Optimize algorithms for maintenance and (CPU) foot-print

r   Stay with a small active selected set of technologies were possible

- Select e.g. one programming language like Java

s   Build on the shoulders of others

- Select and build on open software were useful
- Select open interfaces and standards for portability and reuse

The focus on these sustainability driven principles helps the TaaS team to keep the technology and human resource allocation small. By avoiding cloud provider specific proprietary interfaces TaaS runs in different deployments e.g. legal entities and on different cloud providers – reuse enabled by portability of the software.

Operationalization of sustainability decisions for features and capabilities is realized via their belonging stories and tasks. The evaluation is realized by the acceptance criteria of the stories and in the show and tell sessions. The show and tell sessions combined with the retrospectives are leading to strategic continuous improvement of the sustainability of the deployed service. As sustainability performance indicator the degree of optimization of the deployment foot-print is used. This is a useful metric because it includes also uptimes of secondary deployments like test environments for development and maintenance. Furthermore, it is relative to the past and fosters continuous improvement. About the engineering resources the focus is to reduce operating efforts by smart build time decisions. However the word smart is key, because not all potential possible actions are really sustainable - also in a life-cycle view the amortization of the initial resource invest will not reached. This leads often to trade-off decisions during story refinements.

Over the last years the energy efficiency of TaaS was improved continuously with "foot-print self-benchmarking" – only in the last 12 months we optimized the service delivery efficiency with right-sizing of the infrastructure to the current workload profile, selection of energy optimized compute instances and an optimized caching strategy in a 2-digit percentage value. This shows, that in the fast-changing IT world technology driven opportunities to optimize sustainability are always emerging, too.

The team realized that especially infrastructure is a constraint set for software engineers and pre-defined by the purchased products and services. Only in the pre-defined option set the team can select to optimize the foot-print. However, the Volkswagen AG supplier management acts strategic aligned with the sustainability goals [51], too.

The instantiation of the ISO 14001 aspects are a facilitation for the European Green Deal and the EU Taxonomy Regulation [52] ambitions. The sustainability actions derived from the LoD layer ISO 14001 instantiation directly can mapped to the six objectives of the Taxonomy to indicate that the product or service is a sustainable investment. This can be realized by mapping of indicating sustainability goals and their action to at least one of the 6 objectives and indicating that no other objectives are "harmed" by carry out the service with social and governance standards in the context of the evaluated TaaS setup.

6 Discussion and Limitations

The proposed approach is holistic, because it starts from the global sustainability goals of the UN and can be refined down to individual software products and services within the setting of an organization. With it lean and agile approach based on efiS® framework building blocks it can be adopted directly into the value streams of the delivery teams. It fosters self-determination aligned with [53] *competency, autonomy* and *relatedness*. It helps the value stream team to develop knowledge and competencies about sustainable software engineering the LoD layer and the refinement to the software engineering life-cycle. It fosters autonomy with the LoD approach and its shared-responsibly concept by design. The relatedness is given by the specific product or service focus on which the sustainability aspects are applied. This also offers an additional relatedness dimension in cross-functional sustainability communities of large enterprises etc. The aspect of being part of a global sustainability community also can give purpose and motivation to involved people [54]. The proposed sustainability software engineering approach supports all key indicators needed to foster intrinsic motivation of the involved employees.

A limitation is that the (autonomous agile) teams have to identify which of the SWEBOK mapped sustainability options are the right in the context of the enterprise sustainability strategy or environmental policy and the specific software for the product or service. However, in most practical cases software engineers should be able to make this transfer step with the proposed facilitation.

A further limitation of the biased example evaluation is the instantiation on a modern Group IT service, because it does not cover legacy aspects of software. Sure, legacy software will have more sustainability debts which have to be handled as constraints, but all upcoming maintenance tasks can be aligned with the presented approach. The sustainability debts are a dedicated topic which has to be addressed actively by the devops team to realize improvements over the rest of the life-cycle. Additionally, the biased example is based on the Volkswagen AG sustainability goals and it is not demonstrated that the refinement from all other software companies sustainability goals is possible. However, Volkswagen is not an exclusive software company – it is a mobility company – and this indicates that in most cases the application should be possible.

7 Conclusion and Outlook

To establish systematic sustainability optimization in the software life-cycle aligned with global and enterprise goals and strategies is possible also in lean and agile setups. The generic efiS® framework offers all building blocks to instantiate a ISO 14001 aligned EMS refinement for IT in general and especially for software product teams.

The key contributions *to practice* can be summarized by the following aspects:

– presents an approach guided with the LoD layer ISO 14001 to refine global and enterprise sustainability goals to individual software products and services (RQ1)
– transparency and democratization of ISO 14001 requirements for an EMS to software engineers in autonomous agile teams (RQ2)

- identified generic software sustainability patterns mapped to the SWEBOK for operative instantiation during the software life-cycle (RQ2)
- presents an example of the application of the LoD layer ISO 14001 instantiation and the SWEBOK mapped sustainability patterns in real life enterprise service delivery context in an autonomous agile team setup (RQ1)(RQ2)
- An open point in the EU Taxonomy Regulation [56] for software is addressed and a practical solution is proposed with "foot-print self-benchmarking" (RQ2)

The key contributions *to theory* can be summarized by the following aspects:

- presents the gap of the current research from an EMS view down to specific software products and services (motivates RQ1)
- propose a lean instantiation approach of product specific ISO 14001 refinements (RQ1)
- identified that most for technical sustainable of software is realized during build time; runtime mostly focus on leveling the sustainability benefits – autonomous agile development teams keep the key to sustainable deliverables (RQ2)
- identified generic view for direct and indirect objective of sustainable software engineering: optimize the deployment package; add deployment environment factor and optimize this objectives within autonomous agile teams (RQ2)
- identified that intelligent employment of engineering contributes to the sustainability life-cycle which can be realized in autonomous agile teams (RQ2)

The overall conclusion is, that with the systematic application of the proposed approach it is possible to instantiate enterprise sustainability policies and goals to software driven IT products and services in autonomous agile teams.

A possible future research task is to generalize the LoD layer ISO 14001 to apply it beyond this example in the entire Group IT. Spread the proposed approach to other Group IT teams and create SSKs [55] about "hot topics" for software sustainability enhancements. Make a formal mapping of the software sustainability principles and patterns to the ISO 25010 for a refinement applicable also during quality planning and management. Furthermore, the investigation of low-level optimizations based on compiler flags is needed to see what sustainability improvements are possible with current options. On the highest level investigation can look at the product and service portfolio management and budget allocation – is sustainability selling more when it is driven by an EU Taxonomy mapping and is allocated preferred with money?

References

1. Sustainability Goals of the United Nations. https://sdgs.un.org/goals
2. Volkswagen AG environmental compliance. https://www.volkswagenag.com/en/sustainab ility/environment/environmental-compliance.html
3. Volkswagen AG sustainability strategy. https://www.volkswagenag.com/en/sustainability/ environment.html
4. Volkswagen AG sustainability mission. https://www.volkswagenag.com/presence/nachhalti gkeit/documents/Mission_Statement_Environment_2019-06-20_en_final_hoch.pdf
5. ISO 14001:2015. https://www.iso.org/iso-14001-environmental-management.html
6. Kelly, C., Mangina, E., Ruzelli, A.: Putting a CO 2 figure on a piece of computation. In: 11th International Conference on Electrical Power Quality and Utilisation, pp. 1–7. IEEE, 17 October 2011

7. García-Mireles, G.A., Moraga, M.Á., García, F., Calero, C., Piattini, M.: Interactions between environmental sustainability goals and software product quality: a mapping study. Inf. Softw. Technol. **95**, 108–129 (2018)
8. Naumann, S., Dick, M., Kern, E., Johann, T.: The greensoft model: a reference model for green and sustainable software and its engineering. Sustain. Comput. Inform. Syst. **1**(4), 294–304 (2011)
9. Johann, T., Dick, M., Kern, E., Naumann, S.: Sustainable development, sustainable software, and sustainable software engineering: an integrated approach. In: 2011 International Symposium on Humanities, Science and Engineering Research, pp. 34–39. IEEE, June 2011
10. Albertao, F., Xiao, J., Tian, C., Lu, Y., Zhang, K.Q., Liu, C.: Measuring the sustainability performance of software projects. In: 2010 IEEE 7th International Conference on E-Business Engineering, pp. 369–373. IEEE, November 2010
11. Mahmoud, S.S., Ahmad, I.: Green performance indicators for energy aware it systems: survey and assessment. J. Green Eng. **3**(1), 33–69 (2012)
12. Kipp, A., Jiang, T., Fugini, M., Salomie, I.: Layered green performance indicators. Futur. Gener. Comput. Syst. **28**(2), 478–489 (2012)
13. Sahin, C., Cayci, F., Clause, J., Kiamilev, F., Pollock, L., Winbladh, K.: Towards power reduction through improved software design. In: 2012 IEEE Energytech, pp. 1–6. IEEE, May 2012
14. Sierszecki, K., Mikkonen, T., Steffens, M., Fogdal, T., Savolainen, J.: Green software: greening what and how much? IEEE Softw. **31**(3), 64–68 (2014)
15. Calero, C., Moraga, M.A., Bertoa, M.F., Duboc, L.: Quality in use and software greenability. In: Proceedings of CEUR Workshop, pp. 28–36 (2014)
16. ISO/IEC 25010:2011. https://www.iso.org/standard/35733.html
17. Lago, P., Koçak, S.A., Crnkovic, I., Penzenstadler, B.: Framing sustainability as a property of software quality. Commun. ACM **58**(10), 70–78 (2015)
18. Penzenstadler, B., Femmer, H.: A generic model for sustainability with process-and product-specific instances. In: International Workshop on Green in Software Engineering and Green by Software Engineering at AOSD (2013)
19. Thiry, M., Frez, L., Zoucas, A.: GreenRM: reference model for sustainable software development. In: SEKE, pp. 39–42 (2014)
20. Agarwal, S., Nath, A., Chowdhury, D.: Sustainable approaches and good practices in green software engineering. Int. J. Res. Rev. Comput. Sci. **3**(1), 1425 (2012)
21. Lago, P.: Architecture design decision maps for software sustainability. In: 2019 IEEE/ACM 41st International Conference on Software Engineering: Software Engineering in Society (ICSE-SEIS), pp. 61–64. IEEE (2019)
22. Gupta, S., Lago, P., Donker, R.: A framework of software architecture principles for sustainability-driven design and measurement. In: 2021 IEEE 18th International Conference on Software Architecture Companion, pp. 31–37. IEEE (2021)
23. Venters, C., et al.: The blind men and the elephant: towards an empirical evaluation framework for software sustainability. J. Open Res. Softw. **2**(1), e8, 1–6 (2014). http://dx.doi.org/10.5334/jors.ao
24. Venters, C.C., et al.: Software sustainability: the modern tower of babel. In: CEUR Workshop Proceedings, vol. 1216, pp. 7–12 (2014)
25. Barroso, L.A., Hölzle, U.: The case for energy-proportional computing. Computer **40**(12), 33–37 (2007)
26. Barroso, L.A., Clidaras, J., Hölzle, U.: The datacenter as a computer: an introduction to the design of warehouse-scale machines. Synth. Lect. Comput. Archit. **8**(3), 1–154 (2013)
27. Microsoft Sustainability Engineering. https://docs.microsoft.com/en-us/learn/modules/sustainable-software-engineering-overview/

28. VMware sustainability approach. https://www.heise.de/hintergrund/Sustainability-im-Sof tware-Engineering-Teil-1-ein-Aufruf-6011723.html?seite=all
29. SAP sustainability approach. https://www.heise.de/developer/artikel/Sustainable-Progra mming-Softwarecode-ohne-Stromfresser-4197828.html?seite=all
30. Sustainability approach. https://principles.green/
31. Calero, C., Piattini, M.: Puzzling out software sustainability. Sustain. Comput. Inform. Syst. **16**, 117–124 (2017)
32. Betz, S., et al.: Sustainability debt: a metaphor to support sustainability design decisions (2015)
33. SWEBOK. https://ieeecs-media.computer.org/media/education/swebok/swebok-v3.pdf
34. Hevner, A.R.: A three cycle view of design science research. Scand. J. Inf. Syst. **19**(2), 4 (2007)
35. Avison, D.E., Lau, F., Myers, M.D., Nielsen, P.A.: Action research. Commun. ACM **42**(1), 94–97 (1999)
36. Przybyłek, A., Albecka, M., Springer, O., Kowalski, W.: Game-based Sprint retrospectives: multiple action research. Empir. Softw. Eng. **27**(1), 1–56 (2021). https://doi.org/10.1007/s10 664-021-10043-z
37. Poth, A., Kottke, M., Riel, A.: Orchestrating agile IT quality management for complex solution development through topic-specific partnerships in large enterprises – an example on the EFIS framework. In: Yilmaz, M., Clarke, P., Messnarz, R., Reiner, M. (eds.) EuroSPI 2021. CCIS, vol. 1442, pp. 88–104. Springer, Cham (2021). https://doi.org/10.1007/978-3-030-85521-5_7
38. Poth, A., Kottke, M., Middelhauve, K., Mahr, T., Riel, A.: Lean integration of IT security and data privacy governance aspects into product development in agile organizations. J. Univ. Comput. Sci. **27**(8), 868–893 (2021)
39. Data Center Efficiency. https://e3p.jrc.ec.europa.eu/publications/2021-best-practice-guidel ines-eu-code-conduct-data-centre-energy-efficiency
40. Kruchten, P., Nord, R.L., Ozkaya, I.: Technical debt: from metaphor to theory and practice. IEEE Softw. **29**(6), 18–21 (2012)
41. AMD. https://www.amd.com/system/files/documents/The-Energy-Efficient-AMD-EPYC-Design.pdf
42. Analysis. https://www.servethehome.com/amd-epyc-7002-series-rome-delivers-a-knockout/amd-epyc-7002-power-consumption/
43. Benchmarking. https://www.phoronix.com/scan.php?page=article&item=linux55-xeon-epyc&num=9
44. Intel Xeon 36. https://www.intel.de/content/www/de/de/products/sku/215276/intel-xeon-gold-6342-processor-36m-cache-2-80-ghz/specifications.html
45. Intel Xeon 18. https://www.intel.de/content/www/de/de/products/sku/215273/intel-xeon-gold-6334-processor-18m-cache-3-60-ghz/specifications.html
46. https://www.servethehome.com/ddr4-dimms-system-power-consumption-tested/
47. Poth, A., Urban, H., Riel, A.: Make product and service requirements shippable - from the cloud service vision to a continuous value stream which satisfies current and future user needs. Springer (2022, in print)
48. Volkswagen AG report. https://www.volkswagenag.com/presence/nachhaltigkeit/documents/sustainability-report/2020/Nonfinancial_Report_2020_e.pdf
49. Poth, A., Riel, A.: Quality requirements elicitation by ideation of product quality risks with design thinking. In: 2020 IEEE 28th International Requirements Engineering Conference (RE), pp. 238–249. IEEE, August 2020
50. Poth, A., Kottke, M., Riel, A.: Evaluation of agile team work quality. In: Paasivaara, M., Kruchten, P. (eds.) XP 2020. LNBIP, vol. 396, pp. 101–110. Springer, Cham (2020). https://doi.org/10.1007/978-3-030-58858-8_11

51. Volkswagen AG rating. https://www.vwgroupsupply.com/one-kbp-pub/en/kbp_public/inf ormation/nachhaltigkeit_neu_pub_2019/sustainability_rating__s_rating_2/sustainability_ rating__s_rating_3.html
52. EU Taxonomy. https://ec.europa.eu/info/business-economy-euro/banking-and-finance/sustai nable-finance/eu-taxonomy-sustainable-activities_en
53. Ryan, R.M., Deci, E.L.: Self-determination theory and the facilitation of intrinsic motivation, social development, and well-being. Am. Psychol. **55**(1), 68 (2000)
54. Harackiewicz, J.M., Sansone, C.: Goals and intrinsic motivation: you can get there from here. Adv. Motiv. Achiev. **7**, 21–49 (1991)
55. Poth, A., Kottke, M., Riel, A.: Scaling agile on large enterprise level with self-service kits to support autonomous teams. In: 2020 15th Conference on Computer Science and Information Systems (FedCSIS), pp. 731–737. IEEE, September 2020
56. page 362 "the software gap." https://ec.europa.eu/info/sites/default/files/business_eco nomy_euro/banking_and_finance/documents/200309-sustainable-finance-teg-final-report-taxonomy-annexes_en.pdf#page356

Modeling and Model Transformation as a Service: Towards an Agile Approach to Model-Driven Development

Adel Vahdati and Raman Ramsin(✉) (iD)

Department of Computer Engineering, Sharif University of Technology, Azadi Avenue,
Tehran, Iran
vahdati@ce.sharif.edu, ramsin@sharif.edu

Abstract. Scalability has always been a challenge in software development, and
agile methods have faced their own ordeal in this regard. The classic solution is
to use modeling to manage the complexities of the system while facilitating intra-
team and inter-team communication; however, agile methods tend to shy away
from modeling to avoid its adverse effect on productivity. Model-driven development (MDD) has shown great potential for automatic code generation, thereby
enhancing productivity, but the agile community seems unconvinced that this gain
in productivity justifies the extra effort required for modeling. The challenge that
the MDD community faces today is to incorporate MDD in agile development
methodologies in such a way that agility is tangibly and convincingly preserved.
In this paper, we address this challenge by using a service-oriented approach to
modeling and model transformation that pays special attention to abiding by agile
values and principles.

Keywords: Model-Driven Development · Agile methods · Service-oriented
architecture

1 Introduction

In Model-Driven Development (MDD), models play the primary role throughout the
process of software development [1]. One of the motivations for using this approach is
to automatically create the product from models of the system. In model-driven development, the problem domain is described in terms of models at high levels of abstraction.
By executing a chain of model-to-model transformations, the details of the solution
domain are gradually added, thus producing refined models of the system. The process
culminates in generation of code by using model-to-text transformation.

Agile methods are widely used in the software industry. Although they strive to
expedite software development and delivery as much as possible, they also pay special
attention to enhancing flexibility in order to respond to change in a timely manner [2].
Agile methodologies are lightweight and tend to shy away from modeling, as executable
code is considered the main measure of progress; however, they all incorporate a highly-
disciplined and well-defined process [1].

© Springer Nature Switzerland AG 2022
A. Przybyłek et al. (Eds.): LASD 2022, LNBIP 438, pp. 116–135, 2022.
https://doi.org/10.1007/978-3-030-94238-0_7

It might seem that agile development and model-driven development are poles apart. Agile methods are lightweight, fast, responsive and adaptable, while model-driven approaches are heavyweight and require early investment in modeling [3]. Agile methods focus more on the process and methodological aspects of software development, while model-driven approaches rely on architectural aspects and separation of concerns [4]. Nevertheless, it has been observed that by combining these two approaches, we can take advantage of the strengths of both and cover some of their weaknesses [3]. The goal of both approaches is to manage complexity: model-driven methods reduce accidental complexity by separating design concerns from implementation details [5]; agile methods manage complexity by creating product increments in short iterations and receiving early and fast feedback [6]. Both approaches also try to accelerate development and enhance response to change: agile methods move in this direction by early and continuous delivery of products in short iterations [4]; MDD achieves this goal by raising the level of automation in code generation [2].

There are several reasons for integrating agile methods and model-driven approaches, including [6]: improving agility and minimizing unnecessary tasks, increasing collaboration, enhancing requirements analysis, reducing risks by receiving early feedback, accelerating response to change, increasing the level of automation, managing complexity and building the models in an iterative-incremental fashion, and better understanding of the problem domain [6]. Some very influential agile methods started as model-phobic frameworks; however, it has since been realized that all of them can make use of modeling in some way [7]. One of the potential solutions is Agile Modeling (AM), which provides a means for adding modeling to agile methods without compromising agility [7]. The most important issue in agile MDD is to determine which agile practices, under what circumstances, and how, should be used in MDD [8]. In AM, models are created just in time and just enough for the specific purpose intended [9]. Despite its merits, AM's applicability to MDD should be further explored.

We propose a new agile approach to MDD by using service-oriented concepts. The purpose of this approach is to facilitate participation and collaboration in the modeling process and to improve scalability in terms of model size and the number of modelers involved in the modeling process. To this aim, we introduce the idea of "multilevel modeling as a service" and "model transformation as a service", and propose a new model-driven architecture. For modeling at different levels of abstraction, we propose the concept-based abstract syntax, which allows the description of the problem domain and the solution domain from structural, functional and behavioral perspectives.

The rest of this paper is structured as follows: Sect. 2 provides an overview of the previous works related to this research; Sect. 3 presents the problems currently afflicting agile software development and MDD, and the potential opportunities that will arise as a result of their integration; Sect. 4 describes different approaches for complexity management in modeling processes based on model decomposition; Sect. 5 describes our proposed approach for modeling and model transformation as a service; and Sect. 6 presents the conclusion and explains the next steps in this research.

2 Related Works

Agile development and MDD are both mature domains, and numerous efforts have been made over the years to integrate them. The works mentioned here are meant to provide a brief overview of the related literature.

Matinnejad [1] has evaluated a number of Agile Model-Driven Development (AMDD) methods as to their agility and MDD support. Essebaa and Chantit [4] have proposed a method for combining MDA and agile methods, and have examined how agile methods can benefit from MDA. Alfraihi and Lano [6, 12] have investigated the motivations and challenges of integrating agile development and MDD; lack of a well-defined process and tool support, and the steep learning curves involved, are recognized as the key challenges. Alfraihi and Lano [12] have also conducted a systematic literature review to examine the practices used in agile MDD. To facilitate sprint management in Scrum, Chantit and Essebaa [10] have combined Model-Driven Engineering (MDE) and Model-Based Testing (MBT) to produce a customized V-development life cycle that is integrated into Scrum. Bernaschina [11] has proposed an agile framework for rapid prototyping of model transformations. Asadi and Ramsin [13] have evaluated several MDA-based methods according to general, MDA-related, and tool-related criteria.

3 Integrating Model-Driven and Agile Development Approaches

A prerequisite for integrating agile and MDD methods into agile MDD processes is to be familiar with the strengths and weaknesses of these two areas. Also, the nature of the problems targeted by agile MDD is another issue that should be considered. In this section, we separately examine the deficiencies of agile development and MDD and investigate the challenges and opportunities facing the integration of these two areas.

3.1 Agile Development Challenges

Agile methods have come a long way as to their support for scalability, but scalability is still a serious problem, especially in large and complex projects involving distributed teams [14]. Over-reliance on face-to-face conversation as the sole means for conveying and information, and avoidance of modeling at all costs, can be detrimental to scalability. This poses a challenge to coordination and communication in distributed teams; lack of trust, common ground, language and knowledge base make it difficult for distributed teams to work together and develop a large and complex system [15].

Another problem with agile methods is their attitude towards architecture [2]. Agile approaches are risk-driven rather than architecture-driven, and even though modern, more mature agile methods such as Disciplined Agile Delivery (DAD) [9] pay special attention to architecture, most methods see the main goal as mitigating the risks rather than providing a reliable high-level structure that addresses the quality attributes. As a result, modeling and refining the architecture is not focused upon sufficiently, which in turn adversely affects scalability: it is difficult to assess the effects of architecturally significant design decisions on quality attributes; software evolution is difficult and tedious because the code is the only available means for learning and knowledge sharing; and there will be a steep learning curve for newcomers to the team.

3.2 MDD Challenges

MDD requires early planning, investment and design [3]. Typically, model-driven methodologies have heavyweight processes that have a negative effect on agility. Modeling large and complex systems in an iterative-incremental fashion, and collaboration among teammates during modeling activities in large distributed teams, are other challenges of MDD. The strongest motivation for using MDD is the continuous evolution of software technologies. In MDD, code can be (semi)automatically generated through a series of model transformations [16], but the main problem with this approach is that we need to prepare and take the initial steps before starting the development process [2]. This early investment can add value when the assets produced during these steps can be reused frequently. Therefore, production of reusable artifacts and responding to changes by demand is one of the challenges of MDD [2].

The model-driven architecture (MDA), which has become quite popular in MDD, is a good example of a multi-layered architecture. The three modeling levels of MDA (Computation-Independent Model or CIM, Platform-Independent Model or PIM, and Platform-Specific Model or PSM) enhance reusability through abstraction [16]. For instance, in PIM models, application specifications are platform-independent and ignore implementation technology issues. Therefore, it is possible to reuse these models for different implementation technologies [16].

Research in the field of MDA has focused more on the PIM and PSM levels, and little work has been done on CIM level models. UML, as a popular modeling language, is not suitable for displaying models at higher levels of abstraction such as CIM. Using domain-specific languages (DSL) can improve the expressiveness of the language for displaying models of a particular application domain [16], but in current MDE practices, the process of building DSLs is done on an ad-hoc basis [17].

3.3 Opportunities and Challenges of Integrating Agile and MDD Approaches

Models, as a common language and basis, facilitate communication and interaction between different teams and improve the scalability of agile methods [14]. Model-phobia in some prominent agile methods poses challenges to maintenance, evolution and change tracking. MDD strives to improve productivity by automatically generating code from models, and to provide sufficient detail to assist the maintenance phase by creating models at various abstraction levels. However, MDD is not inherently agile [18]. Therefore, we need to adhere to agile values and use best practices in agile modeling, along with the lessons learnt from hands-on experience and practical expertise in the field, in order to achieve effective agile modeling of software systems [19].

In Agile MDD, instead of modeling the whole system at once, models evolve continuously according to user demands [19]. Agile modeling is done gradually and in small steps, and instead of creating a large and complex model, several models are created and used in parallel. In modeling, unnecessary details are avoided and the focus is on the required aspects. During the modeling process, users are actively involved and simple tools are used to produce the models [6]. By storing artifacts in shared repositories and applying collaborative modeling techniques, communication and interaction between stakeholders is improved and existing artifacts can be reused [20].

One of the gaps in agile methods is the role of architecture in software solutions [14], which is well covered by the use of MDD. Typically, the technologies that are supposed to support a business change faster than the business itself [21]. MDD facilitates software evolution by separating the problem domain from the solution domain. By establishing a mapping between the problem domain and the solution domain, if the problem domain models change, these modifications are propagated to solution domain models through the model transformations and mapping between the two levels, but if the solution domain changes (by adopting a new technology or platform) we only need to modify the mapping (transformations) and the changes will not be propagated to the problem domain models [2].

Despite the opportunities available, integrating agile and model-driven approaches poses its own issues and problems. Most of the proposed methods lack a systematic and well-defined process, and teams usually proceed on an ad-hoc basis based on their experiences [6, 12]. Lack of appropriate tools to take advantage of Agile MDD and the steep learning curve that developers have to face are other problems hindering the integration of these two areas [6]. For example, CI/CD tools are key enablers of agile methodologies, and version control systems play an important role in this pipeline. Current version control systems manage and track changes and resolve conflicts at the code level. Therefore, they can only identify and resolve conflicts at the syntax level, and semantic conflicts caused by changes in modeling artifacts cannot be detected by these tools [20]. This is an interesting research topic, but it will not be addressed in this paper.

The agile approach prioritizes people and their interactions over processes and tools. However, having the right tools to facilitate the use of agile MDD plays an important role in fast product delivery and response to change. In addition to supporting modeling and testing, these tools should also support change and configuration management [6].

4   Complexity Management in Modeling

Software systems are complex in nature, and many are distributed as well. Different teams can be involved in the system development process, but the members of these teams are not necessarily co-located. The key question is how to manage the modeling complexity of the problem domain and improve collaboration in the modeling process. In MDD, the metamodel is first defined by identifying the domain concepts, which are then instantiated to yield the model elements. Accordingly, the model must conform to the syntactic rules and constraints defined in the metamodel. We use model decomposition for managing complexity in modeling processes, and propose three approaches based on the meta-level to which decomposition is applied. As shown in Fig. 1, each approach has its own benefits and liabilities when used in an agile MDD context.

In the first approach, a metamodel is defined for the entire domain and the problem domain is described in the form of a single model. The second approach, similar to the first approach, uses a single metamodel to define the concepts and rules of domain-specific modeling language, but manages model complexity by domain decomposition, breaking up the problem domain model into multiple partial models. The partial models describe different parts of the problem domain, but their modeling language is the same, and an overall model of the problem domain is obtainable by integrating these partial models. In the third approach, breaking up the problem domain takes place at both metamodel and model levels. Therefore, in order to describe the same aspect in different parts (contexts) of the problem, the context-specific metamodel of each part is first defined, and the problem domain is then described from that perspective with the help of models that conform to context-specific aspect-related metamodels.

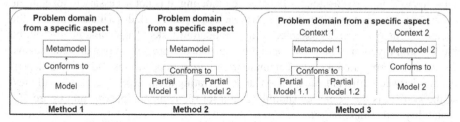

Fig. 1. Three approaches to metamodeling and modeling

4.1 First Approach

This approach is suitable for describing simple problems, but faces serious challenges for large and complex systems. From a scalability point of view, we encounter a large and complex metamodel that contains all the domain concepts and syntactic rules. Validation and maintenance are difficult as it is not possible to get early feedback from the user before defining a heavyweight metamodel. Reusability of the modeling artifacts is also low, as for each aspect, different contexts of the system are described in the form of a single model by using a single modeling language (single metamodel).

This approach lacks agility, and makes iterative-incremental modeling impossible. If the metamodel is modified, these changes should be reflected to a large and complex model, which makes it difficult to keep the model and the metamodel compatible. From the perspective of cooperation and collaborative modeling, this approach also faces various issues. Collaborative modeling requires breaking up the modeling tasks, but this approach lacks a clear strategy for this purpose.

It should be noted that in general, cooperation of team members in the modeling process can be done either synchronously or asynchronously. In synchronous collaboration, all members work on a single shared model, and if a part of the model is modified by a team member, the changes are communicated synchronously to all the members involved in the modeling process. This method usually uses locking mechanisms to maintain consistency. Each modeler must lock the model before making any changes, which interferes with the design process. Locking the elements of a large model and managing and releasing locks is an important problem of this method.

In asynchronous collaboration, each team member has a copy of the remote model and modifies the local version of the model, using version control systems to apply changes to the remote version of the model. Merging the local changes with the remote model is handled automatically in the absence of conflict, otherwise the conflicts must be resolved manually. Pulling all the elements of a large model from the remote repository and storing them locally is not efficient in terms of resource consumption.

4.2 Second Approach

The second approach uses a multitude of models to describe the problem domain. By identifying different areas (subdomains) of the problem domain, it is possible to describe each context consistently and unambiguously. In this approach, the same language (metamodel) is used for describing a specific aspect in different contexts of the problem domain. However, each context (subdomain) can have its own model and model repository, so in asynchronous collaborative modeling, it is not necessary to load all the specifications of the problem domain, but each team can load, describe and modify the specifications of the areas assigned to it as modeling tasks. Thus, subdomains can be the basis for division of modeling activities and task assignment among different teams. However, the operational cost of maintaining multiple repositories and the interdependencies between different subdomains, and integrating them to produce an overall view of the system, is the price that should be paid for reducing complexity, and improving scalability and collaboration.

Reusability at the metamodel level is similar to the first approach. However, if the problem domain is decomposed into cohesive parts with minimal interdependencies, the reusability of partial models will be improved. In this approach, we need to define a heavyweight metamodel before starting the modeling process of different subdomains. Also, making a change in the metamodel can affect the models of multiple subdomains. As a result, iterative-incremental development of models and metamodels becomes challenging and, from this perspective, lacks the necessary agility.

4.3 Third Approach

The third approach manages complexity at both the metamodel and model levels. To describe a specific aspect in different contexts (parts) of the problem domain, the modeling language (abstract syntax) appropriate for each context is created as a metamodel, and the problem domain is then described from that perspective (aspect) by using context-specific languages. In this approach, separation of concerns helps manage complexity. Also, instead of defining a large and complex metamodel for each aspect that considers all context-related concerns and details, several lightweight and context-specific metamodels are developed to describe the different contexts of the problem from that perspective by using different modeling languages (metamodels).

This improves the reusability and maintainability of the metamodel and related models: if one metamodel changes, we only need to maintain the compatibility of its corresponding models. It also allows for gradual and evolutionary modeling and contributes to the agility of the modeling process. By assigning the tasks related to the modeling and metamodeling of each context to a team, different teams can concurrently collaborate in the modeling process, thus enhancing collaborative modeling.

In this approach, the overall view of the problem domain from a specific perspective (aspect) is generated by integrating the partial models of different contexts of the problem domain, and model transformations play a key role in this regard. The complexity of integration is the cost that should be paid to improve cooperation, scalability and mutual independence of teams as to the modeling process. Identifying and distinguishing the different contexts of the problem domain can be challenging: if the logical boundaries between the different contexts of the problem are not well identified, integration will become difficult. There are several strategies for decomposing the metamodel. A coarse-grained metamodel can be decomposed by considering the following goals: increase the cohesion of fine-grained metamodels, form autonomous teams, and improve participation and cooperation in the modeling process. The Bounded Context pattern [22] can be used as a guideline and mechanism to decompose metamodels with respect to these goals.

Specialized fields usually have their own language and literature, which can be the basis for decomposing a coarse-grained metamodel into several fine-grained domain-specific metamodels, thus producing cohesive metamodel and models. The independence of teams in developing different parts of the software system may be the basis for deciding how to break up the metamodel. Reducing inter-team dependencies allows different teams to work in parallel. This improves agility and cooperation in modeling activities. In co-located teams, it is thus possible to exchange information effectively, build trust and promote collaboration. As a rule of thumb, the Bounded Context pattern can be used as a guideline and starting point for decomposing a coarse-grained metamodel. Later on, two context-specific metamodels can be merged and assigned to a single team according to other concerns and criteria, including: reducing inter-team dependencies, saving on integration/operational costs, and reducing the collaboration costs resulting from geographical distribution of the teams. All of these benefits make the third approach a wise choice for agile MDD.

5 Modeling as a Service and Model Transformation as a Service

As seen in the previous section, the third approach to management of modeling complexity improves agility and collaboration in the modeling process. However, the main challenge in this approach is to integrate partial models and provide a high-level view. Although partial models of different contexts describe the problem domain from the same aspect (e.g., the structural aspect), these models are heterogeneous because each partial model conforms to a different metamodel. Therefore, in order to achieve an overall view of the system from a specific aspect, we need to integrate these heterogeneous partial models. To address this problem, we must first determine the types of relationships that exist among the partial models.

5.1 Types of Relationships Between Models

Metamodel/model decomposition should be such that different contexts have the least interdependence. However, in practice, these contexts are not isolated from each other. For example, a model of infrastructure services can be shared and used by other contexts. But at times, the same service is remodeled to enhance team independence and strengthen control over service specification. Inspired by [22], we have identified four categories for classifying the natures and types of relationships between models: separate context, shared context, duplicate context, and conformist context.

Separate Context. The simplest situation is when two partial models have nothing to do with each other and do not need the information of the other model to describe their own domain. Under such circumstances, changes in each of these partial models are not disseminated to the other, and their integration would not provide more information than the pre-integration information.

Shared Context. In this case, part of the information is shared by two partial models and has the same specifications. Describing this shared context requires collaborative modeling (synchronous or asynchronous), and coordination between the teams responsible for each of the partial models. If all of these partial models are stored in a central repository, we will need access control mechanisms so that members of different teams can only access the shared part. However, if each team has its own repository, storing the shared context specifications in a separate, shared repository facilitates access control management and collaboration among team members. However, in this case, each team would need to manage two repositories (one private and one shared), and would also have to integrate the model specifications stored therein. In the Shared Context category, reusing models and avoiding redundancy is the main concern.

Duplicate Context. In this case, some of the information is shared by two partial models, but the burden of coordination and collaborative modeling between the two teams is such that sharing and collaborating in the modeling process (for sake of reuse) costs more than redefining and describing the shared context by each team. In this case, having autonomous teams has a higher priority than reusing artifacts. Although teams can still exchange information through Agile practices such as Scrum-of-Scrums, each team produces its own specifications for the shared context. The price that is paid for this level of flexibility is the possibility of creating semantic inconsistencies.

Conformist Context. In this case, one of the partial models (a downstream model) depends on the information of another model (an upstream model) and these models are defined and maintained by two different teams (supplier and consumer). The supplier has complete independence of action in making design decisions, but the design decisions made by the consumer must be aligned with and conform to the upstream model. Therefore, tracking changes in the upstream model and disseminating it to the downstream model is the responsibility of the consumer. For example, in MDA, CIM models provide information for PIM models, and the relationships between them are conformist. The driving forces behind the CIM models are the rules and constraints that govern the business domain, and PIM models are required to comply with these rules and restrictions, and the design models at the PIM level are in line with the business domain models at the CIM level.

5.2 Loosely Modeled Relationships

As the type and nature of the relationships among the partial models becomes clear, an important question that arises is how the relationships should be modeled in order to facilitate the integration process. Adherence to the two fundamental principles of "high cohesion" and "low coupling" seems to be a suitable strategy. Metamodel decomposition (through the third approach) should first be applied to maximize the cohesion of the conforming model, and in contrast, the relationships between concepts in different models should be loosely modeled in order to minimize coupling. Loosely modeled relationships between two models, or between their elements, promotes inter-team and intra-team collaboration.

Traditional modeling approaches model the relationships among the elements in a tightly coupled manner. Suppose a team of designers intend to model the structural aspects of a system in collaboration with each other in the form of class diagrams. Suppose that there are two classes called *Order* and *Customer* in this model, which are identified by two members of the team. There is an Association relationship between *Order* and *Customer*, but the Association relationship between them cannot be defined before defining the classes themselves. This will tie the design steps of the two team members together because modeling the relationship between the two elements is highly dependent on the presence of both at the moment of relationship definition.

A model can describe a situation, but to do so in the realm of modeling, we should not have to realize all aspects of the constituent elements of that situation. Designers usually model the system from the perspective of an outside observer, while the problem space can be viewed from the perspective of each of its constituent elements. In the previous example, *Order* describes the situation from its perspective as being related to the *Customer*, but the presence or absence of the *Customer* element at the moment of describing this situation does not change the reality of the problem; this is only a technical concern to consistently define the model.

Therefore, relationships should be modeled asynchronously and loosely. The cost of this approach is that the model may sometimes be inconsistent, but this type of inconsistency can be resolved by completing the modeling process. In the long run, it seems that improving flexibility, enhancing participation and collaboration, reducing dependency and increasing scalability outweigh the temporary inconsistency of the domain model. In this regard, we have introduced the idea of modeling and model transformation as a service in which the problem domain is described in terms of different domain concepts, each concept being embodied in the form of a service. This service makes it possible to define a concept from different perspectives. Each concept can be described from three perspectives: structural, functional and behavioral. It also provides essential functionalities required to query the structural, functional, and behavioral specifications of a concept.

The structural dimension expresses the characteristics and relationships of that concept with other concepts. The functional dimension focuses on the functionalities that a concept can provide. The behavioral dimension describes how this concept interacts with other concepts to fulfill its role. The behavioral specification of a concept is described from two perspectives: the responsibilities that the outside observer owes to that concept and the facts about that concept that the outside observer may be interested in knowing. This observer can be another domain concept, or the system as a whole.

In this approach, instead of modeling the problem domain only from the designer's point of view, we describe it from the perspective of each concept in the different contexts that make up the domain. The justifications behind this strategy are: information hiding, reducing unnecessary coupling, managing complexity through domain decomposition, and improving collaboration in the modeling process. For example, if *Order* has a unidirectional relationship with *Customer*, from *Order*'s point of view, there is a specific relationship with a concept called *Customer*, but *Customer* does not need to know anything about this relationship in the *customer management* context. In other words, *Customer* does not even know that a concept called *Order* is present in the problem domain because describing the problem domain from a *customer management* perspective does not require any such knowledge. In addition, *Order* does not need to know about all the *customer*-related attributes defined in the *customer management* context (e.g., date of birth). The loose connection between *Order* and *Customer* can be realized by using an event-driven architecture. *Order* states that it has a specific relationship (with certain name and attributes) with *Customer*. From an event-driven point of view, it can be interpreted that *Order* is interested in being informed when *Customer* is modeled, or if it already exists in the scope of the problem domain. When *Customer* is described in the problem domain, it announces the fact of being existent in the form of a published event. Using the Publisher/Subscriber pattern, it will be possible to model the relationships between two concepts in a loose manner.

This allows for asynchronous modeling, which improves participation and collaboration of team members in the modeling process. On the other hand, problem domain decomposition and describing it from the perspective of each domain concept allows complexity management at fine-grained levels. It is the modeler's responsibility to provide a macro view through the integration of these micro views. Since each domain concept is realized in the form of a self-contained service, it will be possible to provide a high-level view through the integration of services.

By identifying the subdomains, it is possible to model the system in the form of a hierarchical structure from coarse-grained to fine-grained. The problem domain resides at the highest level and consists of one or more subdomains, each of which contains relevant domain concepts. Each subdomain can be considered as a composite service that acts as a wrapper and includes services corresponding to domain concepts.

In other words, a subdomain provides access to these services from the outside world indirectly and is responsible for maintaining the consistency and transactional integrity of its internal concepts. The problem domain acts as a facade over the entire system and ensures consistency and transactional integrity at the system level. This hierarchical structure makes it possible to discover concepts (services) and resolve the relationships between them, similar to what happens in a DNS. The whole process can be done asynchronously by exchanging messages and using the publisher/subscriber pattern.

5.3 Model-Driven Development by Using Service-Oriented Paradigm

MDA is the main architecture adopted in MDD endeavors [23], and several methodologies have been proposed in its support [13]. MDA follows a layered structure (Fig. 2) while our proposed model-driven architecture has an onion structure (Fig. 3).

In current model-driven practices, modelers have focused on design models and usually start their work from the beginning by creating PIM-level models, completely ignoring the CIM-level. Lack of modeling at the CIM level can lead to various problems. Firstly, design models are affected by design decisions and solution issues, so they are less reusable than CIM-level analysis models; secondly, design models are not understandable by the end user, and domain experts cannot validate them; and thirdly, there is a semantic gap between the abstract high-level concepts used by domain experts and the abstract concepts used by modelers and designers, which is a major source of accidental complexity [20, 24]. Due to changes in requirements, bridging the gap manually is not cost-effective in terms of time and effort [24]. Lack of analysis models at the CIM level prevents the automatic production of PIM models based on CIM models. As a result, it is not possible to automatically publish changes in the requirements and analysis models to the design models.

In our proposed architecture, the problem domain is first described in terms of concepts and their interrelationships, and CIM-level models are defined. In line with the idea of "concept as a service", domain concepts are described from structural, functional and behavioral perspectives. A simplified version of the proposed abstract syntax (metamodel) for describing each domain concept is shown in Fig. 4.

Examining a concept from a structural perspective determines what properties that concept has and how it relates to other concepts in the problem domain. Examining a concept from a functional perspective aims to identify the functionalities that it can provide. Concepts in the real world usually need to interact and use the services provided by other concepts to fulfill their roles and tasks. In the behavioral dimension of a concept, the element of time and the sequence of interactions and communications between concepts play a key role. The behavioral specification of a concept expresses the dynamic aspect of that concept, while the structural and functional specifications describe its static aspects.

During the modeling process, the problem domain metamodel is first described by identifying the domain concepts, properties, and the relationships between them in a textual form based on the proposed abstract syntax. This metamodel includes the concepts, domains, and domain concepts of the problem domain. Then, by creating new instances of the domain concepts, domain objects are created to form the domain model.

    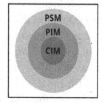

Fig. 2. OMG model-driven architecture   **Fig. 3.** Proposed model-driven architecture

One of the problems with conventional modeling approaches is that existing facilities for defining metamodels cannot be used at the model level as well. So if we need a new type, we have to define it explicitly at the metamodel level. To overcome this drawback, the notion of multilevel modeling was proposed, which allows in-depth definition of a language in more than two levels [25]. Two techniques have been proposed to extend the standard modeling approach: potency-based multilevel modeling [25] and Orthogonal Classification Architectures (OCA) [26, 27].

Potency-based multilevel modeling allows the domain to be described at multiple levels. In this method, the elements in the model have two facets at the same time: type and instance. For this reason, elements are called 'Clabjects', a combination of Class

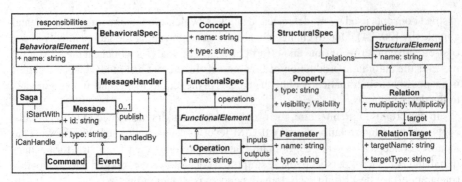

Fig. 4. Describing a concept from three perspectives

and Object that exhibits the characteristics of both. In OCA [26], two orthogonal typing systems are proposed, one based on ontology and the other based on linguistics [27].

In our "multilevel modeling as a service" idea, we extend OCA by adding a third dimension: relational. From an ontological perspective, the elements of the model are logically described as defined in the ontology hierarchy. From a linguistic point of view, the physical dimension of the elements is discussed, which refers to the concepts and structures that are necessary to construct and represent that element in models. The relational dimension focuses on the relationship between two elements of two different models. This dimension is embodied in our proposed solution in the form of an onion architecture: PIM-to-CIM relation, PSM-to-PIM relation, and Code-to-PSM relation.

In Fig. 5, an example of multilevel modeling from ontological (O0, O1, and O2) and linguistic (L0, L1 and L2) dimensions is shown. By analyzing the problem domain and exploring the subdomains ("Domain"s) and concepts, domain concepts are first constructed ("DomainConcept"s). Then, by creating new instances of the domain concepts, domain objects ("DomainObject"s) are created that actually form the domain model. A DomainObject has two facets: it is an instance of its ontological upper level Domain-Concept (e.g., in Fig. 5: *Film* is an instance of *Product*), and it can be considered as a template for instantiation of its ontological lower level, and thus play the role of a DomainConcept for the level below (e.g., in Fig. 5: *Film* is a type for *StarWars*).

Figure 6(b) shows the relational dimension of the proposed multilevel modeling approach. PIM-to-CIM, PSM-to-PIM and Code-to-PSM relations are loosely modeled. In line with the ideas of "modeling as a service" and "concept as a service", each layer provides access to its model elements and their descriptions to its higher layer, through services corresponding to these elements. Therefore, the loosely modeled relationship between the elements of each layer with its lower layer elements can be resolved using service discovery, service call, and the publisher/subscriber pattern.

In our approach (Fig. 6(b)), CIM-level models are created with three objectives:

1. Improve reusability by creating analysis models.
2. Improve understandability: Models at the CIM level are more understandable to the end user and domain experts, and in line with agile values, increase their collaboration and participation in the modeling and validation process.

3. Enable (semi)automated generation of PIM-level models by integrating CIM-level models with the design decisions and concerns described at the PIM level, without polluting CIM-level models with solution domain issues and implementation details.

To promote the participation and cooperation of domain experts and the development team in the modeling process, a common language is required. To this aim, we have introduced a method called CRAC (standing for "Concept-Responsibilities-Asynchronous Collaboration"), which aims to explore the problem space and reach a common language (Ubiquitous Language [22]) between domain experts and the development team. We will further explain this method in the next section. The CRAC analysis model thus produced is transformed into a concept-based model and a set of corresponding structural, functional and behavioral aspects, which constitute the CIM-level models and are represented in the form of self-contained and self-descriptive services at the CIM level. PIM-level services can obtain the specifications of a concept from different perspectives by calling specific concept-related services at the CIM level.

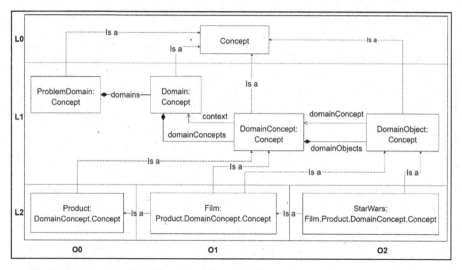

Fig. 5. An example of multilevel modeling from linguistic and ontological perspectives

Next, we enter the realm of the solution domain. To do this, we need to describe design details and solution concerns. However, these specifications do not directly apply to CIM-level models, but are rather expressed using the specific language of the PIM layer (Design-level DomainConcepts). If the partial models described at the PIM level require the specifications of CIM-level concepts, they refer to the concepts and models described at the CIM level (via the relational dimension of the proposed multilevel modeling approach) without the need to redefine this information at the PIM level. Integrating design details at the PIM level with the specifications of CIM-level concepts is done automatically using the built-in or user-defined model transformation services.

The idea of "model transformation as a service" is based on an event-driven architecture that allows reactive model transformations. In other words, model transformations

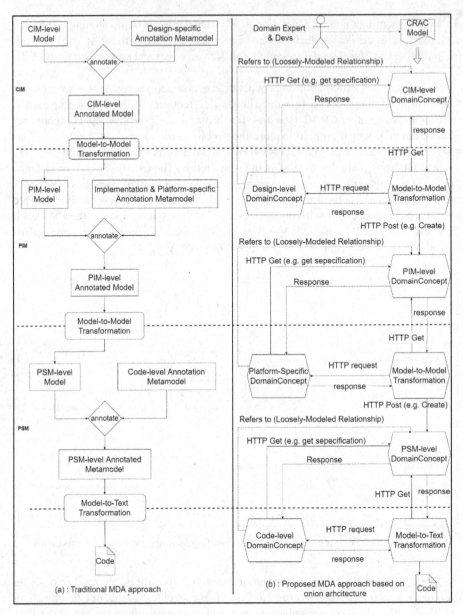

Fig. 6. Traditional MDA vs. proposed MDA approach

can be performed not only at the user's request, but also in response to the creation or modification of domain objects. One of the main components of a model transformation is the source model. When a model transformation service is defined, it declares that it is interested in receiving events related to the domain objects that correspond to its source model (Fig. 7 – A.3: Subscribe to the event based on source model). By creating or modifying a domain object, a relevant event is published (Fig. 7 – B.3: Publish an event) and delivered to the model transformation services that subscribe to the event (Fig. 7 – C.1: Handle the event). Upon receiving this event, the model transformation service initiates the process of de-serializing the event and extracting the domain object identifier, retrieving domain object specifications from corresponding services (Fig. 7 – C.2), performing transformation steps (Fig. 7 – C.3), and creating one or more target domain objects conforming to the destination model (Fig. 7 – C.4).

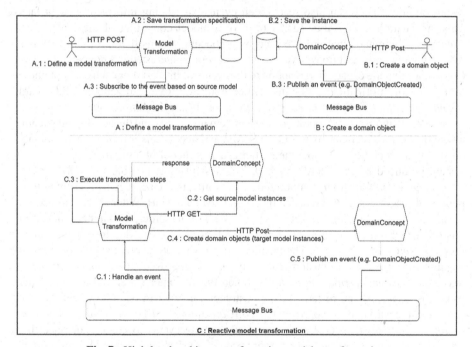

Fig. 7. High-level architecture of reactive model transformation.

In current model-driven practices (Fig. 6(a)), CIM-level model elements are tagged to provide design details that are not present in the CIM-level models, and model transformations use these annotations to conduct transformation steps and produce PIM-level models. This approach contaminates the analysis model with design concerns and reduces its readability and expressiveness. If design decisions change, we will need to re-annotate the analysis model. While in our proposed approach, CIM models remain intact and are not corrupted by solution domain issues. Rather, these details are described separately using PIM-level domain concepts, and are automatically combined with CIM models to generate PIM models. The same scenario exists between the Code, PSM, and PIM layer models, as shown in Fig. 6(b).

5.4 CRAC Method

In this method, we first identify the concepts of the problem domain. Each concept plays a role in the problem space, and other concepts in this context have expectations of it that can be interpreted and expressed in terms of its responsibilities. A concept's responsibilities can be "accomplished" or "failed", and it is possible to deduce a set of facts or events that explain this situation. For example, when a responsibility is successfully performed, it can be inferred that the pre-conditions and post-conditions associated with that responsibility have been met.

Concepts can also be interested in a set of facts and events in order to fulfill their responsibilities. They can also react to an event when being informed about a fact. This information is described in the form of a model consisting of these elements: Concepts, Commands that are executed by a concept, Events that are published as a result of command executions, Events that a concept is interested to know about it, and Commands that are executed in reaction to the events of interest. For each concept, these four pieces of information can be inserted on both sides of a card called a CRAC card (*Commands, Publish Event, Interested in Event,* and *Call for Action* columns).

In order to improve collaboration between domain experts and the development team, a Google Spreadsheet can be used to describe and access this information simultaneously. Figure 8 and Fig. 9 show the partial analysis model of an online food ordering system produced by the CRAC method. The system must be able to receive orders (*'CreateOrder'*). If an order is submitted successfully, the *'OrderCreated'* event will be published. *'Restaurant'* is interested in *'OrderCreated'* events. When this event occurs, it asks the kitchen to issue a ticket (*'CreateTicket'*) for the order; the kitchen can accept this order and issue a receipt (*'TicketCreated'*), or not issue it due to running out of food (*'TicketCreationFailed'*). The identity of the owner of the order should be verified when the order is created; customer identity may be approved (*'CustomerVerified'*) or rejected (*'CustomerVerificationFailed'*). When the customer is verified and the order receipt is issued by the restaurant, the customer's credit card should be checked; at this stage, the card may be approved (*'CreditCardAuthorized'*) or rejected (*'CreditCardAuthorizationFailed'*). *'Order'* is interested in these events to confirm or reject the order: if the *'CreditCardAuthorized'* event occurs, *'Order'* invokes the *'ApproveOrder'* command and the *'OrderApproved'* event is published as a result; otherwise, it invokes *'RejectOrder'* and the *'OrderRejected'* event is published.

Similarly, *'Restaurant'* needs to know if the order is approved or not: if the order is approved, *'Restaurant'* approves the issued receipt by invoking the *'ApproveTicket'* command, which will result in the publication of the *'TicketApproved'* event; but if the order is rejected, *'Restaurant'* rejects the ticket by invoking the *'RejectTicket'* command, and *'TicketRejected'* will be published as a result. Other requirements of the online food delivery system can be analyzed and modeled in the same fashion, but this is not our goal in this paper. As shown in this example, the CRAC method can help better understand the problem domain and express business rules and processes through a chain of commands and events. This modeling approach is understandable to domain experts and end users,

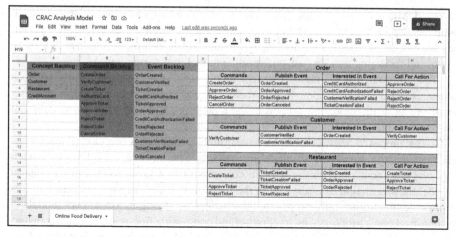

Fig. 8. CRAC analysis model of an online food ordering system

and the terms used for naming the concepts, commands, and events are parts of a language that is common among the development team(s), domain experts and end users.

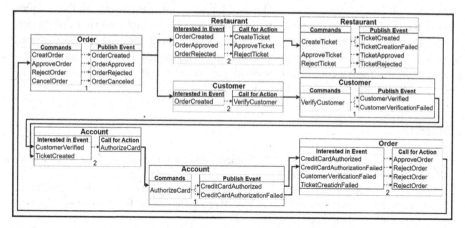

Fig. 9. Analysis model: CRAC cards

6 Conclusion and Future Work

Our preliminary analysis of the proposed approach shows that the idea of modeling and model transformation as a service is in line with the values, principles and best practices of agile modeling. Describing the problem domain in terms of concepts and modeling the relationships among these concepts in a loose manner facilitates collaboration throughout the modeling process and improves scalability in terms of the number of modelers involved. Model decomposition enhances complexity management and addresses scalability challenges in terms of artifact size. It also allows for iterative-incremental modeling and can enhance agility due to loosely-modeled relationships, the onion architecture, multilevel modeling as a service, and reactive model transformation.

The proposed CRAC method fosters mutual and shared understanding between domain experts and development team members, and facilitates collaboration and user involvement in the modeling process at the CIM level. The tool used for modeling at this level is simple and understandable to non-technical users.

In our proposed approach, production of high-level models from lower-level models enhances the reusability of modeling artifacts. Therefore, at each level of modeling, one can focus only on the specific concerns of that level. Realizing the idea of "model transformation as a service" in the form of an event-driven architecture makes it possible to automatically propagate the changes occurring in lower-level models to higher-level ones. Moreover, by integrating and composing fine-grained model transformation services, it is possible to execute reactive model transformations concurrently or as chains.

Applying a service-oriented approach in modeling and model transformation allows for the use of different patterns and architecture styles such as the microservice architecture. Examining the two areas of service-orientation and modeling, and establishing a semantic correspondence between the issues and challenges of these two fields will be one of our future research activities. This will help us apply the patterns and techniques used in the service-oriented paradigm to solve the problems and challenges of model-driven development. Providing a model-driven development platform (MDDPlatform) by using the service-oriented approach has also been planned as a future activity. The goal of MDDPlatform would be to support all the functionalities required to fully realize the ideas of modeling and model transformation as a service.

References

1. Matinnejad, R.: Agile model driven development: an intelligent compromise. In: International SERA Conference, pp. 197–202 (2011)
2. Wegener, H.: Agility in model-driven software development? Implications for organization, process, and architecture. In: OOPSLA Workshop on Generative Techniques in the Context of Model Driven Architecture, vol. 23 (2002)
3. Whittle, J.: Agile versus MDE - friend or foe? In: Workshop on Extreme Modeling, vol. 1089 (2013)
4. Essebaa, I., Chantit, S.: Model driven architecture and agile methodologies: reflexion and discussion of their combination. In: Federated Conference on Computer Science and Information Systems, pp. 939–948 (2018)
5. Mahé, V., Combemale, B., Cadavid, J.: Crossing model driven engineering and agility. In: Workshop on Model-Driven Tool and Process Integration (2010)
6. Alfraihi, H., Lano, K.: Practical aspects of the integration of agile development and model-driven development: an exploratory study. In: Flexible MDE Workshop, pp. 399–404 (2017)
7. Ambler, S.W.: Agile modeling: a brief overview. In: Workshop of the pUML Group, pp. 7–11 (2001). https://dl.gi.de/20.500.12116/30849
8. Zhang, Y., Patel, S.: Agile model-driven development in practice. IEEE Softw. **28**(2), 84–91 (2011)

9. Ambler, S.W., Lines, M.: Choose your WoW: a disciplined agile delivery handbook for optimizing your way of working. Project Management Institute (2020)
10. Chantit, S., Essebaa, I.: Towards an automatic model-based Scrum methodology. Procedia Comput. Sci. **184**, 797–802 (2021)
11. Bernaschina, C.: ALMOsT.js: an agile model to model and model to text transformation framework. In: Cabot, J., De Virgilio, R., Torlone, R. (eds.) ICWE 2017. LNCS, vol. 10360, pp. 79–97. Springer, Cham (2017). https://doi.org/10.1007/978-3-319-60131-1_5
12. Alfraihi, H., Lano, K.C.: The integration of agile development and model driven development: a systematic literature review. In: International Conference on Model-Driven Engineering and Software Development, pp. 451–458 (2017)
13. Asadi, M., Ramsin, R.: MDA-based methodologies: an analytical survey. In: Schieferdecker, I., Hartman, A. (eds.) ECMDA-FA 2008. LNCS, vol. 5095, pp. 419–431. Springer, Heidelberg (2008). https://doi.org/10.1007/978-3-540-69100-6_30
14. Mognon, F., C. Stadzisz, P.: Modeling in agile software development: a systematic literature review. In: Silva da Silva, T., Estácio, B., Kroll, J., Mantovani Fontana, R. (eds.) WBMA 2016. CCIS, vol. 680, pp. 50–59. Springer, Cham (2017). https://doi.org/10.1007/978-3-319-55907-0_5
15. Jolak, R., Wortmann, A., Chaudron, M., Rumpe, B.: Does distance still matter? Revisiting collaborative distributed software design. IEEE Softw. **35**(6), 40–47 (2018)
16. Sebastián, G., Gallud, J.A., Tesoriero, R.: Code generation using model driven architecture: a systematic mapping study. J. Comput. Lang. **56**, 100935 (2020)
17. Kolovos, D., et al.: MONDO: scalable modelling and model management on the cloud. In: CEUR Workshop, pp. 44–53 (2015)
18. da Silva, E., Maciel, R., Magalhães, A.: Integrating model-driven development practices into agile process: analyzing and evaluating software evolution aspects. In: International Conference on Enterprise Information Systems, pp. 101–110 (2020)
19. Schonbock, J., Etzlstorfer, J., Kapsammer, E., Kusel, A., Retschitzegger, W., Schwinger, W.: Model-driven co-evolution for agile development. In: Hawaii International Conference on System Sciences, pp. 5094–5103 (2015)
20. Alam, O., Corley, J., Masson, C., Syriani, E.: Challenges for reuse in collaborative modeling environments. In: MODELS Workshops, pp. 277–283 (2018)
21. Uhl, A.: MDA is ready for prime time. IEEE Softw. **20**(5), 70–72 (2003)
22. Evans, E.: Domain-Driven Design: Tackling Complexity in the Heart of Software. Addison-Wesley Longman, Boston (2003)
23. da Silva, A.R.: Model-driven engineering: a survey supported by the unified conceptual model. Comput. Lang. Syst. Struct. **43**, 139–155 (2015)
24. Combemale, B., Deantoni, J., Baudry, B., France, R., Jézéquel, J.-M., Gray, J.: Globalizing modeling languages. Computer **47**, 68–71 (2014)
25. Atkinson, C., Kühne, T.: The essence of multilevel metamodeling. In: Gogolla, M., Kobryn, C. (eds.) UML 2001. LNCS, vol. 2185, pp. 19–33. Springer, Heidelberg (2001). https://doi.org/10.1007/3-540-45441-1_3
26. Atkinson, C., Kennel, B., Goß, B.: The level-agnostic modeling language. In: Malloy, B., Staab, S., van den Brand, M. (eds.) SLE 2010. LNCS, vol. 6563, pp. 266–275. Springer, Heidelberg (2011). https://doi.org/10.1007/978-3-642-19440-5_16
27. De Lara, J., Guerra, E., Cuadrado, J.S.: When and how to use multilevel modelling. ACM Trans. Softw. Eng. Methodol. **24**(2), 1–46 (2014)

Effort Estimation in Agile Software Development: A Exploratory Study of Practitioners' Perspective

R. C. Sandeep, Mary Sánchez-Gordón(✉) ⓘ, Ricardo Colomo-Palacios ⓘ, and Monica Kristiansen

Østfold University College, Halden, Norway
{sandeep.rc,mary.sanchez-gordon,ricardo.colomo-palacios,
monica.kristiansen}@hiof.no

Abstract. Software is increasingly important for our society. However, software industry presents flaws to meet market demands in a faster and reliable way. Agile methods are a way to tackle this problem. However, this approach also poses several challenges, including effort estimation as one of them. In this scenario, #NoEstimates and #NoProject movements emerged as another way to solve estimation issues. In this new scenario, this study aims to provide further empirical evidence on agile effort estimation techniques in practice. To do so, an online survey was designed based on a literature review. Researchers gathered 53 valid questionnaires from agile practitioners. Result shows the importance of hybrid software development approaches and mixed effort estimation techniques. However, it is important to note that *Story Points* and *Fibonacci series* are often used as well. Moreover, the most perceived benefit of estimation in agile contexts is to *drive the team to complete the project successfully. Complexity and uncertainty* are perceived as key factors in estimation accuracy. Finally, further research should be conducted to gain a better understanding of #NoEstimates and #NoProject movements.

Keywords: Effort estimation · Agile software development · Distributed software development

1 Introduction

Software industry is playing a significant role in fulfilling the increasing demand and extensive use of software in our society [1]. Despite that, software projects are challenged in aspects like cost, quality, time, or expected returns on investment [2]. In this scenario, software development needs careful examination, understanding, support, and improvement [3].

Estimation in software projects contains the assessment of the effort, size, staffing, schedule (time), and cost involved in creating a unit of the software product [4]. Estimation is one of the main concerns for the software development industry [5], playing an important role in software development [6] supporting key software process decisions,

© Springer Nature Switzerland AG 2022
A. Przybyłek et al. (Eds.): LASD 2022, LNBIP 438, pp. 136–149, 2022.
https://doi.org/10.1007/978-3-030-94238-0_8

such as feasibility analysis, resource allocation, risk mitigation, and project planning [7]. However, there is even difficulty in assessing the accuracy of different approaches to effort estimation [8]. Although estimation accuracy directly influences the utility of the estimation results, different software management decisions may require different degrees of accuracy [7]. While, according to [9], effort estimation is not critical for constructing a project's scheduling and planning, it is important to facilitate understanding. Also, software practitioners require effective effort estimation models to facilitate project planning [10] as well as to create baseline budgets and schedules [11].

. In particular, effort estimation in agile software development (ASD) is challenging as the requirements are constantly evolving and they are developed as the project progresses [12]. As a consequence, effort estimations in such environments need to be progressively adjusted for every sprint [4] to ensure delivery in required times [12]. Although different estimation techniques exist in ASD and it was reported as an active research area, accuracy was also reported as a clear gap in this field [13].

In 2014, Usman et al. [13] conducted a systematic literature review on effort estimation in ASD. As a result, 25 primary studies were identified. The four main findings are: i) subjective estimation methods like expert judgment, planning poker, use case points estimation method are often used for agile estimation; ii) Use Case Points (UCP) and Story Points (SP) are the most often used size metrics; iii) Mean Magnitude of Relative Error (MMRE) and Magnitude of Relative Error (MRE) is the frequently used accuracy metrics in ASD, and iv) Team skills, prior experience, and task size are included as the 3 fundamental cost drivers in ASD.

In 2015, a survey on the state of the practice [14] collected data from 16 different countries and 60 agile practitioners that were involved in the effort estimation. The findings revealed that planning poker (63%) was the most used effort estimation technique followed by, analogy (47%) and expert judgment (38%). In 2016, Tanveer et al. [15] carried out a study to understand the accuracy of the estimation process by examining three agile teams that worked on different web applications. The authors conclude that developers' knowledge, experience, and complexity affect it. The same year, a comparative analysis study on effort estimation practice in ASD was carried out by Usman and Britto [16]. In this study, they compared two co-located and globally distributed teams to identify the similarities and differences of effort estimation practice. The result shows that planning poker and story points are the most reported effort estimation technique and size metric for both teams. More recently, Fernández-Diego et al. [10] updated previous works from Usman et al. [13]. In the last years, several intelligent approaches based have also impacted the ASD effort estimation, e.g. [17–20].

According to Duarte [21], in software projects, it is hard to estimate unknown parts. As a response to this challenge, #NoEstimates and #NoProjects movements have emerged. #NoEstimates started back in 2012 promoted by Woody Zuill as a Twitter trend. In this movement, it is claimed to stop estimating backlog because accurate estimation is not possible, and estimations put useless pressure on teams. As a result of this, estimation is seen as waste. #NoProjects concept started back in 2005 [22] and stands for modern management methods to offer proven techniques and tools that go beyond "meeting requirements". These approaches are normally based on continuous value. Both movements are related, #NoEstimate removes the justification of estimation and helps the organization focus on value delivery first [21] whereas #NoProjects is an agile approach towards continuous and market-validated value delivery [22].

In this scenario, despite those previous studies provide valuable insights into effort estimation in ASD, to the best of our knowledge, there is little empirical evidence about the benefits and inaccuracies of effort estimation techniques in actual practice and the impact of #NoEstimates and #NoProjects movements in the software arena. Therefore, this study aims to provide further empirical evidence on agile effort estimation techniques in practice.

The remaining of the paper is structured as follows. Section 2 presents the research method adopted describing formulated research questions. The results of this study are presented in Sect. 3. Section 4 contains the limitations of the study. Finally, some conclusions and future work are given in Sect. 5.

2   Research Method

2.1   Research Questions

The main objective of this study is to better understand the state of the practice on effort estimation in ASD including benefits and challenges. Based on that, four research questions were formulated:

RQ1: What are the effort estimation techniques used in ASD?
RQ2: What are the benefits of estimation techniques in ASD?
RQ3: What are the reasons for inaccurate estimations in ASD?
RQ4: What is the repercussion of #NoEstimates and #NoProjects in ASD?

2.2   Survey Design

Survey research is one possible design choice for quantitative research. Survey research produces quantitative data about trends, attitudes, or opinions among the population under study [23]. There are different approaches for data collection in a survey, such as personal interviews, telephone interviews, direct observation, or self-administered questionnaires [24]. In the study presented in this paper, a draft questionnaire was designed considering the guidelines for software engineering proposed by Molléri et al. [25]. The two first authors developed an initial version in the English language that is informed by previous literature, e.g. [5, 12, 13, 26]. Then, the other authors reviewed it for validity checking. To obtain as many responses as possible, and to not distract participants unnecessarily, it was decided to keep the number of questions to a minimum.

In this study, an online web-based questionnaire tool (Google forms) was used for data collection. The questionnaire contained sections on software development projects as well as demographic information. Questions were presented to subjects with multiple response options. The frequency of use software development approaches (see Fig. 1) and estimation techniques (see Fig. 2) was reported by using a five-point scale *Never Use* (1); *Rarely Use* (2); *Sometimes* (3); *Often* (4); and *Always* (5). In addition, the option *I do not know* (0) was included.

The questionnaire also asks subjects for a set of perceived benefits (see Table 2) and 20 reasons for the inaccuracy (see Table 3). These reasons/factors were grouped into 5 major categories: *Requirement Related Issue (RrI)*, *Project Management Related Issue (PMrI)*, *Team Related Issue (TrI)*, *Over-Optimism (Oo)*, and *Others*. The respondents' agreement regarding benefits and inaccuracies was reported using a five-point scale with the following values: *Strongly Disagree* (1); *Disagree* (2); *Neutral* (3); *Agree* (4); and *Strongly Agree* (5). Additionally, the option *I do not know* (0) was included. Moreover, an additional open question encouraging participants to voice other options was included in each category. Authors also provided a text box at the end to gather any further comments or suggestions from participants.

To get an understanding of the impact caused by #NoEstimates and #NoProjects and their potential benefits and challenges, two types of questions were formulated: one closed-ended question (5-point scale) and one open-ended question. The 5-point scale was: *I've never heard of it* (0); *I've HEARD of it and Not interested* (1); *I've HEARD of it and WOULD like to learn it* (2); *I've USED it before, and would NOT use it again* (3); *I've USED it before, and would use it again* (4).

Survey Execution and Sampling Strategy. Participants were identified among the networks of researchers. An e-mail was sent out to contacts detailing the purpose of the study and inviting software practitioners to participate. Authors underlined that the questionnaire was anonymous. The period to answer the questionnaire was about two weeks starting from the 24th of June 2019 to the 8th of July 2019 and one email reminder invitation was sent out after one week of the survey being open. In consequence, recruiting participants was based on availability – a convenience sampling. Despite the drawbacks and bias in such a sample, it does not mean that is inappropriate. Indeed, such a sampling method is reported as the dominant survey approach in software engineering [27, 28].

Data Analysis and Synthesis Approach. As mentioned before, the survey primarily contained questions with predefined lists from which participants could choose a value (e.g., job role, gender, and ASD approach), or code simple data such as integers or strings (e.g., country and years of experience). After reviewing the raw data, 53 out of 62 questionnaires were considered valid. These respondents provided relevant and reliable answers since they were involved in the effort estimation process. In this phase, anonymous IDs were assigned to the respondents and their data records, i.e., we used the "Pi" format [P1 to P62].

To investigate benefits and accuracy challenges in ASD estimation as well as statistical differences between years of experience, the data was analyzed using statistical tests chosen based on certain pre-conditions. In addition, *"I do not Know-0"* answers are excluded from the analysis. For all reported statistical tests, we used a significance level of 0.05. Before the actual test, we tested each skill for normality with the Shapiro-Wilk test. The results of the tests of normality indicated that our sample was not normally distributed. Therefore, we used a non-parametric statistical test called Wilcoxon signed-rank test. Results were analyzed using SPSS.

3 Results

In this section, first, an overview of the study population is presented then the results of the survey answer the research questions.

Study Population. A total of 53 valid responses were collected from seven countries, however, almost 70% of them come from Nepal (22, 41.5%) and Norway (15, 28.3%). Most of the responses were male participants (83%) while females made up 15% (8), and one participant preferred not to say (2%). Regarding years of experience, most of the respondents have more than 3 years of agile experience (33, 62.3%), whereas 32.1% (17) have 1–3 years and 5.7% (3) have less than a year. Most of the respondents also were software developers (31, 58.5%). 50.9% (27) of respondents work in a team size of 6–10 people while 41.5% (22) are in teams of 1–5 people. The project length was reported longer than 1 year by most of the respondents (77.4%, 41). The business domain most reported was e-commerce (56.6%, 30).

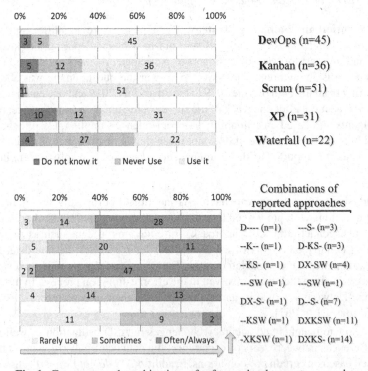

Fig. 1. Frequency and combinations of software development approaches

Figure 1 shows the frequency and combinations of software development approaches. Although **Scrum** and Kanban are the most frequently practiced approaches in ASD, it is worth noting that many combinations of them are reported, e.g., *DevOps and Scrum* (DS, 7) or *DevOps, XP, Kanban, and Scrum* (*DXKS*, 14) or all of them along with *W*aterfall

(**DXKS**, 11). This result is aligned with a large previous survey, namely HELENA [29] in which mixed approaches were reported as commonly used.

Finally, the perceived importance of the estimation process by most respondents (75.8%, 43) was that *estimation is very important in ASD* whereas 7 perceived it as important and only 3 were neutral. Moreover, participants who reported that they were not involved in estimation processes, perceived it as very important (4) and important (5).

RQ1: What are the effort estimation techniques used in ASD?

The descriptive analysis of seven effort estimation techniques reported in this study is shown in Fig. 2.

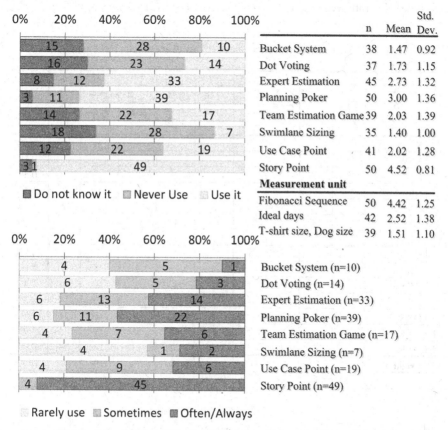

	n	Mean	Std. Dev.
Bucket System	38	1.47	0.92
Dot Voting	37	1.73	1.15
Expert Estimation	45	2.73	1.32
Planning Poker	50	3.00	1.36
Team Estimation Game	39	2.03	1.39
Swimlane Sizing	35	1.40	1.00
Use Case Point	41	2.02	1.28
Story Point	50	4.52	0.81
Measurement unit			
Fibonacci Sequence	50	4.42	1.25
Ideal days	42	2.52	1.38
T-shirt size, Dog size	39	1.51	1.10

Fig. 2. Descriptive statistical results of the effort estimation techniques

In this study, we included *Bucket system, Dot Voting, Expert estimation, Planning Poker, Team estimation game, Swimlane sizing, Use case point*. According to [30], *Planning Poker* is an estimation technique similar to the *Team estimation game* so we considered each technique separately. Moreover, *Story points* were included in the group of effort estimation techniques, although, *Story points* are a unit of measurement used to represent an estimate of the entire effort necessary to completely perform a piece of software work. It was decided because *Story points* are usually expressed either in numbers that follow the Fibonacci series, t-shirt sizes, or even dog sizes that were included as measurement units.

As we expected, more than 90% of the respondents reported that "Often/Always use" *Story points* while *Planning Poker* and *Expert Estimation Method* were the most common estimation techniques. *Story point* has the highest mean value (4.52) followed by *Planning Poker* (3.00) and *Expert Estimation Method* (2.73). However, it is worth noting that one respondent stated—using the open question—that "*the organization uses COCOMO for estimation*".

Based on the mean values of the measurement units, the *Fibonacci Sequence* was preferred (4.42) followed by *Ideal days* (2.52) and *T-shirt size/Dog size* (1.51).

Table 1. Overview of estimation techniques by software development approaches

N	A S D	Swimlane Sizing	Bucket System	Dot Voting	Team Estimation Game	Use Case Point	Expert Estimation	Planning Poker	Story Point	Frequency	%
1	K								1	1	0.5%
1	KSW					1				1	0.5%
1	D							1		1	0.5%
1	KS			1					1	2	1.1%
1	DXS					1			1	2	1.1%
1	SW						1	1	1	3	1.6%
1	XKSW				1	1	1		1	4	2.1%
3	S			1	1		2	2	3	9	4.8%
3	DKS	1	1		1	1		2	3	9	4.8%
4	DKSW		1	2	1	2	4	2	2	14	7.4%
7	DS				1	1	3	6	7	18	9.6%
4	DXSW		2	2	3	4	3	3	4	21	11.2%
11	DXKSW	3	2	5	4	4	7	9	11	45	23.9%
14	DXKS	3	4	4	4	4	12	13	14	58	30.9%
53	**Frequency**	7	10	14	17	19	33	39	49	188	100%
	%	3.7%	5.3%	7.4%	9.0%	10.1%	17.6%	20.7%	26.1%	100%	

Table 1 shows the frequency of the use of estimation techniques by software development approaches. The first column contains the frequency (#) followed by the (14) combinations of software development approaches (see Table 1), estimation techniques—*Swimlane sizing (SS), Bucket System (BS), Dot voting (DV), Team estimation game (TEG), Use case point (UCP), Expert Estimation (EE), Planning Poker (PP),* and *Story point (SP)*—, and finally Total and Percentage (%).

As it was expected, *Story point* (26.1%) is the most used estimation technique as it has the highest percentage of usage followed by *Planning Poker* (20.7%), *Expert Estimation* (17.6%), and *Use Case Point* (10.1%). These findings are in line with the previous studies [14, 16, 31] that mentioned *Story point* as the most frequently used size metrics. On the other hand, the large survey—1319 full responses—carried out by VersionOne [32] reveals that 61% of respondents chose Planning poker/team estimation as agile techniques that their companies use. In addition, the findings also reveal that not only hybrid software development approaches are used but also mixed effort estimation techniques.

RQ$_2$: What are the benefits of estimation techniques in ASD?

The six categories of perceived benefits are shown in Table 2. More than 75% (41) respondents "agree/strongly agree" with them. Moreover, *"To gain accuracy"* is the only benefit in which 20% are neutral responses followed by *"To create transparency"* (13.2%) and *"Helps to identify important issues earlier"* (9.4%).

Table 2. Descriptive statistical results of the estimation benefits

	Benefits	n	Less than 3 years Mean	Std. Dev.	n	More than 3 years Mean	Std. Dev.	n	Total Mean	Std. Dev.
1	Drive the team to complete the project successfully	20	4.35	0.67	33	**4.39**	0.70	53	**4.38**	0.69
2	Identify the resources and project scope*	20	**4.50**	0.61	33	4.27	0.63	53	4.36	0.62
3	Helps to identify important issues earlier*	20	4.30	0.73	33	4.09	0.88	53	4.17	0.83
4	Monitors project progress	20	4.20	0.62	33	4.27	0.67	53	4.25	0.65
5	To create transparency	20	4.20	0.70	33	4.21	0.65	53	4.21	0.66
6	To gain accuracy	20	3.90	0.85	33	4.18	0.73	53	4.08	0.78

Based on the highest mean value, the most perceived benefit is to *Drive the team to complete the project successfully* (4.38) followed by *identifying the resources and project scope* (4.36) and *Monitors project progress* (4.25). Thus, effort estimation is one of the essential factors of the software development process since it drives the team to complete the project successfully [33]. For two benefits—*Identify the resources and project scope* and *Help to identify important issues earlier*, less experienced respondents reached a higher agreement than more experienced ones (marked as *in Table 1, higher mean values are bolded).

On the other hand, it would be interesting to explore if there is a significant difference between the answers based on the experience of the respondents. To do so, the respondents were grouped into two categories "less than 3 years of experience" (n = 20) and "more than 3 years of experience" (n = 33). We tested the null hypotheses H_0: μ_{Bx}(<3 years) = μ_{Bx}(3 years+) using Wilcoxon signed-rank test. We used that non-parametric statistical test method because it does not require the data sets to follow a normal distribution. The results show that there is no significant difference in the respondents' perceived value of the benefits based on their experience. Although the practitioners in this study rated benefits in a similarly positive way, it is worth noting that 13% of respondents from the 2019 VersionOne survey [32] pointed out that estimation accuracy is one measure of success.

RQ$_3$: What are the reasons for inaccurate estimations in ASDSD?
To get insights about the inaccuracy in the estimation, 20 potential factors/reasons were analyzed. These factors were grouped into 5 major categories: *Requirement Related Issue (RrI), Project Management Related Issue (PMrI), Team Related Issue (TrI), Over-Optimism (Oo)*, and *Others*. Table 3 shows the lists of the descriptive statistical results of each factor.

Table 3 also shows that less experienced respondents reached a higher agreement than more experienced ones for 3 out of 20 factors—*Unstructured group estimation process, Distributed team*, and *Knowledge sharing problem in team* (marked as *). The descriptive statistical analysis result shows that most reported inaccurate estimates based on the mean values are two *Complexity and Uncertainty* (4.25) and *Missing and changing requirements* (4.06). Both are in category RrI. The higher mean values in the other categories are *Knowledge sharing problem in the team* TrI (3.96), *Considering best case scenario* OO (3.96), *Ignoring Testing Effort* Others (3.94), and *Poor change control* PMrI (3.86).

On the other hand, one can see differences in the hindering factors influencing accuracy based on the experience of the respondents. In consequence, we tested the null hypotheses H_0: μ_{Ax}(<3 years) = μ_{Ax}(3 years+) using a Wilcoxon signed-rank test. The results show that there are two significant differences:

- *Poor user stories* (U = 199.5, p = 0.02)
- *Poor change control* (U = 191.00, p = 0.045)

RQ$_4$: What is the repercussion of #NoEstimates and #NoProjects in ASD?
The result shows that around 85% of the respondents (45 and 47) *have never heard of* #NoEstimate and #NoProject. Moreover, three respondents claim that they *"have heard of it and are not interested"* in both movements. While less than 10% *heard of it* and *wanted to know about* #NoEstimate (5) and only one of them about #NoProject. Despite that fact, 3 participants provided valid answers related to the benefits of #NoEstimate— *1. Faster, 2. Overshadow Project Scope, and 3. Provide a clear timeline for delivery*—. However, no valid responses were received for #NoProject.

The aforementioned reveals the scarce impact of these movements on the effort estimations among the respondents in this study. Although, a previous study [34] about "agile uncertainty assessment for benefit points and story points" highlights that *"the #NoEstimates movement is gaining attention of agile practitioners"*, our findings rather

Table 3. Descriptive statistical results of the inaccurate estimates

	Inaccurate	Less than 3 years			More than 3 years			Total		
		n	Mean	Std. Dev.	n	Mean	Std. Dev.	n	Mean	Std. Dev.
RrI	Complexity and Uncertainty	19	**4.16**	0.76	33	**4.30**	0.68	52	**4.25**	.71
	Missing and changing requirements	19	3.84	1.12	33	4.18	0.77	52	4.06	.92
	Overlooking non-functional requirements	17	3.88	0.86	33	4.06	0.83	50	4.00	.83
	Poor user stories	19	3.53	1.17	33	4.24	0.79	52	3.98	1.00
PMrI	*Poor change control*	19	3.58	0.90	31	**4.03**	0.66	50	**3.86**	0.78
	Scope creep	19	3.58	1.07	30	3.93	0.83	49	3.80	0.93
	Scrum Master not guiding the team	20	3.20	1.06	33	3.76	1.09	53	3.55	1.10
	Unstructured group estimation process*	20	**3.85**	0.99	32	3.69	1.09	52	3.75	1.05
TrI	Distributed teams*	19	3.42	0.90	33	2.88	1.22	52	3.08	1.13
	Dominant Personalities	20	3.35	0.93	33	3.48	0.94	53	3.43	0.93
	Inexperience	20	3.50	1.10	33	3.82	1.07	53	3.70	1.08
	Knowledge sharing problem in team*	20	**4.00**	1.03	33	3.94	0.97	53	**3.96**	0.98
	Pressure of timeline	20	3.55	1.05	33	3.79	0.93	53	3.70	0.97
	Unskilled team members	20	3.90	0.72	33	**3.97**	0.98	53	3.94	0.89
OO	Considering best case scenario	20	**3.90**	0.72	32	**4.00**	0.80	53	**3.96**	0.76
	Purposely underestimating to obtain work	20	3.50	1.15	32	3.56	1.01	52	3.54	1.06
Others	Hardware	20	3.30	1.03	33	3.33	0.96	53	3.32	0.98
	Ignoring testing effort	20	**3.65**	1.09	33	**4.12**	0.74	53	**3.94**	0.91
	Insufficient customer involvement during estimation process	20	3.15	1.09	33	3.67	0.96	53	3.47	1.03
	Lack of formal estimation process	20	3.35	1.09	33	3.88	0.93	53	3.68	1.01

point out little attention. The authors also mention that it could not offer enough benefit-over-cost optimization in the context of large agile projects however our findings neither support nor deny such a claim.

4 Limitations

In this study, authors followed the survey guidelines for software engineering proposed by Molléri et al. [25]. However, this study still has some limitations:

The researchers' bias is always a threat. To reduce that bias, the survey questionnaire was iteratively designed and updated by the authors based on the results of the literature review, and its completeness and readability were validated by one senior researcher. However, further research should make clear that story points are a unit of measurement and include man-hours as measurement units, as well. In this sense, it is worth noting that *Fibonacci numbers* are just numbers so that they can refer to *ideal days* or *man-hours*.

Irrelevant respondents could introduce a systematic error or bias in the study results. To reduce that threat some steps were taken. Firstly, respondents were assured of their anonymity to avoid evaluation apprehension. Secondly, it was explicitly stated in the survey introduction that only practitioners with experience in ASD should participate.

Additionally, respondents were asked about their experience in ASD and effort estimation to ensure that all respondents were agile practitioners and active participants in the effort estimation process. Although 62 agile practitioners were involved in this study, 53 of them reported work experience on effort estimation. Therefore, only 53 were valid answers that could provide relevant and reliable insights on this area. Thirdly, some respondents might have misinterpreted the questionnaire, or they could be confused. To ensure the correct understanding of the questionnaire, 2 rounds of pilot testing were done. Moreover, although multiple options were added to the questionnaire, respondents might not get the answer they want. To reduce this threat, "Other" option was included at the end of all the questions.

The sample is small, which limits the generalization of the results, and a large part of the sample coming from Nepal, meaning that it is not representing a generic population. Although we believe that such a sample is quite heterogeneous in terms of experience, job role, and country, the sample size should be expanded to a larger group to increase the generalizability of the results. The statistical significance is threatened by the small sample size. Finally, it is worth noting that the *"I do not Know-0"* answers are excluded from the analysis.

5 Conclusion and Future Work

This paper presents the findings of our exploratory study that aims to identify agile effort estimation techniques in practice including their benefits and challenges related to inaccuracy. To identify the effort estimation techniques a previous literature review was carried out. Based on those results, a questionnaire was designed to get the answers to our research questions. Most of the questions were formulated using a six-point scale however the questions were divided into both open and closed-ended. It means that our survey was intentionally designed to explore effort estimation in agile contexts.

Therefore, a subjective evaluation made by the respondents based on a predefined list of options and agile artifacts such as user stories were considered.

After inviting agile practitioners, 62 answers were collected but only 53 were valid since those practitioners were involved in the effort estimation process. The most used effort estimation technique based on the higher value mean is *Planning Poker* (3.00) along with *Story Point* (4.52). In this context, the most frequently used measurement unit also is the *Fibonacci series* (4.42). In addition, most of the respondents agree that *Drive the team to complete the project successfully* (4.38) was the top perceived benefit.

Regarding the reasons for inaccuracy, 20 factors were grouped into five categories. By each category, the factors most agreed were *Complexity and Uncertainty* "RrI" (4.25), *Knowledge sharing problem in the team* "TrI" (3.96), *Considering best case scenario* "OO" (3.96), *Ignoring Testing Effort* "Others" (3.94), and *Poor change control* "PMrI" (3.86). The respondents were also grouped into two categories "less than 3 years of experience" (n = 20) and "more than 3 years of experience" (n = 33) to identify if there are significant differences.

A richer investigation of agile artifacts to estimate effort accurately should be conducted. The most obvious opportunity for further research in the context of this study is to collect more responses. Moreover, although #NoEstimate and #NoProject are promoted as practitioners' movements, more than 84% of the respondents *did not know about it*, so further research is also needed to better understand the principles behind those movements and their impact in practice.

References

1. Stankovic, D., Nikolic, V., Djordjevic, M., Cao, D.-B.: A survey study of critical success factors in agile software projects in former Yugoslavia IT companies. J. Syst. Softw. **86**, 1663–1678 (2013). https://doi.org/10.1016/j.jss.2013.02.027

2. Kulathunga, D., Ratiyala, S.D.: Key success factors of scrum software development methodology in Sri Lanka. Am. Sci. Res. J. Eng. Technol. Sci. (ASRJETS) **45**, 234–252 (2018)

3. Fuggetta, A., Di Nitto, E.: Software process. In: Proceedings of the on Future of Software Engineering, pp. 1–12. ACM (2014)

4. Jorgensen, M., Shepperd, M.: A systematic review of software development cost estimation studies. IEEE Trans. Softw. Eng. **33**, 33–53 (2007). https://doi.org/10.1109/TSE.2007.256943

5. Popli, R., Chauhan, N.: Agile estimation using people and project related factors. In: 2014 International Conference on Computing for Sustainable Global Development (INDIACom), pp. 564–569 (2014)

6. Usman, M., Mendes, E., Weidt, F., Britto, R.: Effort estimation in agile software development: a systematic literature review. In: Proceedings of the 10th International Conference on Predictive Models in Software Engineering, Turin, Italy, pp. 82–91. ACM (2014)

7. Qi, K., Boehm, B.W.: Process-driven incremental effort estimation. In: 2019 IEEE/ACM International Conference on Software and System Processes (ICSSP), pp. 165–174 (2019)

8. Sommerville, I.: Software Engineering, 9th edn. Addison-Wesley, Boston (2010)

9. Altaleb, A., Altherwi, M., Gravell, A.: A pair estimation technique of effort estimation in mobile app development for agile process: case study. In: Proceedings of the 2020 The 3rd International Conference on Information Science and System, pp. 29–37. Association for Computing Machinery, New York (2020)

10. Fernández-Diego, M., Méndez, E.R., González-Ladrón-De-Guevara, F., et al.: An update on effort estimation in agile software development: a systematic literature review. IEEE Access **8**, 166768–166800 (2020). https://doi.org/10.1109/ACCESS.2020.3021664

11. Rosa, W., Clark, B.K., Madachy, R., Boehm, B.: Empirical effort and schedule estimation models for agile processes in the US DoD. IEEE Trans. Softw. Eng. 1 (2021). https://doi.org/10.1109/TSE.2021.3080666

12. Tanveer, B., Guzmán, L., Engel, U.M.: Effort estimation in agile software development: case study and improvement framework. J. Softw. Evol. Process **29**, e1862 (2017). https://doi.org/10.1002/smr.1862

13. Usman, M., Mendes, E., Weidt, F., Britto, R.: Effort estimation in agile software development: a systematic literature review. In: Proceedings of the 10th International Conference on Predictive Models in Software Engineering, pp. 82–91. ACM, New York (2014)

14. Usman, M., Mendes, E., Börstler, J.: Effort estimation in agile software development: a survey on the state of the practice. In: Proceedings of the 19th International Conference on Evaluation and Assessment in Software Engineering, p. 12. ACM (2015)

15. Tanveer, B., Guzmán, L., Engel, U.M.: Understanding and improving effort estimation in agile software development: an industrial case study. In: Proceedings of the International Conference on Software and Systems Process, pp. 41–50. ACM (2016)

16. Usman, M., Britto, R.: Effort estimation in co-located and globally distributed agile software development: a comparative study. In: 2016 Joint Conference of the International Workshop on Software Measurement and the International Conference on Software Process and Product Measurement (IWSM-MENSURA), pp. 219–224. IEEE (2016)

17. Arora, M., Sharma, A., Katoch, S., et al.: A state of the art regressor model's comparison for effort estimation of agile software. In: 2021 2nd International Conference on Intelligent Engineering and Management (ICIEM), pp. 211–215 (2021)

18. Sinha, R.R., Gora, R.K.: Software effort estimation using machine learning techniques. In: Goar, V., Kuri, M., Kumar, R., Senjyu, T. (eds.) Advances in Information Communication Technology and Computing. LNNS, vol. 135, pp. 65–79. Springer, Singapore (2021). https://doi.org/10.1007/978-981-15-5421-6_8

19. Weflen, E., MacKenzie, C.A., Rivero, I.V.: An influence diagram approach to automating lead time estimation in Agile Kanban project management. Expert Syst. Appl. **187**, 115866 (2022). https://doi.org/10.1016/j.eswa.2021.115866

20. Ramessur, M.A., Nagowah, S.D.: A predictive model to estimate effort in a sprint using machine learning techniques. Int. J. Inf. Technol. **13**(3), 1101–1110 (2021). https://doi.org/10.1007/s41870-021-00669-z

21. Duarte, V.: NoEstimates: How To Measure Project Progress Without Estimating (2015). https://www.amazon.com/NoEstimates-Measure-Project-Progress-Estimating-ebook/dp/B01FWMSBBK. Accessed 25 Feb 2019

22. Leybourn, E., Hastie, S.: # noprojects: A Culture of Continuous Value. Lulu.com (2018)

23. Creswell, J.W.: Research Design: Qualitative, Quantitative, and Mixed Methods Approaches, 3rd edn. Sage Publications, Thousand Oaks (2009)

24. Scheaffer, R.L., Mendenhall, W., Ott, L.: Elementary Survey Sampling, 4th edn. PMS-KENT Publishing Company, Boston (1990)

25. Molléri, J.S., Petersen, K., Mendes, E.: Survey guidelines in software engineering: an annotated review. In: Proceedings of the 10th ESEM 2016, pp. 58:1–58:6. ACM, New York (2016)

26. Usman, M., Börstler, J., Petersen, K.: An effort estimation taxonomy for agile software development. Int. J. Softw. Eng. Knowl. Eng. **27**, 641–674 (2017). https://doi.org/10.1142/S0218194017500243

27. Sánchez-Gordón, M.-L., O'Connor, R.V.: Understanding the gap between software process practices and actual practice in very small companies. Softw. Qual. J. **24**(3), 549–570 (2015). https://doi.org/10.1007/s11219-015-9282-6

28. Sjoeberg, D.I.K., Hannay, J.E., Hansen, O., et al.: A survey of controlled experiments in software engineering. IEEE Trans. Softw. Eng. **31**, 733–753 (2005). https://doi.org/10.1109/TSE.2005.97

29. Kuhrmann, M., Tell, P., Klünder, J., et al.: HELENA Stage 2 Results (2018)

30. Dalton, J.: Team estimation game. In: Dalton, J. (ed.) Great Big Agile: An OS for Agile Leaders, pp. 255–257. Apress, Berkeley (2019)

31. Pozenel, M., Hovelja, T.: A comparison of the planning poker and team estimation game: a case study in software development capstoneproject course. Int. J. Eng. Educ. **35**, 195–208 (2019)

32. VersionOne: 13th Annual State of Agile Report (2019). https://explore.versionone.com/state-of-agile/13th-annual-state-of-agile-report

33. Schweighofer, T., Kline, A., Pavlic, L., Hericko, M.: How is effort estimated in agile software development projects? In: SQAMIA, pp. 73–80 (2016)

34. Hannay, J.E., Benestad, H.C., Strand, K.: Agile uncertainty assessment for benefit points and story points. IEEE Softw. **36**, 50–62 (2018)

Towards Agile Mutation Testing Using Branch Coverage Based Prioritization Technique

Sangharatna Godboley[1]([⊠])[iD] and Durga Prasad Mohapatra[2][iD]

[1] National Institute of Technology Warangal, Warangal, India
sanghu@nitw.ac.in
[2] National Institute of Technology Rourkela, Rourkela, India
durga@nitrkl.ac.in

Abstract. The agile model is the present reality for any software development process. Its main objective is to produce good quality software in optimal time. Programmers do unit testing to ensure that the software unit or module they are developing should be bug-free and check that the module is doing what it is supposed to do. On the other hand mutation testing is an important technique to show that the quality of test cases is good. But, industrial practitioners do not follow it in practice because of the computational expenses and huge amount of effort required. In this paper, we introduce a technique to make mutation testing faster, so that the continuous integration (CI) which is the main process of agile can be performed. This way we are towards achieving principles of agile testing. We compute Line and Branch Coverages for a program and utilize them in mutation testing. Using Line coverage information we eliminate the Dead Mutants upfront. Next, using Branch coverage information we set the priority by assigning a rank to each test case and running on reachable mutants. In this paper, we have obtained better results for **45 out of 60** Programs i.e. **75%**. Experimentally, we show that our proposed prioritization approach consumes approx. **1036** s less mutation testing time as compared to the baseline (without prioritization). Since we perform mutation testing in less time to achieve agility, we call this technique Agile Mutation Testing.

Keywords: Agile mutation testing · Prioritization · Line coverage · Branch coverage

1 Introduction

Information Technology (IT) industry experienced several innovative techniques and practices in the last few years at different levels. It ranges from different development phases to complete projects, also from testing to verification of products. A good number of studies have been conducted to investigate the impact of using agile principles in the testing process. At present, agile based software development is the reality [3].

© Springer Nature Switzerland AG 2022
A. Przybyłek et al. (Eds.): LASD 2022, LNBIP 438, pp. 150–169, 2022.
https://doi.org/10.1007/978-3-030-94238-0_9

Traditionally Software Testing is considered to be the expensive and crucial phase of Software Development Life Cycle (SDLC). Fundamentally, software testing identifies the bugs present in the program [27]. Software testing doesn't guarantee a 100% bug free software, but it helps find the defects which can cause failure of the software system [13–17].

Using fault-based testing approach, we can populate test cases that identifies the recurring bugs [1]. These are faults which are repeatedly committed by different programmers while developing a software. This testing technique deals with problems in the absence of pre-specified faults (artificial faults created for analysis). Fault injection or Error seeding [28] and mutation testing [60] are two different types of fault-based testing techniques. Basically, mutation testing is a unit-testing approach to compute the quality and efficiency of the targeted test cases [9,10].

In 1978, DeMillo et al. [5] proposed mutation testing. Later, several researches were done by different researchers. Walsh [59] showed that mutation testing is more powerful and effective than branch coverage and statement coverage based testing techniques [27]. Offutt et al. [32] and Frankl et al. [12] concluded that mutation testing is better than data-flow based testing. Offutt et al. [34] presented that mutation testing is useful in accessing and comparing new testing techniques.

At present time, there is a need of mutation analysis within the computer science community and majorly in industries. Mutation testing is a well-known but costly approach for determining test adequacy. The logic behind the approach is to generate mutants, which are small syntactic variants of the program under test, and then to measure for a given set of test cases, how many mutants they kill. The effectiveness of mutation testing in computing the quality of test cases relies on the ability to apply it using a large number of mutants. However, running many tests against many mutants is time consuming. Another issue with mutation testing, obstructing its industrial adoption, is the information overload that follows from running a mutation analysis. A poor developer might end up with 1000 s of individual results to assess. Mutation testing often does not provide actionable results.

The Continuous Integration (CI) is an important approach for the Agile process. It is the process of developing software iteratively with small chunks of program being integrated into the main program body repeatedly following all the phases. In this process Software Requirements are divided into tasks and assigned to team members. The programmers work on code and tests the logic of the feature on this system via Unit testing. The program is updated in repository (mostly in cloud) empowered with a Version Control System. This process starts with several tests that can be either automated or manual. These tests target to check the functionalities of software every time new module is added via Integration Testing. Integration Testing checks that new code does not break existing features. The code is certified as ready for deployment once all tests pass. Here, the frequency of testing gets increases, also we have to maintain the quality of test cases to check newly implemented modules. So, faster approach of mutation testing will be beneficial to quickly check the quality of test cases so that the product release can be deployed with lesser time. Hence, in this paper we propose a technique to reduce mutation testing time using test case prioritization technique.

In the literature, we have observed that there are approx. ten agile principles[1] such as Provide continuous feedback, Deliver value to the customer, Enable face-to-face communication, Have the courage Keep it simple, Practice continuous improvement, Respond to change, Self-organize, Focus on people, and Enjoy. Among these principles, our propose technique closely adheres to *Provide continuous feedback, Practice continuous improvement,* and *Respond to change.*

In this paper, we propose a mechanism to reduce the time cost of mutation analysis, which also adheres to agile testing principles. The idea is to prioritize the test cases based on the branch coverage. This prioritization technique sorts the test cases according to the branch coverage contributed for the original program.

The rest of the paper is organized as follows. Section 2 discusses certain basic concepts. Section 3 explains our proposed approach. Section 4 presents the experimental results. Comparison with Related work is presented in Sect. 5. Section 6 concludes the paper.

2   Basic Concepts

In this section, we discuss a few basic concepts which are important to understand our proposed approach.

Mutation Testing: In this technique, the program under test is mutated to check whether the designed test suite is able to expose the induced faults or not. The main objective of mutation testing is to assess the quality of the test suite. In order to kill a mutant, a test input must satisfy the following three criteria [6,31,64]:

1. *Reachability*: A Mutant m is similar to the program P except the mutated statement s. Hence, if the statement s is not covered by a test case tc (tc ∈ TestSuite), then the execution of mutant program m with test case tc will generate the same output as that of the program P. For any tc (tc ∈ TestSuite), if s is not executed by tc, then it is guaranteed that tc will not be able to kill mutant m.

2. *Necessity*: To kill a mutant m, the test case tc (tc ∈ TestSuite) must reflect difference in the internal states of m and P immediately after the invocation of statement s. It is because, all the other instructions present in m and P are exactly the same. Otherwise, there will be no difference in the states of remaining statements in P and m during their executions, and both the programs will result in the same output at the end of program execution.

---

[1] https://enlabsoftware.com/agile-management/agile-testing-principles-for-tester-and-agile-software-development-team.html.

3. *Sufficiency*: To kill a mutant m, the test case tc ($tc \in$ TestSuite) must generate different outputs for the mutant m and the original program P. Different internal states result by satisfying the necessity criterion but the change must be propagated through the program's execution to the final state and yield different output.

It is stated that a test case tc *strongly kills* a mutant m, only if tc satisfies the *reachability*, *necessity*, and *sufficiency* criteria for mutation testing. The mutation ratio (MR) metric for program P with test suite T is calculated using Eq. 1.

$$MR = \frac{|mt| * 100}{|MT|} \tag{1}$$

where, mt and MT are two sets. mt contains the killed mutants and MT keeps the total mutants generated for the program P.

Killed Mutants: Mutants for which any of the test case from the complete test suite gives different result from the original program is known as the "killed" mutants [24,25].

Alive Mutants: Mutants for which all the test cases present in the given test suite generate same output as the original program, are known as "alive" mutants [24,25].

Line coverage: Line coverage is a basic and simple metric which determines whether a line of program or code is reachable and executed or not. The number of executed lines divided by the total number of lines is the Line Coverage of a program as shown in Eq. 2.

$$LineCoverage = \frac{No.\ of\ Executed\ Statements}{Total\ No.\ of\ Statements} \tag{2}$$

Branch coverage: The portion of independent code pieces that were executed is referred to as branch coverage [18]. The term *"independent code pieces"* refers to segments of code that have no branches leading into or out of them. To cover all branches of the control flow graph, the branch coverage method is implemented. At least, it covers all possible outcomes (true and false) once of each decision point condition. The branch coverage is a white box testing technique which guarantees that each decision point's branches are all tested and is shown in Eq. 3.

$$BranchCoverage = \frac{No.\ of\ Executed\ Branches}{Total\ No.\ of\ Branches} \tag{3}$$

3 Proposed Approach

In this section, we discuss about the traditional approach[2] and our proposed approach i.e. use of prioritization to achieve the agility for measuring mutation score, which means the continuous integration would be faster.

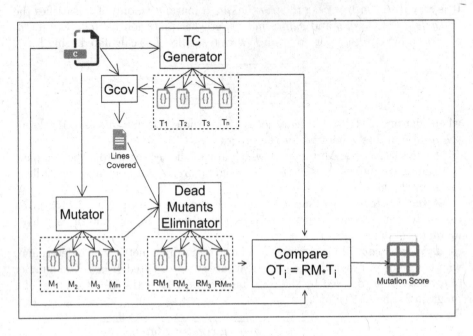

Fig. 1. Framework for traditional approach

Figure 1 shows the framework for traditional approach. Firstly, a C-Program is supplied into a *TC Generator* component to produce test cases (T_1, T_2, T_3, and T_n). For this paper, we have considered C Bounded Model Checker (CBMC)[3] to generate the test cases for input *C-Program*. Next, these test cases are replayed with *C-Program* using *Gcov*[4] tool to produce the lines covered. On the other hand, the *C-Program* is supplied into *Mutator* component to produce mutants (M_1, M_2, M_3, and M_m). In the literature survey, we have observed that there are more than 22 fault classes. But, to show our idea of this paper we have selected five fault classes, and we assume that it is enough for a good observation. Since, researchers have realized that a large set of mutation operators may cause to generate too many mutants. The large number of mutants may exhaust time or space resources without providing comparable benefits. Therefore, researchers

---

[2] Here, traditional approach represents the automated technique without manual intervention.

[3] https://www.cprover.org/cbmc/.

[4] https://gcc.gnu.org/onlinedocs/gcc/Gcov-Intro.html#Gcov-Intro.

start to find subsets of mutation operators that can achieve approximately the same effectiveness in indicating the quality of test inputs. Offutt et al. [32,33] found the five mutation operators are approximately as effective as all the 22 mutation operators of Mothra [4], a mutation-testing tool.

It might be the situation that some of the mutants are non-reachable. So, trying to kill these mutants will be waste of efforts. Hence, as they are not reachable and will be alive by the test cases, if executed, so we can eliminate them from the set of mutants. The *Dead Mutants Eliminator* component in Fig. 1 takes a set of mutants (M_1, M_2, M_3, and M_m) along with the lines covered as inputs and produces a set of reachable mutants (RM_1, RM_2, RM_3, and RM_m).

Next, *Compare* component takes the set of test cases (T_1, T_2, T_3, and T_n)[5] along with the *C-Program* and a set of reachable mutants (RM_1, RM_2, RM_3, and RM_m). Here, using the test cases we get the outputs for original and mutated versions of the *C-Program*. Table 1 shows the full comparison of the test cases running over reachable mutants. In Table 1, each row shows different mutants and each column shows different test cases. Each cell represents the comparison process of the outputs for original and the specific mutant when running with particular test case. It is to be noted that the mutation process will kill the mutants by executing test case if the outputs are found to be different for original and mutated versions. Finally, mutation score can be computed using the killed and alive mutants results produced by *Compare* component as shown in Fig. 1.

Table 1. Full comparison of all test cases (in the order they have been generated) with all reachable mutants. Notations: OT_i shows the output for original program with i^{th} test case. RM_*T_i shows the output for all mutants (1st to m^{th} mutant) with i^{th} test case.

$OT_1 = RM_1T_1$	$OT_2 = RM_1T_2$	$OT_3 = RM_1T_3$	...	$OT_n = RM_1T_n$
$OT_1 = RM_2T_1$	$OT_2 = RM_2T_2$	$OT_3 = RM_2T_3$	...	$OT_n = RM_2T_n$
$OT_1 = RM_3T_1$	$OT_2 = RM_3T_2$	$OT_3 = RM_3T_3$	...	$OT_n = RM_3T_n$
...	...	...	...	...
$OT_1 = RM_mT_1$	$OT_2 = RM_mT_2$	$OT_3 = RM_mT_3$	...	$OT_n = RM_mT_n$

Table 2. Full comparison of all prioritized test cases with all reachable mutants. Notations: OPT_i shows the output for original program with i^{th} prioritized test case. RM_*PT_i shows the output for all mutants (1st to m^{th} mutant) with i^{th} prioritized test case.

$OPT_1 = RM_1PT_1$	$OPT_2 = RM_1PT_2$	$OPT_3 = RM_1PT_3$	...	$OPT_n = RM_1PT_n$
$OPT_1 = RM_2PT_1$	$OPT_2 = RM_2PT_2$	$OPT_3 = RM_2PT_3$	...	$OPT_n = RM_2PT_n$
$OPT_1 = RM_3PT_1$	$OPT_2 = RM_3PT_2$	$OPT_3 = RM_3PT_3$	...	$OPT_n = RM_3PT_n$
...	...	...	...	...
$OPT_1 = RM_mPT_1$	$OPT_2 = RM_mPT_2$	$OPT_3 = RM_mPT_3$	...	$OPT_n = RM_mPT_n$

---

[5] Order of the test cases is ordered as they have been generated from TC Generator.

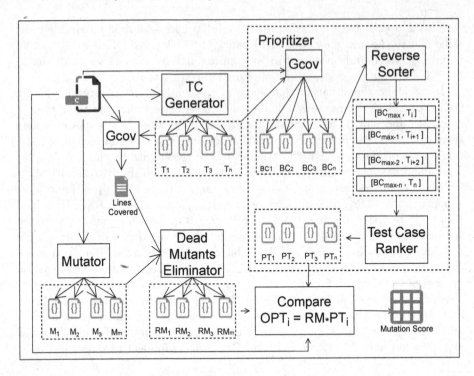

Fig. 2. Framework for our proposed approach

Figure 2 shows the framework for our proposed approach. It is to be noted that the functionalities of *TC Generator, Gcov, Mutator,* and *Dead Mutants Eliminator* are same as explained above for the traditional approach. In this framework, we introduce a component named *Prioritizer* which takes a *C-Program* and a set of test cases (T_1, T_2, T_3, and T_n) as input and produces a set of prioritized test cases (PT_1, PT_2, PT_3, and PT_n) as output. As shown in Fig. 2, *Prioritizer* uses *Gcov* tool to compute Branch Coverages (BC_1, BC_2, BC_3, and BC_n) for the corresponding test cases (T_1, T_2, T_3, and T_n). The component *Reverse Sorter* re-arranges the order of Branch Coverages with their respective test cases based on the maximum value. We use the order [BC_{max}, T_i], [BC_{max-1}, T_{i+1}], [BC_{max-2}, T_{i+2}], and [BC_{max-n}, T_n][6].

Next, the *Test Case Ranker* component takes the ordered array, and allocates a rank to each test case. Finally, *Prioritizer* produces the order of test cases from maximum to minimum branch coverages and as call them prioritized test cases (PT_1, PT_2, PT_3, and PT_n).

Table 2 shows the full comparison of the prioritized test cases running over reachable mutants. In Table 2, each row shows different mutants and each column shows prioritized test cases. Each cell represents the comparison process of the

---

[6] BC_{max-1} decreasing with 1 is just to show that we take the lesser value, but in real execution the actual branch coverage value will be considered.

outputs for original and the specific mutant when running with the ranked test case. It is to be noted that the mutation process will kill the mutants by executing any test case if the outputs are found different for original and mutated version. Finally, the mutation score can be computed using the killed and alive mutants produced by *Compare2* component as shown in Fig. 2.

4   Experimental Results

In this section, we discuss the setup, benchmark tested, result evaluation in detail, and inference of proposed approach.

4.1   The Set Up

We used an Intel Core i7-9700 CPU @ 3.00 GHz × 8 Linux box (64-bit Ubuntu 16.04) with 64 GB RAM. All the input programs considered for our study are written in ANSI-C format. We consider *CBMC* [2] as test case generator. The baseline we consider is the mutation analysis without prioritization to show the effectiveness.

4.2   Benchmarks Tested

Reactive systems appear everywhere, e.g. as Web services, decision support systems, or logical controllers. The testing techniques are diverse due to their complex structure. Rigorous Examination of Reactive Systems (RERS) programs are automatically synthesized to exhibit chosen properties, and then enhanced to include dedicated dimensions of difficulty, ranging from conceptual complexity of the properties such as reachability, full safety, liveness etc. over size of the reactive systems (a few hundred lines to millions of them), to exploited language features (arrays, arithmetic at index pointer, and parallel message passing). We have considered the RERS programs that replicate the real-world applications from Avionics, Banking, Medical and Railways etc. [49]. They are from RERS challenge competition in years 2012 [39], 2013 [40–43], 2014 [44], 2016 [45], 2017 [46–48], 2018 [50,51], 2019 [52], and 2020 [53]. These programs are from the small and moderate size group and easy to hard categories. The codes contain a lot of Boolean expressions, plain assignments, arithmetic operations, and data structures.

4.3   Result Evaluation

Table 3 shows the detailed result analysis of our experimental study for traditional and proposed approaches. Columns 1 and 2 show the Sl. No. and name of program respectively, as described in Sect. 4.2. It is to be noted that each program is suffixed with *-B1* or *-B2* which signify the loop bound considered in program because all were unbounded originally. We considered a set of 30 C-Programs with 2 different loop bounds which makes the structure and characteristics different. So, 30 X 2 = **60** programs we tested in this paper. Column 3 (#TC) shows the total number

Table 3. Experimental Results for traditional and our proposed approaches. Note: #TC is Total test cases generated, LC is Line Coverage, BC is Branch Coverage

Sl. No	Program	#TC	LC	BC	#Total Mutants	#Alive Mutants	#Killed Mutants	Mutation Score%	Traditional Time (Sec)	Proposed Time (Sec)
1	PS-P10-L-T-R16-B1	6	8.08	8.19	926	616	310	33%	94.40	93.97
2	PS-P10-L-T-R16-B2	10	15.87	19.51	1972	1151	821	41%	217.71	213.03
3	PS-P2-L-T-R16-B1	11	6.98	7.54	926	617	309	33%	105.51	110.06
4	PS-P2-L-T-R16-B2	13	12.61	14.28	1628	956	672	41%	194.28	192.79
5	PS-P3-L-R16-B1	11	3.40	4.10	993	815	178	17%	179.10	173.98
6	PS-P3-L-R16-B2	14	5.14	6.59	1524	1132	392	25%	281.25	279.90
7	PS-P3-L-R18-B1	19	2.10	3.41	1181	762	419	35%	382.32	370.83
8	PS-P3-L-R18-B2	21	5.20	9.38	3151	1977	1174	37%	1041.80	1018.34
9	PS-P3-L-T-R19-B1	11	7.18	9.00	910	557	353	38%	106.96	103.93
10	PS-P3-L-T-R19-B2	19	18.71	23.69	2306	1251	1055	45%	297.02	289.14
11	PS-P3-L-T-R20-B1	7	6.29	5.66	340	162	178	52%	28.61	28.55
12	PS-P3-L-T-R20-B2	27	16.83	16.57	905	297	608	67%	103.33	96.83
13	PS-P3-T-R17-B1	11	2.81	4.39	1350	992	358	26%	358.83	357.29
14	PS-P3-T-R17-B2	15	5.65	7.89	2508	1609	899	35%	679.25	645.90
15	PS-P55-GB-R13-B1	7	13.27	9.09	984	619	365	37%	119.72	120.35
16	PS-P55-GB-R13-B2	34	34.47	27.65	2075	858	1217	58%	341.81	360.99
17	PS-P56-GB-R13-B1	5	10.88	8.20	1641	1268	373	22%	242.92	238.20
18	PS-P56-GB-R13-B2	17	21.14	16.92	2976	1967	1009	33%	543.49	545.00
19	PS-P57-GB-R13-B1	41	14.35	8.98	1477	1051	426	28%	303.09	323.21
20	PS-P57-GB-R13-B2	217	43.73	32.01	3787	2173	1614	42%	2497.78	2449.10
21	PS-P7-L-T-R16-B1	6	10.96	10.68	736	446	290	39%	59.95	58.88
22	PS-P7-L-T-R16-B2	9	21.24	25.44	1582	882	700	44%	140.23	134.64
23	PS-P8-L-T-R16-B1	6	7.62	8.37	802	555	247	30%	58.90	57.98
24	PS-P8-L-T-R16-B2	10	12.54	15.36	1159	659	500	43%	89.94	92.72
25	PS-P9-L-T-R16-B1	5	5.58	7.66	1288	1014	274	21%	170.16	176.41
26	PS-P9-L-T-R16-B2	12	9.81	12.67	1925	1260	665	34%	278.10	270.28
27	PS-Prob1-IO-R14-B1	7	26.20	22.31	872	513	359	41%	81.60	89.85
28	PS-Prob1-IO-R14-B2	47	83.86	71.16	1996	662	1334	66%	380.91	356.83
29	PS-Prob16-R12-B1	7	33.30	24.35	10326	9686	640	6%	1593.43	1552.47
30	PS-Prob16-R12-B2	23	35.29	37.52	10442	9360	1082	10%	1825.43	1828.04
31	PS-Prob2-IO-R14-B1	6	14.87	12.82	2468	2034	434	17%	405.05	400.03
32	PS-Prob2-IO-R14-B2	20	27.47	26.44	4361	3070	1291	29%	1051.82	964.58
33	PS-Prob3-IO-R14-B1	22	18.16	15.16	2051	1660	391	19%	371.90	350.03
34	PS-Prob3-IO-R14-B2	192	58.00	56.46	5710	3563	2147	37%	3793.54	3487.52
35	PS-Prob3-LTL-DS-SEQ-B1	11	6.87	9.00	910	561	349	38%	108.76	108.53
36	PS-Prob3-LTL-DS-SEQ-B2	18	18.44	23.69	2306	1241	1065	46%	340.52	310.52
37	PS-Vp1-B1	7	11.55	9.39	1072	657	415	38%	118.74	117.28
38	PS-Vp1-B2	28	24.89	19.55	1754	773	981	55%	264.80	262.62
39	PS-Vp2-B1	7	13.05	9.04	2175	1737	438	20%	340.82	344.72
40	PS-Vp2-B2	39	37.56	30.31	5264	3504	1760	33%	1418.10	1396.41
41	PS-Vp3-B1	26	11.50	8.49	1629	1142	487	29%	294.57	305.00
42	PS-Vp3-B2	172	38.02	30.53	4773	2820	1953	40%	2438.46	2392.75
43	PS-Wtest10-B1	6	38.29	34.07	1118	935	183	16%	73.55	75.59
44	PS-Wtest10-B2	21	45.00	53.23	1119	789	330	29%	137.60	131.83
45	PS-Wtest11-B1	6	43.13	37.63	3814	3383	431	11%	287.85	282.93
46	PS-Wtest11-B2	13	47.95	59.30	3918	3102	816	20%	521.22	485.36
47	PS-Wtest12-B1	7	34.01	28.36	7036	6356	680	9%	907.71	850.00
48	PS-Wtest12-B2	36	45.01	61.70	7471	5480	1991	26%	1656.76	1616.84
49	PS-Wtest22-B1	6	5.21	5.85	899	699	200	22%	94.98	94.06
50	PS-Wtest22-B2	7	9.08	12.80	1556	1038	518	33%	173.66	164.96
51	PS-Wtest23-B1	11	2.91	4.37	1350	992	358	26%	339.47	344.48
52	PS-Wtest23-B2	13	5.77	7.88	2508	1618	890	35%	742.69	761.84
53	PS-Wtest31-B1	11	4.96	6.13	194	93	101	52%	15.57	15.21
54	PS-Wtest31-B2	12	6.90	8.43	260	81	179	68%	19.53	19.53
55	PS-Wtest7-B1	7	38.31	36.47	4538	4076	462	10%	467.73	449.25
56	PS-Wtest7-B2	12	40.50	40.37	4550	3944	606	13%	505.09	486.04
57	PS-Wtest8-B1	7	30.21	25.09	14712	14068	644	4%	2634.35	2659.80
58	PS-Wtest8-B2	15	32.13	32.11	14877	13801	1076	7%	3268.40	3067.94
59	PS-Wtest9-B1	7	39.80	30.98	1215	1021	194	15%	92.08	86.24
60	PS-Wtest9-B2	7	39.80	30.98	1215	1021	194	15%	116.98	103.15

of test cases generated by *CBMC*. It ranges from **5** to **217** also shown in Fig. 3a. Except 3 programs all others programs have less than **50** test cases. Column 4 (LC) shows the Line Coverage information. It ranges from **2.1% to 83.86%**, also shown in Fig. 3b. Except 2 programs, all the programs have less than **50%** Line Coverage. Column 5 (BC) shows the Branch Coverage information. It ranges from **3.41% to 71.16%**, also shown in Fig. 3c. Except 5 programs, all the other programs have less than **50%** Branch Coverage.

Columns 6 to 9 in Table 3 show the information about the mutation analysis. Column 6 (#Total Mutants) shows the total number of reachable mutants after eliminating the dead mutants from the original set of mutants. It ranges from **194 to 14877** mutants. Column 7 (#Alive Mutants) shows the total number of survived or alive mutants which could not found with entire set of test cases exhausted. It ranges from **81 to 14068** mutants. Column 8 (#Killed Mutants) shows the total number of killed mutants which got detected/found with at least a test case from the entire set of test cases. It ranges from **101 to 1953** mutants. Column 9 (#Mutation Score) shows the ratio of killed and total mutants. It ranges from **4% to 68%** also shown in Fig. 3d. Except 7 programs, all the programs have less than **50%** Mutation score.

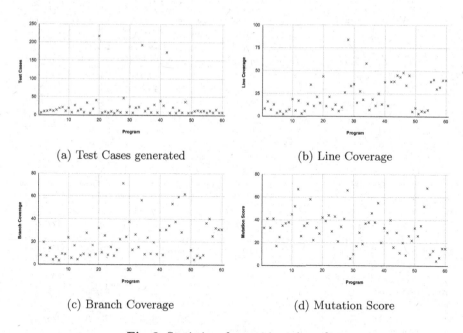

(a) Test Cases generated

(b) Line Coverage

(c) Branch Coverage

(d) Mutation Score

Fig. 3. Statistics of experimental results

Next, we explain the main contribution of this paper i.e. minimising the time cost to show the agility in mutation testing. Column 10 and Column 11 in Table 3 show the mutation testing time for Traditional and Proposed approaches in seconds. The time cost varies from **15.57 to 3793.54** s for Traditional approach.

Table 4. Five classes of mutants considered in experimental analysis. Note: To show killed mutants we have use prefix #K* and for total mutants prefixed with #T*. LOF is Logical Operator Fault, AOF is Arithmetic Operator Fault, ROF is Relational Operator Fault, CNF is Conditional Negation Fault, PNF is Predicate Negation Fault.

Sl. No.	Program	#KLOF/ #TLOF	#KAOF/ #TAOF	#KROF/ #TROF	#KCNF/ #TCNF	#KPNF/ #TPNF	#Killed/ #Total
1	PS-P10-L-T-R16-B1	54/115	0/84	177/580	62/130	17/17	310/926
2	PS-P10-L-T-R16-B2	116/247	53/176	458/1240	162/277	32/32	821/1972
3	PS-P2-L-T-R16-B1	31/117	0/72	196/590	66/131	16/16	309/926
4	PS-P2-L-T-R16-B2	82/193	16/224	408/970	141/216	25/25	672/1628
5	PS-P3-L-R16-B1	23/120	1/116	99/605	38/135	17/17	178/993
6	PS-P3-L-R16-B2	27/173	50/264	213/870	79/194	23/23	392/1524
7	PS-P3-L-R18-B1	57/143	0/136	258/725	86/159	18/18	419/1181
8	PS-P3-L-R18-B2	179/385	79/352	646/1935	222/431	48/48	1174/3151
9	PS-P3-L-T-R19-B1	41/114	0/68	221/580	73/130	18/18	353/910
10	PS-P3-L-T-R19-B2	131/274	49/300	619/1380	216/312	40/40	1055/2306
11	PS-P3-L-T-R20-B1	19/30	0/92	99/150	40/48	20/20	178/340
12	PS-P3-L-T-R20-B2	61/96	43/136	332/485	125/141	47/47	608/905
13	PS-P3-T-R17-B1	73/153	4/232	193/770	66/173	22/22	358/1350
14	PS-P3-T-R17-B2	122/267	134/560	452/1345	155/300	36/36	899/2508
15	PS-P55-GB-R13-B1	168/397	0/0	28/30	88/476	81/81	365/984
16	PS-P55-GB-R13-B2	506/824	0/0	141/145	428/964	142/142	1217/2075
17	PS-P56-GB-R13-B1	158/405	0/168	54/505	81/483	80/80	373/1641
18	PS-P56-GB-R13-B2	350/642	41/612	242/860	265/751	111/111	1009/2976
19	PS-P57-GB-R13-B1	178/412	0/68	79/425	88/491	81/81	426/1477
20	PS-P57-GB-R13-B2	591/922	28/628	356/1015	488/1071	151/151	1614/3787
21	PS-P7-L-T-R16-B1	28/93	0/56	185/470	64/104	13/13	290/736
22	PS-P7-L-T-R16-B2	70/193	18/180	433/970	155/215	24/24	700/1582
23	PS-P8-L-T-R16-B1	55/109	0/0	129/550	45/125	18/18	247/802
24	PS-P8-L-T-R16-B2	101/158	0/0	277/795	97/181	25/25	500/1159
25	PS-P9-L-T-R16-B1	48/147	0/220	154/740	54/163	18/18	274/1288
26	PS-P9-L-T-R16-B2	95/199	91/472	337/1005	116/223	26/26	665/1925
27	PS-Prob1-IO-R14-B1	170/345	0/0	29/30	83/420	77/77	359/872
28	PS-Prob1-IO-R14-B2	488/758	0/0	196/210	514/892	136/136	1334/1996
29	PS-Prob16-R12-B1	181/1953	0/64	79/5705	54/2278	326/326	640/10326
30	PS-Prob16-R12-B2	359/1953	19/180	214/5705	164/2278	326/326	1082/10442
31	PS-Prob2-IO-R14-B1	130/370	13/432	124/1140	88/447	79/79	434/2468
32	PS-Prob2-IO-R14-B2	296/611	128/1072	471/1855	289/716	107/107	1291/4361
33	PS-Prob3-IO-R14-B1	123/334	2/368	99/865	91/408	76/76	391/2051
34	PS-Prob3-IO-R14-B2	448/799	213/1828	787/2020	566/930	133/133	2147/5710
35	PS-Prob3-LTL-DS-SEQ-B1	42/115	0/68	217/580	73/130	17/17	349/910
36	PS-Prob3-LTL-DS-SEQ-B2	132/275	49/300	629/1380	216/312	39/39	1065/2306
37	PS-Vp1-B1	196/437	0/0	28/30	106/520	85/85	415/1072
38	PS-Vp1-B2	430/696	0/0	114/120	315/816	122/122	981/1754
39	PS-Vp2-B1	141/415	9/204	117/985	92/492	79/79	438/2175
40	PS-Vp2-B2	529/943	80/1208	514/1880	491/1087	146/146	1760/5264
41	PS-Vp3-B1	174/432	0/152	80/455	153/510	80/80	487/1629
42	PS-Vp3-B2	679/1049	56/1028	440/1325	616/1209	162/162	1953/4773
43	PS-Wtest10-B1	0/0	0/0	0/0	46/981	137/137	183/1118
44	PS-Wtest10-B2	0/0	0/0	0/0	192/981	138/138	330/1119
45	PS-Wtest11-B1	175/809	0/68	66/1855	53/945	137/137	431/3814
46	PS-Wtest11-B2	311/809	12/172	198/1855	158/945	137/137	816/3918

(*continued*)

Table 4. (*continued*)

Sl. No.	Program	#KLOF/ #TLOF	#KAOF/ #TAOF	#KROF/ #TROF	#KCNF/ #TCNF	#KPNF/ #TPNF	#Killed/ #Total
47	PS-Wtest12-B1	330/1449	2/84	106/3690	59/1630	183/183	680/7036
48	PS-Wtest12-B2	735/1449	46/516	649/3690	375/1630	186/186	1991/7471
49	PS-Wtest22-B1	37/114	0/64	109/575	37/129	17/17	200/899
50	PS-Wtest22-B2	75/186	27/196	289/940	102/209	25/25	518/1556
51	PS-Wtest23-B1	73/153	4/232	193/770	66/173	22/22	358/1350
52	PS-Wtest23-B2	122/267	134/560	443/1345	155/300	36/36	890/2508
53	PS-Wtest31-B1	12/22	0/12	54/110	20/35	15/15	101/194
54	PS-Wtest31-B2	25/30	3/12	96/150	35/48	20/20	179/260
55	PS-Wtest7-B1	161/951	0/0	68/2285	57/1126	176/176	462/4538
56	PS-Wtest7-B2	205/951	0/12	130/2285	95/1126	176/176	606/4550
57	PS-Wtest8-B1	160/2059	0/128	126/9875	62/2354	296/296	644/14712
58	PS-Wtest8-B2	284/2059	29/292	317/9875	149/2354	297/297	1076/14877
59	PS-Wtest9-B1	0/0	0/0	8/10	56/1075	130/130	194/1215
60	PS-Wtest9-B2	0/0	0/0	8/10	56/1075	130/130	194/1215

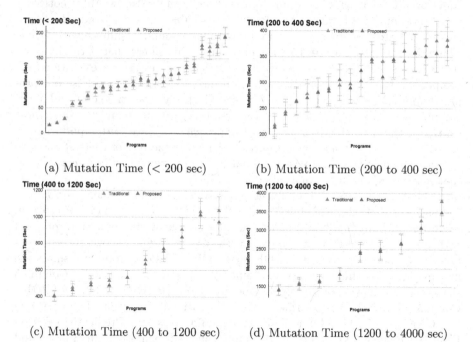

(a) Mutation Time (< 200 sec)   (b) Mutation Time (200 to 400 sec)

(c) Mutation Time (400 to 1200 sec)   (d) Mutation Time (1200 to 4000 sec)

Fig. 4. Mutation testing time analysis for traditional and proposed approaches. The programs have been sorted as per the time of traditional technique (min to max)

Similarly, time cost varies from **15.21 to 3487.52** s for Proposed approach. The green color cells in Table 3 highlights the better performance by either Traditional or Proposed approach. From the results, it is observed that Traditional approach performs better in **15 out of 60** programs. Similarly, our proposed approach performs better in **44 out of 60** programs. There was only **1** program for which both the approaches have equal time cost, it is highlighted with blue colored cell. Figure 4 shows the Mutation Testing time analysis for Traditional and Proposed Approaches. We categorise the time results in four groups for better presentation. Group1 shows the mutation time for the programs having the time less than **200 s** as shown in Fig. 4a. Group2 shows the mutation time for the programs having the time **200 s** to **400 s** as shown in Fig. 4b. Group3 shows the mutation time for the programs having the time from **400 s** to **1200 s** as shown in Fig. 4c. Group4 shows the mutation time for the programs having the time from **1200 s** to **4000 s** as shown in Fig. 4d.

Now, let us understand why our proposed approach has no better performance on 15 programs as compared to traditional approach. Firstly, the total number of test cases are very less to show a time difference between both the approaches, that is why some times our proposed approach is winning or loosing with marginal time difference. Secondly, the tie between test cases due to having equal branch coverage makes our approach inefficient. Also, we have noticed a trend from our experimental results shown in Table 3 that the traditional approach has better results if the program is with loop bound 1 (suffixed with *-B1*). There are total **10 out of 15** such programs. This shows that if the program structure is small, the code coverage and test cases are less, so the execution time comparison for the programs is not significant. This is a fact because our proposed approach avoids executing test cases which saves our time cost and hence our proposed approach is faster. If the test cases are more and avoiding these cases will be more then our proposed approach will have better performance as compared to the traditional approach. To avoid the rest of the test cases to execute, the particular test case candidate should have highest code coverage so that maximum number of mutants can be killed.

Table 4 shows the details of mutation analysis. In our experiment we consider **5 classes** of mutants. Columns 1 and 2 show the Sl. No. and name of program respectively. Columns 3 to 7 show the information of killed mutants prefixed with $\#K^*$ and total mutants prefixed with $\#T^*$. Column 3 shows the information of Logical Operator Fault (LOF) ($\#KLOF/\#TLOF$). Column 4 shows the information of Arithmetic Operator Fault (AOF) ($\#KAOF/\#TAOF$). Column 5 shows the information of Relational Operator Fault (ROF) ($\#KROF/\#TROF$). Column 6 shows the information of Conditional Negation Fault (CNF) ($\#KCNF/\#TCNF$). Column 7 shows the information of Predicate Negation Fault (PNF) ($\#KPNF/\#TPNF$). Column 8 shows the information of killed and total mutants processed ($\#Killed/\#Total$). The $\#Killed$ mutants can be computed by using Eq. 4. and $\#Total$ mutants can be computed by using Eq. 5.

$$\boxed{\#Killed = \#KLOF + \#KAOF + \#KROF + \#KCNF + \#KPNF} \quad (4)$$

$$\boxed{\#Total = \#TLOF + \#TAOF + \#TROF + \#TCNF + \#TPNF} \quad (5)$$

Table 5. Summary of experimental results

Aggr. TC	Avg. LC	Avg. BC	Aggr.-TMutants	Aggr.-Alive	Aggr.-Killed	Avg. Score	Aggr.-Time Traditional	Aggr.-Time Proposed
1400	21.51%	20.76%	171511	131126	40385	31.51%	35800.13	34764.54

4.4 Inference

In this section, we discuss about the inferences drawn from the experimental results. Table 5 shows the summary of experimental results. In total we tested **60** programs and generated **1400** test cases. From 60 programs, we got **21.51%** Line Coverage and **20.76%** Branch Coverage[7]. There were a total number of **171511** reachable mutants, out of which **40385** have been killed and the rest **131126** were alive or survived. So, from 60 programs on average we obtained **31.51%** mutation score. Now, total time consumed by traditional approach was **35800.13** s, however our proposed approach consumed **34764.54** s. In total we saved **1035.59** s using our proposed agile mutation testing approach.

Table 6 shows the summary of mutant classes considered in this paper. There were total **29721** LOF type mutants out of which **10587** were killed, score achieved is **35.62%**. There were total **14468** AOF type mutants out of which **1433** were killed, score achieved is **9.90%**. There were total **83340** ROF type mutants out of which **13784** were killed, score achieved is **16.54%**. There were total **38585** CNF type mutants out of which **9184** were killed, score achieved is **23.80%**. There were total **5397** CNF type mutants out of which **5397** were killed, score achieved is **100.00%**. Finally, total mutants were **171511** and got **40385** killed, final score we achieved is **23.55%**. We can observe that, there is a full score for PNF type mutants, it means the set of test cases is of very good quality. Secondly, LOF, ROF, CNF have some scores but not significant. The reason being that the test cases generated from CBMC was using the *Condition Coverage* criterion, if we use more stronger criterion such as *Modified Condition/Decision Coverage (MC/DC)* or *Multiple Condition Coverage (MCC)* then the test cases will be capable of killing these types of mutants effectively. Also, AOF type mutants has poor performance in our experiment which can be recovered with the test cases generated by *Fuzzing* approach. Fuzzing has been proven as a most popular dynamic test case generation technique to find the exploitable bugs which lead to crashes. We plan to add Fuzzing as our test case generator component, so that we can observe improvements in mutation scores. Overall, here we present the quality of test cases using agile mutation testing.

---

[7] For more clarity it is to be noted that these values are for both traditional and our proposed approaches. So improvement for our proposed work is not due to uncovered elements of the programs rather dependent on ordering of test cases so that high ranked test case can kill the mutant and most of the mutants can be avoided.

Table 6. Summary of mutants classes

Types	LOF	AOF	ROF	CNF	PNF	#Total
#Killed	10587	1433	13784	9184	5397	40385
#Total	29721	14468	83340	38585	5397	171511
Scores	35.62%	9.90%	16.54%	23.80%	100.00%	23.55%

5   Comparison to Related Work

DeMillo et al. [5] proposed mutation testing for revealing the bugs/faults in the software. Traditional mutation testing was expensive and non-scalable. A better version of mutation testing was proposed [22] and called as Weak Mutation Testing. Original mutation testing is also known as Strong Mutation Testing. It is recommended to use this version which is practical for test suite quality. Papadakis et al. [36] proposed a technique to populate the test cases as per the mutation specifications. They have combined mutation schemata with dynamic symbolic execution to produce quality test cases. They also minimize the overhead of mutation testing. They have used strong mutation [5] and weak mutation [30]. Zang et al. [63] presented few techniques to minimise the cost of mutation testing. They have used prioritizing and test case reduction techniques to more quickly find the mutants. They have shown the effective and efficient technique by experiment. In this paper, we consider weak mutation testing type. We first generate the test cases from CBMC which is a verifer and then apply dead mutants elimination and prioritization techniques using coverage information to make the technique efficient.

Ayari et al. [1] used ant colony optimization (ACO) [8] based evolutionary approach for mutation-based test case generation. They introduced a fitness function to evaluate the closeness of a test case to kill any specific mutant. Experiments show that the proposed ACO based test generation method is effective than other searching strategies such as random, hill climbing [20], and genetic algorithm [21]. In this paper, we have not used any learning algorithm rather computed the branch coverage for each test case and sorted them in max to min order. We have shown that this approach is beneficial.

Mutation testing is a popular technique for test case generation and bug prediction, but it is rarely used for fault localization [26,35]. It was believed that mutation is very expensive and difficult to scale. However, mutation testing has a strong capability to replicate real-world bugs. Now-a-days, several open-source mutation testing tools such as MILU [29], PIT [38], Javalanche [23] are available. Also, the computational capability of computers has increased phenomenally. In this paper, we have developed our own mutator with five fault types.

Zhang et al. [64] proposed a test generation technique using dynamic symbolic execution (DSE) [19,55] for effective mutation testing. They named their approach and tool as PexMutator. PexMutator transforms the input program into a meta program which contains mutant killing constraints. The instrumented meta program is supplied to the dynamic symbolic executor engine Pex [57] to generate test cases. Experimental results show that PexMutator generated test cases can kill 80% more mutants for five different subject programs undertaken for the study. In this paper, we have considered CBMC as test case generator but in future we plan to extend this work using DSEs.

Parsai [37] shows the techniques for mutation testing from theory to practice. Software industries still use simple coverage metrics to assess the quality of their tests. Literature in academic has done a good progress in mutation testing to assess and improve the quality of software tests. After several efforts in this domain it is not yet widely adopted in industry. Parsai [37] identifies three main problems: the performance overhead, lack of domain knowledge in tool providers, and lack of tool support. Parsai [37] addresses these three problems and shows that it is practical to abide the process of mutation testing based on industrial needs. Vercammen et al. [58] proposed an approach based on fine-grained traceability links at method level (named focal methods). This technique reduces the execution time of mutation testing and verifies the quality of the test cases for each individual method, instead of the usually verified overall test suite quality. In this paper, we also focus of reducing mutation testing time by ordering the test cases.

Testura [56] is an open source tool available that support mutation testing in a Continuous Integration (CI) context. This is a mutation testing tool/visual studio extension for C# that verifies the quality of unit tests by injecting different mutations in production code and then checks whether unit tests catch them or not. Our work is mostly align with this work because our work also abide the agile principles.

Yang et al. [61] reported survey on code-coverage based testing tools. They have included 17 different tools and compared them based on their functionalities such as coverage criteria, code coverage measurement, and reporting and automation. They observed that each tool has its pros and cons based on its domain of application. In this paper, we have used CBMC for test case generation and Gcov to compute the line and branch coverage. We have developed our in house mutator which is currently supporting 5 classes of faults.

Zhang et al. [62] introduced unified models for test case prioritization. These subsume the total and additional strategies as extreme cases. Their approach contains a spectrum of strategies between the two strategies. In this paper, we have not considered any unified models but we ordered the test cases based on the ranking given to each test case.

Rothermel et al. [11,54] proposed test case prioritization techniques viz. based on the number of code elements they covered and the number of additional elements they covered. Do et al. [7] showed an analysis to compare the traditional test case prioritization techniques by simulating real faults to show the usability of mutation faults. In this paper, we have also used the code element such as covered branches. In future we plan to do more study on other code coverage criteria to improve the mutation testing time.

6   Conclusion

Agility in software development phase is an essential requirement. Agility improves the development process with respect to the quality and time cost. Mutation testing is a proven power full technique to show the quality of test cases. But due to it's expensive process makes this technique non-popular. We propose a technique towards agile mutation testing by branch coverage based prioritization. In this paper, we experimented 60 programs and considered 5 types of fault classes. Our results are promising and showed that **45 out of 60 Programs** i.e. **75%** have better performance for the proposed approach as compared to the traditional approach. Also, we saved approx. **1036** s time using our proposed approach.

In future, we will consider other stronger coverage criteria to produce more meaningful test cases to analyse the mutation testing. Also, we try to club more test case generators to focus on all aspects of mutation testing. We target to propose new prioritization algorithm using other code elements so that we can improvise the time efficiency.

References

1. Ayari, K., Bouktif, S., Antoniol, G.: Automatic mutation test input data generation via ant colony. In: Proceedings of the 9th Annual Conference on Genetic and Evolutionary Computation, pp. 1074–1081 (2007)
2. Clarke, E., Kroening, D., Lerda, F.: A tool for checking ANSI-C programs. In: Jensen, K., Podelski, A. (eds.) TACAS 2004. LNCS, vol. 2988, pp. 168–176. Springer, Heidelberg (2004). https://doi.org/10.1007/978-3-540-24730-2_15
3. Crispin, L., Gregory, J.: Agile Testing: A Practical Guide for Testers and Agile Teams. Addison-Wesley Professional, 1 edn (2009)
4. DeMillo, R., Martin, R.: The mothra software testing environment user's manual. Software Engineering Research Center, Tech. Rep (1987)
5. DeMillo, R.A., Lipton, R.J., Sayward, F.G.: Hints on test data selection: help for the practicing programmer. Computer **11**(4), 34–41 (1978)
6. DeMillo, R.A., Offutt, A.J.: Constraint-based automatic test data generation. IEEE Trans. Softw. Eng. **17**(9), 900–910 (1991)
7. Do, H., Rothermel, G.: On the use of mutation faults in empirical assessments of test case prioritization techniques. IEEE Trans. Softw. Eng. **32**(9), 733–752 (2006). https://doi.org/10.1109/TSE.2006.92
8. Dorigo, M., Birattari, M., Stutzle, T.: Ant colony optimization. IEEE Comput. Intell. Mag. **1**(4), 28–39 (2006)
9. Dutta, A., Godboley, S.: MSFL: a model for fault localization using mutation-spectra technique. In: Przybyłek, A., Miler, J., Poth, A., Riel, A. (eds.) LASD 2021. LNBIP, vol. 408, pp. 156–173. Springer, Cham (2021). https://doi.org/10.1007/978-3-030-67084-9_10
10. Dutta, A., Srivastava, S.S., Godboley, S., Mohapatra, D.P.: Combi-FL: Neural network and SBFL based fault localization using mutation analysis. J. Comput. Lang. **66**, 101064 (2021)
11. Elbaum, S., Malishevsky, A.G., Rothermel, G.: Test case prioritization: a family of empirical studies. IEEE Trans. Softw. Eng. **28**(2), 159–182 (2002)

12. Frankl, P.G., Weiss, S.N., Hu, C.: All-uses vs mutation testing: an experimental comparison of effectiveness. J. Syst. Softw. **38**(3), 235–253 (1997)

13. Godboley, S., Dutta, A., Mohapatra, D.P., Das, A., Mall, R.: Making a concolic tester achieve increased MC/DC. Innovations Syst. Softw. Eng. **12**(4), 319–332 (2016)

14. Godboley, S., Dutta, A., Mohapatra, D.P., Mall, R.: J3 model: a novel framework for improved modified condition/decision coverage analysis. Comput. Stand. Interfaces **50**, 1–17 (2017)

15. Godboley, S., Dutta, A., Mohapatra, D.P., Mall, R.: Gecojap: a novel source-code preprocessing technique to improve code coverage. Comput. Stand. Interfaces **55**, 27–46 (2018)

16. Godboley, S., Dutta, A., Mohapatra, D.P., Mall, R.: Scaling modified condition/decision coverage using distributed concolic testing for java programs. Comput. Stand. Interfaces **59**, 61–86 (2018)

17. Godboley, S., Mohapatra, D.P., Das, A., Mall, R.: An improved distributed concolic testing approach. Softw. Pract. Exp. **47**(2), 311–342 (2017)

18. Godboley, S., Sahani, A., Mohapatra, D.P.: ABCE: a novel framework for improved branch coverage analysis. Proc. Comput. Sci. **62**, 266–273 (2015). https://doi.org/10.1016/j.procs.2015.08.449

19. Godefroid, P., Klarlund, N., Sen, K.: Dart: directed automated random testing. In: Proceedings of the 2005 ACM SIGPLAN conference on Programming language design and implementation, pp. 213–223 (2005)

20. Greiner, R.: PALO: a probabilistic hill-climbing algorithm. Artif. Intell. **84**(1–2), 177–208 (1996)

21. Harik, G.R., Lobo, F.G., Goldberg, D.E.: The compact genetic algorithm. IEEE Trans. Evol. Comput. **3**(4), 287–297 (1999)

22. Howden, W.E.: Weak mutation testing and completeness of test sets. IEEE Trans. Softw. Eng. **4**, 371–379 (1982)

23. Javalanche: (2012). http://www.javalanche.org/

24. Kaminski, G., Ammann, P., Offutt, J.: Better predicate testing. In: Proceedings of the 6th International Workshop on Automation of Software Test, pp. 57–63 (2011)

25. Kaminski, G., Ammann, P., Offutt, J.: Improving logic-based testing. J. Syst. Softw. **86**(8), 2002–2012 (2013)

26. Li, X., Li, W., Zhang, Y., Zhang, L.: Deepfl: Integrating multiple fault diagnosis dimensions for deep fault localization. In: Proceedings of the 28th ACM SIGSOFT International Symposium on Software Testing and Analysis, pp. 169–180 (2019)

27. Mall, R.: Fundamentals of Software Engineering. PHI Learning Pvt Ltd, New Delhi (2018)

28. Meek, B., Siu, K.: The effectiveness of error seeding. ACM Sigplan Not. **24**(6), 81–89 (1989)

29. MILU: (2018). https://github.com/yuejia/Milu

30. Offutt, A.J., Lee, S.D.: How strong is weak mutation? In: Proceedings of the symposium on Testing, analysis, and verification, pp. 200–213 (1991)

31. Offutt, A.J., Pan, J.: Automatically detecting equivalent mutants and infeasible paths. Softw. Testing, Verification Reliab. **7**(3), 165–192 (1997)

32. Offutt, A.J., Pan, J., Tewary, K., Zhang, T.: An experimental evaluation of data flow and mutation testing. Softw. Pract. Exp. **26**(2), 165–176 (1996)

33. Offutt, A.J., Rothermel, G., Zapf, C.: An experimental evaluation of selective mutation. In: Proceedings of 1993 15th international conference on software engineering, pp. 100–107. IEEE (1993)

34. Offutt A.J., Untch R.H.: Mutation 2000: uniting the orthogonal. In: Wong, W.E., (eds) Mutation Testing for the New Century. The Springer International Series on Advances in Database Systems, vol. 24. Springer, Boston (2001)

35. Papadakis, M., Le Traon, Y.: Metallaxis-FL: mutation-based fault localization. Softw. Testing Verifi. Reliab. **25**(5–7), 605–628 (2015)

36. Papadakis, M., Malevris, N.: Automatic mutation test case generation via dynamic symbolic execution. In: 2010 IEEE 21st International Symposium on Software Reliability Engineering, pp. 121–130. IEEE (2010)

37. Parsai, A.: Mutation testing: from theory to practice. Ph.D. thesis, University of Antwerp (2019)

38. PIT (2020). https://pitest.org/

39. RERS12 (2012). http://rers-challenge.org/2012/

40. Regular extrapolation of reactive systems (rers-2013): Problem28 (2013), http://rers-challenge.org/2013ase/problems/challengeProblems/White/Problem28/Problem28.c

41. Regular extrapolation of reactive systems (rers-2013): Problem29 (2013), http://rers-challenge.org/2013ase/problems/challengeProblems/White/Problem29/Problem29.c

42. Regular extrapolation of reactive systems (rers-2013): Problem30 (2013). http://rers-challenge.org/2013ase/problems/challengeProblems/White/Problem30/Problem30.c

43. Regular extrapolation of reactive systems (rers-2013): Problem32 (2013). http://rers-challenge.org/2013ase/problems/challengeProblems/White/Problem28/Problem32.c

44. RERS14 (2014). http://rers-challenge.org/2014/

45. RERS16 (2016). http://rers-challenge.org/2016/

46. Rigorous examination of reactive systems (rers-2017): Sequential ltl problems (2017). http://www.rers-challenge.org/2017/index.php?page=ltlProblems

47. Rigorous examination of reactive systems (rers-2017): Sequential reachability problems (2017). http://www.rers-challenge.org/2017/index.php?page=reachProblems

48. Rigorous examination of reactive systems (rers-2017): Sequential training problems for rers 2017 (2017). http://www.rers-challenge.org/2017/index.php?page=trainingphase

49. RERS (2018). http://rers-challenge.org/

50. RERS18 (2018). http://rers-challenge.org/2018/

51. Rigorous examination of reactive systems (rers-2018): Sequential training problems for rers 2018 (2018). http://www.rers-challenge.org/2018/index.php?page=trainingphase

52. RERS19: Sequential Reachability Problems (2019). http://rers-challenge.org/2019/index.php?page=reachProblems

53. RERS20: Sequential Reachability Problems (2020). http://rers-challenge.org/2020/index.php?page=reachProblems

54. Rothermel, G., Untch, R.H., Chu, C., Harrold, M.J.: Prioritizing test cases for regression testing. IEEE Trans. Softw. Eng. **27**(10), 929–948 (2001)

55. Sen, K., Marinov, D., Agha, G.: Cute: a concolic unit testing engine for c. ACM SIGSOFT Softw. Eng. Not. **30**(5), 263–272 (2005)

56. Testura.mutation (2021). https://github.com/Testura/Testura.Mutation

57. Tillmann, N., de Halleux, J.: Pex–White box test generation for .NET. In: Beckert, B., Hähnle, R. (eds.) TAP 2008. LNCS, vol. 4966, pp. 134–153. Springer, Heidelberg (2008). https://doi.org/10.1007/978-3-540-79124-9_10

58. Vercammen, S., Ghafari, M., Demeyer, S., Borg, M.: Goal-oriented mutation testing with focal methods. In: Proceedings of the 9th ACM SIGSOFT International Workshop on Automating TEST Case Design, Selection, and Evaluation, pp. 23–30 (2018)

59. Walsh, P.J.: A measure of test case completeness (software, engineering) (1985)

60. Woodward, M., Halewood, K.: From weak to strong, dead or alive? an analysis of some mutation testing issues. In: Workshop on software testing, verification, and analysis, pp. 152–153. IEEE Computer Society (1988)

61. Yang, Q., Li, J.J., Weiss, D.M.: A survey of coverage-based testing tools. Comput. J. **52**(5), 589–597 (2007). https://doi.org/10.1093/comjnl/bxm021

62. Zhang, L., Hao, D., Zhang, L., Rothermel, G., Mei, H.: Bridging the gap between the total and additional test-case prioritization strategies. In: 2013 35th International Conference on Software Engineering (ICSE), pp. 192–201 (2013). https://doi.org/10.1109/ICSE.2013.6606565

63. Zhang, L., Marinov, D., Khurshid, S.: Faster mutation testing inspired by test prioritization and reduction. In: Proceedings of the 2013 International Symposium on Software Testing and Analysis, p. 235–245. ISSTA 2013, Association for Computing Machinery, New York, NY, USA (2013). https://doi.org/10.1145/2483760.2483782

64. Zhang, L., Xie, T., Zhang, L., Tillmann, N., De Halleux, J., Mei, H.: Test generation via dynamic symbolic execution for mutation testing. In: 2010 IEEE International Conference on Software Maintenance, pp. 1–10. IEEE (2010)

Agility Based Coverage Improvement

Swadhin Kumar Barisal[1,2]($\boxtimes$), Arpita Dutta[3], Sangharatna Godboley[4], Bibhudatta Sahoo[1], and Durga Prasad Mohapatra[1]

[1] National Institute of Technology, Rourkela, India
{bdsahu,durga}@nitrkl.ac.in
[2] Siksha 'O' Anusandhan deemed tobe University, Bhubaneswar, India
swadhinbarisal@soa.ac.in
[3] National University of Singapore, Singapore, Singapore
[4] National Institute of Technology Warangal, Warangal, India
sanghu@nitw.ac.in

Abstract. Recent source code transformation techniques are adopted for coverage-driven testing to ensure software quality. However, due to the limitations present in constraint solvers of concolic testing, they lag to meet desired satisfaction level for testing safety avionics softwares. Particularly, they have the limitation of generating required number of qualitative test cases. So, we propose an agile-based automated test case augmentation technique that flips concolic based test cases that are obtained through source code transformation techniques to achieve high "Modified Condition/Decision Coverage" (MC/DC) score. This work has four technical contributions. The first contribution is code instrumentation of the input program to make it tool supportive. The second contribution is to propose a technique that can generate new effective test cases through agile process by augmenting concolic test cases. The third contribution is to propose a minimizer that can remove redundant and infeasible test cases. The fourth contribution is to propose a framework for MC/DC computation. To validate the proposed technique, it is experimented on two recent source code transformation techniques such as JPCT and JEXNCT and achieved 16.69% and 19.47% increase on MC/DC score respectively than existing technique using some benchmark input Java programs.

Keywords: Agile testing · Source code transformation · Concolic testing · MC/DC · BVA

1 Introduction

Automated testing approach speeds up testing process as compared to manual testing for generating test cases [3]. This automated testing approach uses testing tools to generate test cases. Concolic testing or dynamic symbolic execution technique generates the test cases automatically. Thus, it reduces the effort of generating test cases manually. In this regard, concolic testing is increasingly

A. Przybyłek et al. (Eds.): LASD 2022, LNBIP 438, pp. 170–186, 2022.
https://doi.org/10.1007/978-3-030-94238-0_10

used by the research community. Concolic testing is a testing technique that is designed to test on self guided inputs, with symbolic execution [20]. It executes program variables as symbolic variables. The software under test (SUT) is executed concretely with test inputs to obtain the execution trace. The execution trace is then fed to a Symbolic Execution Engine (SEE) for symbolic execution. The SEE re-executes the concrete trace symbolically. A constraint solver can find suitable concrete values to complete the execution traces.

Testing automation is a critical technique in software development under this environment, and several software development methodologies emphasise its importance. It is, for example, regarded as the cornerstone of agile testing, and its long-term benefits in a software project can be seen even with a small initial investment. Agile techniques stand out because they can quickly adapt to changes in the original objectives and prioritise functional development through executable code rather than voluminous written documentation [5]. Instead than following rigid strategies and contract negotiations, they collaborate with the customer.

The standard DO-178C/ED-12C, for Airborne Systems is the international standard jointly published by the RTCA and EUROCAE [17]. This new standard approves all commercial software-based aerospace systems such as the "Federal Aviation Administration" (FAA, USA) and the "European Aviation Safety Agency" (EASA).

Test-driven development (TDD) is a agile-based software development process. The software requirements are being converted to test cases before software developed. It repeatedly tests the software against all these test cases. Here, JUnit is used as a Java TDD unit test framework.

Source code transformation technique is used to automate code refactoring. This deals with computing source code metrics and transforms a code segment to another form of the same code. It targets to catch bugs and faults in the software. Some of the code transformation techniques such as BCT (Boolean Code Transformer) [6], JPCT (Java Program Code Transformer) [7] and JEXNCT (Java Ex-NOR Code Transformer) [7,8] are commonly used for achieving high code coverage.

JPCT [7] is a source code transformation technique that transforms the given input Java program into a equivalent version without changing syntax and meaning. It tries to explore additional paths, due to which the code coverage increases. JPCT inserts additional conditional code blocks. These code blocks are rule based statements generated against each predicates present in the input program. These extra code blocks facilitates the concolic tester to generate new test data. These new test data help to visit maximum number of possible nodes and edges of execution tree. Thus, it covers more number of branches that leads to explore more paths too. As many paths are traversed means that new test data help us to toggle individual clauses independently. Therefore, more number of independent clause gives us an opportunity to achieve high MC/DC.

JEXNCT [7,8] uses a source code transformation technique. Here, the code transformation is nothing but one kind of code instrumentation of the input Java program. It adds extra conditional code blocks. These conditional code blocks try to explore new paths by generating new test data. This leads us to achieve better coverage.

JEXNCT uses the concept of Boolean expression derivative method. It uses Exclusive-NOR logic operation to evaluate the predicate under test. In fact, JEXNCT adds empty nested if-else conditional code blocks to original program against each predicate. It is to note that transformed program is semantically same with respect to original program. The added code blocks are removed to regain the original code.

XCT technique uses the Boolean derivative method [15]. Here, boolean means that it uses $Ex - OR$ logic to determine the independent conditions (ICs). Additional conditional code blocks are inserted just above the identified predicate of the original program. The objective is to generate more test data without changing the semantics of the original program. This process helps us to achieve high MC/DC.

Boundary value analysis (BVA) is a testing technique to generate test data. BVA testing is used in black-box testing and mostly used in cases where tester deals with a large volume of test cases. It is used to generate test cases for the test variables based on their domain values as shown in Fig. 1. This is a very useful technique to mutate test cases to generate a new set of test data.

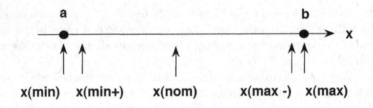

Fig. 1. Working of BVA

This technique motivated us to accelerate code coverage by combining both kind of generated test cases. For example, let us consider that a program has a condition (mark > 50). This condition carries a single variable named `mark`. Use of BVA generates new test cases (49, 50, 51) these additional test cases help to increase code coverage.

This motivates us to set our objectives to target some existing code transformation techniques and accelerate their performance in terms of code coverage. In particular, this work targets JPCT and JEXNCT code transformation techniques to accelerate their performance, that is the cases where they fail to achieve good MC/DC score.

MC/DC percentage is calculated using test cases generated by any of the mentioned code transformation approaches. Using these obtained test cases and predicates from the input program, we compute boolean truth table. This table helps us to determine independent conditions (ICs). Using ICs and total number of conditions, MC/DC percentage is computed using Eq. 1.

$$MC/DC\% = \frac{\#Total\_ICs}{\#Total\_Conditions} \tag{1}$$

The remaining sections of this paper are structured as follows. Section 2 highlights some of the existing literature related to code coverage, concolic testing and MC/DC. Section 3 discusses the problem description. Section 4 presents implementation details and obtained results. Section 5 does a comparative study with the performance of existing code transformation techniques. Section 6 summaries the conclusion and future insights on the context of improving code coverage score.

2   Literature Review

Bokil et al. [3] developed a tool called AutoGen, which generated test data. AutoGen was developed using C Language. This tool helped to reduce one third execution time over manual execution time. They used DART and CUTE for testing. They used a program analysis methodology with algorithmic advancement, increased computational power and constraints solver technology.

Qu and Robinson [19] compared many existing concolic testing tools and highlighted their advantages as well as limitations. On the other hand, DART (Directed Automated Random Testing) finds standard bugs from the program under test. Likewise, SAGE (Scalable Automated, Guided Execution) is designed using DART. The jCUTE (Java Concolic Unit Testing Engine), CUTE (Concolic Unit Testing Engine) and CREST are concolic testing tools. CUTE and CREST are mainly designed for C programs while jCUTE is for programs written in Java. The KLEE, EXE (Execution generated Executions) and RWSET (Read Write SET) belongs to the different family of concolic testing tools designed for C programs. The RWSET tracks the memory location which is either read or written and indicates the pruned redundant execution paths.

Ammann et al. [1] proposed a method for the generation of the test-suite which can give clause the ability to toggle the predicate's result. Particularly, they used the Exclusive OR logic for the calculation of these conditions. But, the process was not completely automated.

Mjeda et al. [16] had proposed a testing tool named CMT model. For the development of the CMT model, they used tools like Simulink, Stateflow and MATLAB. They evaluated the MC/DC score for the programs fed by the user. Jones et al. [13] proposed a technique for reducing the test cases count and also prioritizing so that their importance can be observed. They had developed their prototype tools using C++ language. They have processed C program to compute MC/DC score.

Woodward et al. [24] proposed a relationship that exists between two coverage criteria such as 'MC/DC' and 'all Jump to Jump paths (JJ-paths)'. These criteria are based on the concept of comparatively sophisticated control flow.

However, it was marked by them that the 'MC/DC' and 'all JJ-paths' are generally incomparable. But, it is seen that for few programs, that are written under specific constraints, the 'all JJ-path' criteria incorporates 'MC/DC' criteria.

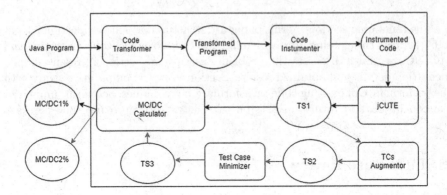

Fig. 2. Proposed model diagram

3   Proposed Approach

This section describes the proposed problem and its representation. The problem is to increase MC/DC score using agility based testing. The proposed idea is represented in the form of block diagram as shown in Fig. 2.

3.1   Setup

This work is implemented on win64 bit machine with core i5 processor and 4 GB RAM. jCUTE tool is used to carry out concolic testing with random search up to 1000 iterations. All the user defined algorithms are implemented using Java language.

3.2   Detail Description

The proposed approach is mainly consist of six modules that are implemented by us. The first module is   `code transformer` that translates the input Java program into its another form without changing its behaviour. The second module is `code instrumenter` that adds the required add-on to this Java code such that it can be taken as input for jCUTE. Then, jCUTE executes the instrumented code to generate concolic based test cases (TS1). Subsequently, these test cases are used by the `MC/DC Calculator` module to compute MC/DC score (MC/DC1%). Our third important module named `Test case Augmenter` is used to toggle these test cases in an iterative way using agile approach so as to find new sets of feasible test cases and combines all these test cases to form TS2. Now, TS2 is used by the fourth module called `minimizer` to remove infeasible and redundant test cases and produces TS3. TS3 is used by the fifth module named MC/DC calculator to find MC/DC2%.

```
1  void weight(int p, int q, int r){
2    if((p>30) && ((q<40) || (r<50)))
3    {
4      Do something;
5    }
6    else
7    {
8      Do otherwise;
9    }
10 }
```

Listing 1.1. Sample Program

In this work, we have experimented on two existing code transformation techniques namely JPCT and JEXNCT. Both these techniques were used increase MC/DC score. But, they could not meet the satisfaction level of testers. Therefore, we apply a greedy algorithm named TCs Augmenter to toggle the generated test cases.

Consider a sample java program as shown in Listing 1.1. To this additional conditional statements are inserted to form a JPCT transformed program, as presented in Listing 1.2.

```
1  void weight(int p, int q, int r){
2    if((p>30))
3    {
4        if((q<40)){}
5        else{}
6    }
7    else{}
8    if((p>30))
9    {
10       if((r<50)){}
11       else{}
12   }
13   else{}
14   if((p>30) && ((q<40) || (r<50)))
15   {
16       Do something;
17   }
18   else
19   {
20       Do otherwise;
21   }
22 }
```

Listing 1.2. JPCT transformed Program

Algorithm 1. JPCT: //Code transformation for Java Programs

Require: Java Program (J) //Input program
Ensure: (J') //Transformed program
1: **for** each instruction s ∈ J **do**
2:    **if** && or ||or unary ! found in s **then**
3:        Predicate_List ← s
4:    **end if**
5: **end for**
6: **for** each obtained predicate p **do**
7:    Generate equivalent SOP form
8:    Generate Minterm(SOP)
9:    Minimization using QM
10:   List_code ← Additional if-else statements of Minterm(SOP)
11:       J' ← List_code
12: **end for**
13: **return**(Transformed program (J'))

Algorithm 1 identifies the predicates and generates SOPs against each predicate. SOP is then converted into their Minterms for each identified predicates. Then SOP is further simplified using Quine McCluskey technique. This procedure collects all additional conditional statements inserted into original program and returns as the final transformed program. Here, it is to note that, these conditional code blocks do not the program behaviour. Rather, the main objective of these code blocks is to produce new test cases for exploring the new paths.

The second code transformer is JEXNCT. It has two modules: first one is `Identification of predicates` and second one is `Code bolck generator`. First module identifies all predicates with boolean logical operator. It uses Exclusive-Nor operation on each predicate to generate code blocks that leads to produce a transformed program. For the considered sample program, its corresponding JEXNCT transformed code is shown in Listing 1.3.

```
1  void testLogical(bool p, bool q, bool r)
2  {
3      if(!(q<40) && !(r<50))
4      {
5          if(p>30){}
6          elseif(!(p>30)){}
7      }
8      if(!(p>30) || (r<50))
9      {
10         if(q){}
11         elseif(!(q<40)){}
12     }
13     if(!(p>30) || (q<40))
14     {
15         if((r<50)){}
16         elseif(!(r<50)){}
```

```
17    }
18    if((p>30)&&((q<40)||(r<50)))
19    {
20        do;
21    }
22     else
23    {
24        otherwise;
25    }
26 }
```

Listing 1.3. JEXNCT Transformed Program

Algorithm 2. JEXNCT

Require: M // Input program
Ensure: M' // Transformed program
 1: **for** read input statement of M **do**
 2:    **if** && **or** || found **then**
 3:       Make a $P\_list \leftarrow$ statement //
 4:    **end if**else
 5: **end for**
 6: **for** each predicate $p \in P\_list$ **do**
 7:    $Code\_list = Produce\_XNOR\_code\_block$
 8:    $M' =$ Insert $Code\_list$ to M
 9: **end for**
10: **return** (M') // transformed program

Algorithm 2 represents step wise description of JEXNCT. It takes M as input i.e. original program. and produces M' as the output i.e. the transformed code. Lines 1 to 5 are used to find predicates. Here, each statement of the input program is checked to filter the available predicates. and added to P_list. Lines 6 to 10 represents the transformed program using X-NOR operation.

TCs Augmenter (TCA) module plays a key role in this work. The obtained test cases from jCUTE fail to achieve target level of coverage that may due to some limitations of constraint solver of symbolic execution. Some conditions of a predicate found that they are unable to toggle the outcome a that predicate. So to achieve this, TCA checks the boundary values of a variable within its domain and produces new test cases. These new test cases help to achieve more coverage.

These conditions are passed through TCs Augmenter to find the possibility of new feasible test cases. The generated new set test cases checked further for theit feasibility and effectiveness. Then, it results in an increase in the MC/DC percentage. Finally, the new test set is inserted to original test suite (TS1). The updated test suite becomes (TS2).

Algorithm 3 presents step wise description of the pseudocode of test case augmenter module. It takes the original test cases as input and produces a test

---

Algorithm 3. TCs Augmenter (TCA)

Require: TS1 //Original test cases
Ensure: TS2
1: **for** each $Clause \in PredicateP$ **do**
2:     **if** Not contributing towards MC/DC **then**
3:         Compute boundary values of the operand //
4:     **end if**   // else do nothing
5: **end for**
6: TS2 $\leftarrow$ TS1
7: **for** each new test generated **do**
8:     **if** feasible to add **then**
9:         Append to TS2
10:    **end if**
11: **end for**
12: **return** (TS2) // added new test cases

Algorithm 4. TCs Minimizer

Require: Test cases (TS2)
Ensure: TS3
1: **for** each predicate p $\in$ PUT **do**
2:     Initialize T= Extended Truth table for predicate p
3:     **for** each Condition C $\in$ P **do**
4:         **for** each testcase $t_c \in$ TS2 **do**
5:             Initialize truthVal = ""
6:             **for** each clause c $\in$ C **do**
7:                 truthVal += Evaluate truthValue for c
8:                 Insert truthVal in truthVector
9:             **end for**
10:        **end for**
11:        **for** each testcase **do**
12:            **if** truthVector of t_c == truthVector of t_c' and t_c != t_c' **then**
13:                Remove non contributing t_c
14:            **end if**
15:        **end for**
16:    **end for**
17:    Reduced TestSet = add minimized test cases for P
18:    TS3= TS3 $\cup$ ReducedTestSet
19: **end for**
20: **return**(TS3) // MinimizedTestCases

---

suite that contains original test cases with additional new test cases. Steps 1 to 5 find the variables that do not contribute towards forming MC/DC pair. Steps 6 to 11 are used to generate additional test cases and append to original test suite (TS1). Step 12 returns the updated test suite (TS2).

Algorithm 5. MC/DC Calculator

Require: TS Original test cases and TS3
Ensure: MC/DC% MC/DC1% and MC/DC2%
1: Prepare boolean truth table using TS
2: **for** each test case from input TS **do**
3:    **if** found as IC **then**
4:        Add to IC_List
5:    **else**
            Add to C_list
6:    **end if**
7: **end for**
8: Total_ICs=IC_List
9: Total_Conditions=C_list
10: Compute MC/DC score using Eq. 1.
11: **return MC/DC%**

TCs Minimizer module demons traits the process of test case minimization. The updated test suite (TS2) is minimized by removing test cases that are not feasible and redundant.

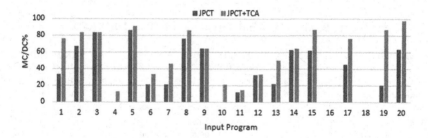

Fig. 3. Increase in MC/DC for JPCT and JPCT+TCA

It is note that, non contributing test cases refers to the test cases that do not form a MC/DC pair. Such test cases should be removed from TS2. On the other hand, a redundant test case is nothing but a test case that gives a truth value for the clauses and for the same clause with same truth value we encounter a different test case. So, redundant test cases are of no use and should be removed from TS2. Both these steps are followed to make TS3.

Algorithm 4 demonstrates the step wise description of test case minimizer module. Steps 1 to 10 select each test case from TS2 and fired at each clause of a predicate. Here, it evaluates truth value of each clause and also prepares the whole truth table. Then steps 11 to 16 are used to check whether each is capable enough to toggle the net outcome of a predicate. If it toggles the predicate's output the it is treated as a IC. If any test case is found non contributing then that test case is removed. This process is repeated until it processes all test cases of TS2 to finalize TS3.

Table 1. Characteristics of Test programs

Program no.	Program name	SLOC	No. of functions	Predicates	Clauses	IC Orig	IC JPCT	IC JEXNCT
1	SwitchTest1	75	2	2	6	2	2	4
2	Largest_Number	34	1	3	6	4	4	6
	Bank	65	2	4	12	9	10	10
4	WBS	273	1	4	8	0	0	1
5	Conditio0lDemo1	41	1	6	16	12	14	14
6	Bubblesort	122	3	7	14	2	3	2
7	InsertionSort	142	3	7	14	3	3	4
8	AssetTest2	72	1	7	21	16	18	18
9	StringBuffer2	520	8	7	14	7	9	9
10	Math_Cal	141	3	7	14	0	0	3
11	WildLife2	174	3	13	41	5	5	6
12	MarketSales2	321	3	24	55	14	18	15
13	Problem2_RERS2015	737	3	26	148	34	41	68
14	Problem5RV_2014	917	9	42	153	47	96	98
15	Problem4_RERS2017	644	9	74	242	149	209	205
16	Problem1-RERS2013	940	2	77	466	90	CTF	298
17	Problem12_RER2016	687	11	79	274	85	207	211
18	Problem3-RERS2016	1051	13	91	511	163	CTF	372
19	Problem5-RERS2015	803	3	104	240	34	209	211
20	Problem11-RERS2019	855	35	127	453	265	446	442

Table 2. MC/DC computation for JPCT and JEXNCT

Program name	MC/DC Orig	MC/DC JPCT	MC/DC JEXNCT	MCDC JPCT+TCA	MCDC JEXNCT+TCA	INC JPCT	INC JEXNCT
SwitchTest1	33.33	33.33	66.66	76.19	76.19	42.86	9.53
Largest_Number	66.66	66.66	66.66	83.33	66.66	16.67	0
Bank	33.33	83.33	83.33	83.33	83.33	0	0
WBS	0	0	12.5	12.5	25	12.5	12.5
Conditio0lDemo1	75	85.71	85.71	90.9	90.9	5.19	5.19
Bubblesort	14.28	21.42	14.28	33.33	54.65	11.91	40.37
InsertionSort	21.42	21.42	28.57	45.95	63.33	24.53	34.76
AssetTest2	66.66	76.19	76.19	85.71	85.71	9.52	9.52
StringBuffer2	50	64.28	64.28	64.28	71.42	0	7.14
Math_Cal	0	0	21.42	21.42	22.97	21.42	1.55
WildLife2	12.19	12.19	14.63	14.16	21.95	1.97	7.32
MarketSales2	25.45	32.72	27.27	33.33	42.85	0.61	15.58
Problem2_RERS2015	22.97	22.29	17.56	50	64.28	27.71	46.72
Problem5RV_2014	30.72	62.74	64.05	64.05	65.36	1.31	1.31
Problem4_RERS2017	61.57	61.57	38.84	86.64	87.6	25.07	48.76
Problem1-RERS2013	19.31	CTF	63.94	CTF	64.8	0	0.86
Problem12_RER2016	31.02	44.89	35.77	76.19	79.56	31.3	43.79
Problem3-RERS2016	31.9	CTF	72.79	CTF	73.19	0	0.4
Problem5-RERS2015	14.16	20	22.08	87.08	87.08	67.08	65
Problem11-RERS2019	58.49	63.35	59.16	97.57	98.45	34.22	39.29

CTF: Code Transformation Failed

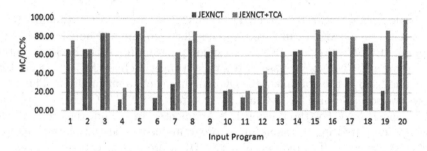

Fig. 4. Increase in MC/DC for JEXNCT and JEXNCT+TCA

MC/DC calculator is the fourth contribution of this work that computes MC/DC percentage. Algorithm 5 demonstrates step wise description of MC/DC calculator module. Steps 1 is used to prepare boolean truth table using input test cases and predicate from the original program. Steps 2 to 7 are used find out number of independent conditions and total number of conditions present in the input program. Steps 8 to 10 are used to store number of independent conditions, total conditions and computes MC/DC%. Finally, Step 11 returns MC/DC score.

4   Implementation

This section analyzes the obtained results. Here, twenty benchmark Java programs are experimented using this approach. These programs are of various size and complexity that validates our approach. The program complexity refers to number of conditions in that program. These programs are collected from various sources. First twelve Programs (Sl. No. 1–12) are taken from *Github*[1] and programming sites[2]. For example, "String buffers" program is used by the compiler to implement the binary "*" string concatenation operator. The rest eight programs (Sl. No. 13–20) are taken from Rigorous Examination of Reactive Systems (RERS) challenge TOOLympics event [2013–2019][3]. These RERS programs contain large number of complex predicates with 6 to 511 clauses in total that create complex execution trees during execution. These programs are targeted for reachability, full safety, and liveliness problems of the reactive systems.

During execution of list of input programs, several parameters are evaluated through our experiment that are shown in Table 1. Specifically, we obtained the parameter values such as number of functions executed, number of predicates found, total number of clauses found in each program. This table also shows the number of independent clauses (ICs) obtained during execution of original, JPCT and JEXNCT version of each input program.

---

[1]   https://github.com/osl/jCUTE/tree/master/src/tests.

[2]   http://www.programmingsimplified.com/java-stheproposedce-codes.

[3]   http://rers-challenge.org/.

Table 1 shows that for `Problem11-RERS2019` program, maximum of 511 clauses are executed that in turn produces 265, 446 and 442 number of ICs for original, JPCT version and JEXNCT version program respectively. So, from this we infer that if there is increase in ICs then it must increase MC/DC score too.

Table 2 shows the obtained MC/DC score for each input program. This table shows two scenarios like first scenario, we compute the MC/DC score for original, JPCT and JEXNCT without using TCs Augmenter. In second scenario, MC/DC score is computed for the same input programs using the test suite generated by `TCs Augmenter`. The difference in MC/DC score between these two scenario validates the increase in MC/DC for each input program. For JPCT, there is a minimum of zero up to a maximum of 67.08% increase of MC/DC score, which is shown in Fig. 3. Here, zero percentage increase indicates that JPCT+BVA could not generate effective test case for that particular program as in case of `Bank program`. Similarly, for JEXNCT, there is a minimum of zero up to a maximum of 48.76% increase of MC/DC score, which is shown in Fig. 4. Both JPCT and JEXNCT achieved 16.69% and 19.47% average increase in MC/DC%. In Fig. 3, we can see that there is an average increment of 16.69% in MC/DC score for 20 programs considered for our study. Also, we can infer from Fig. 4, that there is an average increment of 19.47% in MC/DC score for 20 programs considered for our study. For all the 20 programs, either the MC/DC score is going up or is equal to previous one. The result of the 20 programs justify the effectivity of our technique in achieving a higher MC/DC score. To further justify our proposed approach, below we discuss some proposed research questions.

RQ: Why does source code transformation techniques help increase MC/DC score?

Justification: Source code transformation technique converts the input program into a different version without changing semantics. It is to note that, existing limitations of constraint solvers leads to less code coverage. So, we use TCA with code transformation technique that generates new set of test cases to improve MC/DC. Code transformation inserts additional conditional code blocks. These extra code blocks support the concolic tester to explore more nodes and edges in execution tree. Since more paths are covered, so coverage increases. This justifies that more number of effective test cases are generated. Hence, we can achieve high MC/DC.

RQ: How does TCs Augmenter help increase MC/DC score?

Justification: Tcs Augmenter uses the concept of BVA, where it toggles the given test data to generate new sets of test data. These test data are treated as additional test cases.

Table 3. Comparison with state-of-the-art works

Sl. no	Authors name	Testing type	Testing tool	Code transformer	Coverage analyzer	Input type	Output type
1	Das et al. [6]	Concolic testing, MC/DC	CREST	BCT	CA	C Program	MC/DC% -
2	Godboley et al. [7]	Concolic testing MC/DC	jCUTE	JPCT	JCA	Java	Improved MC/DC
3	Godboley et al. [8]	Concolic testing MC/DC	jCUTE	JEXNCT	JCA	Java	Improved MC/DC
4	Harman et al. [10]	Evolutionary testing	Evolutionary tester	TeTra	-	Evolutionary testing	Improved test data generation
5	Harman et al. [11]	Search based testing	Search based testing tool	TeTra	Coverage module	Open problems	Improved coverages
6	Jiang et al. [12]	Regression Testing	RETORT	-	-	Old model graph	New model graph
7	Majumdar et al. [20]	Hybrid concolic testing	CUTE	-	-	C Editor	Test cases
8	Tiwari et al. [21]	Concolic MC/DC	Test Cases Generator	Leveling, CDG module	Coverage module	C Program	MC/DC
9	Wegener et al. [22]	Structural testing	Evolutionary Test Tester	-	-	C Program	Code coverage
10	Proposed approach	Concolic testing MC/DC	jCUTE	JPCT, JEXNCT, BVA	MC/DC Calculator	Java	Improved MC/DC

5   Comparison Study

Harman et al. [11] proposed a code-to-code transformation technique termed as testability transformation. Their objective is to improve the quality of the test data generation technique for the original program provided by the user. They had defined an algorithm for flag removal which identify their technique which illustrated that their algorithm improved the test data performance [23,25]. The testability transformation plays a significant role in improving the test generation process. They [11] had applied testability transformation on evolutionary testing. After concluding the experiment, they [11] had concluded that, it was really difficult to generate test data for MC/DC testing.

Pandita et al. [18] proposed a code instrumentation algorithm for logical coverage criteria. They automated the boundary value and applied symbolic execution. They used symbolic execution and an automated boundary value. For symbolic testing, *PEX* was used. An algorithm was proposed by them which will accomplish the test-generation process for branch or block coverage criterion. The test input generated by them achieved a higher Line Coverage (LC) as well as Boundary Value Coverage (BVC). Upon evaluating the five subject programs, they observed that there is 26% maximum (21.5% average) increment in LC and 0.5% maximum (23% average) increment in BVC of the considered subject programs. But, they had not evaluated MC/DC percentage using the concolic testing.

Harman [9] proposed an approach of testability transformation for effective for search-based test case generation. This technique helps to attain high code-coverage. He has also suggested few interesting and challenging open problems on which testability transformation could be applied and effective solutions can be thought off. Some of the problems are related with mutation testing, exception raising, state variable problems, temporal testing, mutation testing, stress testing, subsumption relation, dynamic symbolic execution, and directed random testing. He had also mentioned in this article that researchers and software industries are interested in concolic testing recently.

Das et al. [6] proposed a novel source-code augmentation technique for MC/DC specific test data generation. It is based on Boolean condition mapping and their simplification using K-map . They have implemented their approach for C-programs.

Tiwari et al. [21] proposed two techniques viz. levelling module and CDG module to convert an original C program to generate useful test cases. They generated test cases using their developed tool called concolic testing by extending a module called coverage module, which measured MC/DC percentage for a C program. They compared their strategies with "DFS", "CFG" etc.

Baluda et al. [2] reported an approach to improve code-coverage for input programs. They have illustrated the effectiveness of their technique over a set of experimental data with a ARC-B tool. They have introduced an abstraction refinement and coarsing (ARC), which combines the automatic test data generation and feasibility analysis to obtain high code coverage. Coarsing technique improves the scalability of the analysis by dynamically balancing memory requirements and precision. On the other hand, in our proposed approach, we extended concolic testing to obtain MC/DC specific test case to attain high MC/DC percentage.

Majumdar et al. [20] proposed a Hybrid Concolic testing technique. They have developed a tool called CUTE. They have used C language to generate test cases for an editor written in C language. Burnim et al. [4] proposed Heuristic Concolic testing. They have used CREST tool as concolic tester to generate test cases. Finally, they have measured branch coverage percentage. In our proposed approach, we improved Java distributed concolic testing to achieve higher MC/DC for a multithreaded Java program. In our experimental study, we have considered distributed environment and multithreaded concept to achieve higher MC/DC.

Kim et al. [14] developed a tool and named it SCORE. SCORE generates branch coverage targeted test cases in distributed environment for the procedural programs. On the other hand, we have targeted for MC/DC specific test data generation. We have used jCUTE concolic tester to generate the test cases.

Harman et al. [10] had done a survey of existing work and written a section focusing on the introductory part of testability transformation. They had introduced two novel code-transformation techniques called Fine-Grain transformation technique and Coarse-Grain transformation technique [11].

The above literature work are summarised in Table 3 for a quick observation and comparison. The basic thing is to note that every work is trying to increase code coverage score using different approach. Thus, our work keeps a quality space in the ongoing research trend.

6   Conclusion and Future Work

This paper demonstrates a MC/DC test case generation using agile process that increases MC/DC score. Being a coverage metric, achieving high MC/DC score assures safety crticality nature in Avionics software. High MC/DC score is achieved by toggling the test case values that are obtained through different code transformation techniques. We have also minimize the obtained test suite to reduce the overhead of unwanted test cases. We have evaluated our proposed approach over twenty open-source Java programs. Our experimental results show 16.69% and 19.47% improvement in the obtained MC/DC% over existing code transformation techniques JPCT and JEXNCT respectively.

In future, we plan to extend our approach in distributed environment to speed-up the test generation process using agile computing such that we can minimize execution time. Distributed environment can be setup in star topology with master-slave framework. The master will instrument the program and distribute to slaves (clients) to perform symbolic execution to generate non-redundant test cases. More number of test cases can be generated with lesser time and the higher code coverage can be achieved. Here, time is an agile factor that can be focused to achieve the agility. We also experiment on the multi-threaded program for analyzing execution time. Further, we prioritize the test cases to guide the tester for effective and efficient test case selection.

References

1. Ammann, P., Offutt, J., Huang. H.: Coverage criteria for logical expressions. In: 14th International Symposium on Softare Reliability Engineering, 2003. ISSRE 2003, pp. 99–107. IEEE (2003)
2. Baluda, M., Braione, P., Denaro, G., Pezzè, M.: Enhancing structural software coverage by incrementally computing branch executability. Softw. Qual. J. **19**(4), 725–751 (2011)
3. Bokil, P., Darke, P., Shrotri, U., Venkatesh, R.: Automatic test data generation for C programs. In: 2009 Third IEEE International Conference on Secure Software Integration and Reliability Improvement, pp. 359–368. IEEE (2009)
4. Burnim, J., Sen, J.: Heuristics for scalable dynamic test generation. In: 2008 23rd IEEE/ACM International Conference on Automated Software Engineering, pp. 443–446. IEEE (2008)
5. Collins, E., Dias-Neto, A., de Lucena Jr., V.F.: Strategies for agile software testing automation: an industrial experience. In: 2012 IEEE 36th Annual Computer Software and Applications Conference Workshops, pp. 440–445. IEEE (2012)
6. Das, A., Mall, R.: Automatic generation of MC/DC test data. Int. J. Softw. Eng. **2**(1) (2013)
7. Godboley, S., Dutta, A., Mohapatra, D.P., Mall, D.: J3 model: a novel framework for improved modified condition/decision coverage analysis. Comput. Stand. Interf. **50**, 1–17 (2017)

8. Godboley, S., Dutta, A., Mohapatra, D.P., Mall, R.: GECOJAP: a novel source-code preprocessing technique to improve code coverage. Comput. Stand. Interf. **55**, 27–46 (2018)

9. Harman, M.: Open problems in testability transformation. In: 2008 IEEE International Conference on Software Testing Verification and Validation Workshop, pp. 196–209. IEEE (2008)

10. Harman, M., et al.: Testability transformation – program transformation to improve testability. In: Hierons, R.M., Bowen, J.P., Harman, M. (eds.) Formal Methods and Testing. LNCS, vol. 4949, pp. 320–344. Springer, Heidelberg (2008). https://doi.org/10.1007/978-3-540-78917-8_11

11. Harman, M., Lin, H., Hierons, R., Wegener, J., Sthamer, H., Baresel, A., Roper, M.: Testability transformation. IEEE Transa. Softw. Eng. **30**(1), 3–16 (2004)

12. Jiang, B., et al.: Assuring the model evolution of protocol software specifications by regression testing process improvement. Softw. Pract. Exp. **41**(10), 1073–1103 (2011)

13. Jones,J.A., Harrold. M.J.: Test-suite reduction and prioritization for modified condition/decision coverage. IEEE Trans. Softw. Eng. **29**(3), 195–209 (2003)

14. Kim,Y., Kim, M.: Score: a scalable concolic testing tool for reliable embedded software. In: Proceedings of the 19th ACM SIGSOFT Symposium and the 13th European Conference on Foundations of Software Egineering, pp. 420–423 (2011)

15. Richard Kuhn, D.: Fault classes and error detection capability of specification-based testing. ACM Trans. Softw. Eng. Methodol. (TOSEM) **8**(4), 411–424 (1999)

16. Mjeda, A., Hinchey, H.: Ctmcontrol: addressing the MC/DC objective for safety-critical automotive software (2013)

17. Nordhoff, S.: Do-178c/ed-12c⸴ SQS Software Quality Systems, Cologne, Germany, Undated. White Paper 24 (2012). http://www.sqs.com/us/_download/DO-178C_ED-12C.pdf

18. Pandita, R., Xie, T., Tillmann, N., De Halleux. J.: Guided test generation for coverage criteria. In: 2010 IEEE International Conference on Software Maintenance, pp. 1–10. IEEE (2010)

19. Qu, X., Robinson, B.: A case study of concolic testing tools and their limitations. In: 2011 International Symposium on Empirical Software Engineering and Measurement, pp. 117–126. IEEE (2011)

20. Sen, K., Agha, G.: A race-detection and flipping algorithm for automated testing of multi-threaded programs. In: Bin, E., Ziv, A., Ur, S. (eds.) HVC 2006. LNCS, vol. 4383, pp. 166–182. Springer, Heidelberg (2007). https://doi.org/10.1007/978-3-540-70889-6_13

21. Tiwari, S.: Automatic Generation of Testcases for High MCDC Coverage. M. Tech Thesis, IIT Kanpur (2014)

22. Wegener, J., Baresel, A., Sthamer, H.: Evolutionary test environment for automatic structural testing. Inf. Softw. Technol. **43**(14), 841–854 (2001)

23. Williams, N., Marre, B., Mouy, P., Roger, M.: PathCrawler: automatic generation of path tests by combining static and dynamic analysis. In: Dal Cin, M., Kaâniche, M., Pataricza, A. (eds.) EDCC 2005. LNCS, vol. 3463, pp. 281–292. Springer, Heidelberg (2005). https://doi.org/10.1007/11408901_21

24. Woodward, M.R., Hennell, M.A.: On the relationship between two control-flow coverage criteria: all IJ-paths and MCDC. Inf. Softw. Technol. **48**(7), 433–440 (2006)

25. Yoo, S., Harman, M.: Pareto efficient multi-objective test case selection. In: Proceedings of the 2007 International Symposium on Software Testing and Analysis, pp. 140–150 (2007)

Short Paper

A Complete Unit Test Framework for Agile Software Development

Arpita Dutta[✉]

National University of Singapore, Singapore, Singapore
`arpita@comp.nus.edu.sg`

Abstract. Testing is an inevitable part of software development. Agile software development model follows a quick build, test, fix, and deliver methodology. In agile framework, testing is considered as a light-weight task as compare to the plan-driven methodologies where testing is exhaustively performed. To bridge the gap between traditional and agile testing frameworks, we propose a Blue-Box testing (BBT) technique. BBT includes both white-box and black-box test cases to generate a robust test suite which ensures the maximum coverage. Code coverage is one of the best metrics to determine the quality of a software system. In the article, we use Modified Condition/Decision Coverage (MC/DC) for evaluation of test cases and programs undertaken. Our experimental results show, on an average, 22.79% better code coverage is obtained as compare to other considered white-box and black-box testing techniques using our BBT method.

Keywords: Agile testing · MC/DC · Pairwise testing · Concolic execution

1 Introduction

In recent times, almost all the software development companies follow agile methodology. Major benefit of agile is its quick delivery and continuous communication with the costumers [10]. In agile, each and every stakeholder of the software have a constant look on the software development process and can give his feedback at any point of time. Agile follows an incremental delivery approach. However, to ensure the credibility of any software, quality measurement is a pivotal task. Software testing is one of the best methods to measure the quality of a software. But, due to the demand of quick delivery in agile framework, testing is not done as exhaustively as it is done in any traditional software development method [19]. Since, developer himself has to play the role of tester, it may possible that he may miss a good number of quality test cases when verifying the software. It ultimately leads to undetected bugs in the delivered software which can cause failure in the later stages [3].

Exhaustive software testing ensures reachability of different program elements such as branch, statements, predicates etc. It also provides indication of the dead codes residing in the program. Software testing techniques are broadly

© Springer Nature Switzerland AG 2022
A. Przybyłek et al. (Eds.): LASD 2022, LNBIP 438, pp. 189–197, 2022.
https://doi.org/10.1007/978-3-030-94238-0_11

classified into two categories viz., white-box testing [10] and black-box testing. In white-box testing, we have knowledge of the internal structure of the program whereas in black-box testing, only the system functionality is known. Also, there is a mid-way technique available, known as grey-box testing. In grey box testing, partial knowledge of the internal structure of the code is available to the tester.

As per the requirement of agile development, both tester and customer collaboratively tests the software. In this scenario, the developer team has the knowledge of the internal structure of the system. On the other hand, customers provide the test cases based on the functional knowledge/requirements of the software. Therefore, to take the best of this situation, we propose a new testing methodology called Blue-Box testing (BBT). In BBT, we generate white-box test cases using the most effective test generation technique called Concolic testing by the help of developer team. In addition to this, black-box test cases are created by the customers. We use pairwise testing technique on the black-box test cases to generate all possible 2-way combinations of the input values in a minimalist way. Finally, we combine both the white-box and 2-way combined black-box test cases to generate another test suite which helps to thoroughly test the complete software. At present, we consider only the unit testing of a system, however other testing techniques (integration, performance, interface, stress, etc.) are also equally important. But the other testing phases will be less error prone if the unit testing is carried in a fair manner. We use Modified Condition/ Decision Coverage (MC/DC) testing to measure the quality of test cases. MC/DC is the second strongest coverage criterion [7]. It requires (n+1) number of test cases to test a predicate of size n. We have not considered the strongest coverage criterion Multiple Condition Coverage (MCC) as it require 2^n number of test cases for a predicate of size n. In practical usage, exponential number of test cases are not suggestible to use for testing any system [5,6].

Rest of the article is organized as follows. Few basic concepts are discussed in Sect. 2 to understand the proposed approach. In Sect. 3, we present the related literature. Proposed method with example is discussed in Sect. 4. Experimental setup and obtained results are presented in Sect. 5. We finally conclude this article in Sect. 6 with some future insights.

2   Basic Concepts

In this section, we discuss few important concepts which helps to understand our proposed technique.

Concolic Testing [15,16]: It is a combination of symbolic as well as concrete execution to generate the test inputs which covers all possible paths present in a program execution tree. Symbolic execution treats the program variables as symbolic variables and with the help of constraint solvers generate different input values. Concrete execution uses concrete input values while executing the program under test.

Pairwise Testing [2,17]: It is a type of combinatorial testing and also known as 2-way testing. It creates all possible combinations of input values for each pair of variables present in the input space in a minimalist manner. For example, we have a system with 3 variables, say, A, B, and C. The values for these variables are {0,1}. The possible test cases generated using pairwise testing is {0,0,0}, {0,1,0}, {1,0,0}, and {1,1,1}.

Modified Condition/Decision Coverage (MC/DC) [7,11]: It is a predicate based testing technique and is considered as the second strongest coverage criterion. It aims to satisfy the following four norms in order to obtain 100% MC/DC coverage.

1. All the exit and entry points must be covered at least once.
2. Every condition must satisfy all the possible outcomes.
3. Every decision must satisfy all the possible outcomes.
4. Every condition present in the decision independently affect the final outcome of the decision.

We compute the MC/DC% of a predicate using Eq. 1.

$$MC/DC\% = \frac{Number\ of\ independently\ affecting\ conditions}{Total\ number\ of\ Conditions} * 100 \qquad (1)$$

3   Literature Review

Tripathi et al. [18] reported the challenges and important factors which are critical in agile testing. Basically, agile testing practices are light-weight as compare to the exhaustive testing practices performed in the traditional software development. Authors have suggested to establish good communication among developers, testers and the customers. Early report of any flaw or bug is recommended. Since, agile focuses on early delivery of software, there must be automation of testing activity. Automated testing practices are important for improving the regression testing results and efficiency. It is the quite important because agile follows the policy of incremental release.

Virtanen [21] presented a brief review on the available automation models used in agile testing. He classified the models based on the domains of software application. They are frequently used in safety-critical applications, customer facing, open-source development, and acceptance testing. Among these four, the first two domains are mostly used. The commonly used test automation models are Chameleon model, and behavior-driven automation framework [9]. He also found that earlier when the 50–60% of total software development effort goes to the testing process is reduced to 25% in agile methodology. Some of the available agile software testing tools are CI, Apache Maven, Travis Cruise Control, Robot Framework, Perforce, Git, Subversion, Hudson CI, JMeter, CDash, TestLink, Mantis Bug Tracker, CMake and Doxygen [1].

In the earlier days, random testing was quite popular. But due to increase in size and complexity of software systems, bug remains undetected. To handle this issue, symbolic testing was proposed. However, very often when the constraints are complex, the solver simply returns the false positives. Therefore to mitigate these issues, concolic testing came into force which combines the positives of both concrete random and symbolic executions. Some of the available concolic testing tools are jCUTE, Score, LCT etc. [15,16].

Hayrust et al. [7] was the first to introduce the concept of MC/DC testing. It is a predicate based testing and mandatory for the safety-critical systems. Different variations of MC/DC testing are available such as unique-clause MC/DC testing, masking MC/DC etc. Several code transformation techniques are developed to achieve high MC/DC coverage [5,6].

Pairwise Testing [2,17] is an economical way to check all possible combinations of a set of variables. In this technique a set of test cases is generated that covers all combinations of the selected test data values for each pair of variables. This is also referred as all-pairs testing and 2-way testing. It can be extended to all-triples (3-way) or all-quadruples (4-way) testing, but the size of the higher order test sets grows very rapidly.

The Pairwise Independent Combinatorial Testing tool (PICT) [12] help to efficiently design test cases and test configurations for software systems. With PICT, we can generate tests that are more effective than manually generated tests and also the creation time is in fractions as compared to the time required by hands-on test case design. PICT generates a compact set of parameter value choices that represent the test cases we should use to get comprehensive combinatorial coverage of the input parameters.

Vilkomir et al. [20] reported the MC/DC coverage of combinatorial test cases. Later, Dutta et al. [4] used concolic test cases to generate effective pairwise test suite. Also, they have calculated the MC/DC coverage of the improved test suite. Dutta et al.[4] have not taken separately generated Black-Box test alike in our proposed approach. Table 1 show the comparison of different related work. Columns 3–5 show the techniques considered in the proposed approaches.

Table 1. Comparison of related work

S. No.	Authors	White-box testing	Black-box testing	MC/DC
1	Bach et al. [2]	No	Yes	No
2	Godboley et al. [5]	Yes	No	Yes
3	Godboley et al. [6]	Yes	No	Yes
4	Vilkomir et al. [20]	Yes	No	Yes
5	Dutta et al. [4]	Yes	Yes	Yes
6	Proposed work	Yes	Yes	Yes

4 Proposed Approach: Blue-Box Testing (BBT)

In this section, we first discuss our proposed framework in detail. Subsequently, we understand the working of Blue-Box Testing (BBT) using a sample program.

4.1 Framework

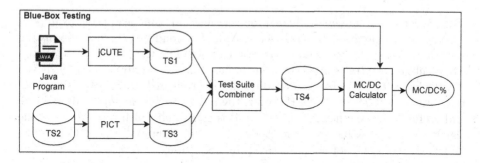

Fig. 1. Complete framework of Blue-Box Testing (BBT)

Figure 1 shows the flow diagram of proposed Blue-Box Testing (BBT) approach. The input to this framework is a Java program to test and a set of black-box test cases written by the customer based on the functional requirements of the software. The output is the MC/DC% of the input Java program. We first supply the Java program to a concolic tester jCUTE (Java Concolic Unit Testing Engine) to generate the white-box test cases. The test suite generated by jCUTE is marked as TS1 in the Fig. 1. On the other hand, the black-box test cases are given by the customers or can be by developers which are created based on the functional knowledge of the system is marked as TS2. We supply the black-box test suite TS2 to PICT (Pairwise Independent Combinatorial Tool) to create possible 2-way combinations of variable values and create another test suite called TS3. Subsequently, these two test suites (TS1 and TS3) are imparted to the Test Suite Combiner (TSC) module. TSC combines both the test suites and generates a more effective and efficient test suite called TS4 using the input test suites. Test Suite Combiner basically integrates both the input test suites. The input Java program along with the test suite TS4 is supplied to the MC/DC calculator. The MC/DC calculator first detects the predicated present in the program and then creates a extended truth table (ETT) for each predicate. The ETT is completed by the run-time execution information of test cases. It finally computes the MC/DC percentage of the program using the Eq. 1.

In our proposed framework, we have combined both the black-box and white-box test cases. Also, the black-box test cases are strengthen using pairwise testing technique. This approach includes inputs from all the stakeholders of the software under test. Because of all these reasons, we termed Blue-Box testing is framework for the complete unit agile testing. The proposed model is also used for large and complex system since it considers both the Black-Box and White-Box test cases. However, the Black-box test cases are required to be created more cautiously. The time cost of proposed technique depends on the execution time of White-Box test case generator jCUTE as well as the manual creation time of Black-Box test cases along with PICT.

4.2   Working Example

In this section, we understand the proposed method using a working example.

The sample program with one decision and five conditions is shown in Listing 1.1. After supplying the sample program to jCUTE, the generated test suite TS1 contains the test cases shown in Listing 1.2. Using only TS1, we achieved MC/DC% as 60. The black box test suite is given in Listing 1.3. Using TS2, the obtained MC/DC% is 40. However, the test suite TS2 is imparted on PICT and useful test case (shown in Listing 1.4) is generated which helps to prove the clause (m < 25) as independent clause. After combining all the test cases the MC/DC percentage obtained for this program is 100%.

```
1  void prog(int a, int b, int c, int d, int m){
2    if(((((a<10)  ||  ((b>20)) && ((c!=5) ||(d>=100))) && (m<25)
       )
3    {
4      True Block;
5    }
6    else
7    {
8      False Block;
9    }
10  }
```

Listing 1.1. Sample Program

```
1  TC1: a=9,  b=10, c=4, d=99, m=24
2  TC2: a=11, b=10, c=4, d=99, m=24
3  TC3: a=11, b=21, c=4, d=99, m=24
4  TC4: a=11, b=21, c=5, d=99, m=24
```

Listing 1.2. TS1: Test Cases generated from jCUTE

```
1  TC1': a=20, b=25, c=5, d=90,  m=22
2  TC2': a=30, b=25, c=4, d=95,  m=10
3  TC3': a=40, b=25, c=6, d=100, m=15
```

Listing 1.3. TS2: Black Box Test cases

```
1  TC1'': a=40, b=25, c=6, d=100, m=22
```

Listing 1.4. TS3: Black Box Test case obtained on passing TS2 to PICT

5   Experimental Study

In this section, we first discuss the used experimental setup. Subsequently, we present the characteristics of programs used and obtained results. We also discuss the threats to the validity of the obtained results from our proposed approach.

5.1   Used Setup

All the experiments are performed on 16 GB of RAM, Intel (R) Core(TM) i7 CPU 650 @ 3.20 GHz 3.19 GHz, and 64 bit operating system. Input programs are written in Java [13,14]. jCUTE [8] and PICT [12] are open source tools. We have developed MC/DC calculator to compute the MC/DC percentage. The MC/DC calculator is written in Java.

5.2   Obtained Results

We have evaluated our approach over six open source programs taken from different repositories [13,14]. Table 2, Columns 3–5 show the characteristics of the programs used in terms of LOC, Conditions and Decisions respectively. Columns MC/DC1, MC/DC2, and MC/DC3 show the MC/DC percentage obtained using TS1, TS2 and TS4 respectively. The last two columns of the table, Diff1 and Diff2, show the improvement obtained over the white-box and black-box test cases on using our proposed blue-box testing technique respectively. Diff1 and Diff2 are calculated using Eqs. 2 and 3. Average MC/DC1, MC/DC2, and MC/DC3 are 67.71%, 55.27% and 84.28% respectively. Using BBT method, we have obtained 16.57% and 29.01% improvement over white-box and black-box testing methods.

$$Diff1 = MC/DC3 - MC/DC1 \tag{2}$$

$$Diff2 = MC/DC3 - MC/DC2 \tag{3}$$

Table 2. Obtained results

S. No.	Program	LOC	Condition	Decision	MC/DC1	MC/DC2	MC/DC3	Diff1	Diff2
1	BSTree	307	13	3	76.92	61.54	92.31	15.38	30.77
2	Dsort1	136	20	2	80.00	35.00	90.00	10.00	55.00
3	BubbleSort	142	14	7	78.57	85.71	100.00	21.43	14.29
4	AssertTest1	75	7	3	57.14	42.86	71.43	14.29	28.57
5	Demo	76	8	3	62.50	62.50	87.50	25.00	25.00
6	Problem11-RERS2019	3214	450	126	51.11	44.00	64.44	13.33	20.44

5.3   Discussion

From the obtained experimental results, it can be observed that both the white-box and black-box test cases alone are not sufficient enough to prove each of the conditions present in a predicate as independent. On the other hand, the combined set of both the test suites are comparatively much better than the individual test suites. The combined test suite proved almost all the conditions present in the program as independent. Columns 6, 7, and 8 of Table 2 are directly proportional to the number of independent conditions proved using TS1, TS2, and TS4 respectively. Hence, it can be concluded that the BBT approach is better than the individual base techniques used.

5.4   Threats to the Validity

In this section, we discuss some of the important threats to the validity of obtained results.

1. We have experimented over limited set of programs. It is possible that our approach may not work equally well on another programs. However, to mitigate this threat, we have considered programs from different domains with different characteristics.
2. For MC/DC computation, a program must contain at least one predicate (decision) with minimum two conditions.
3. For better evaluation of proposed method, other methods such as fault based testing can be considered.

6   Conclusion

Testing is one of the most important phase of software development life cycle. With day-by-day increasing software size and complexity, it is quite important to give large attention to the testing phase. However, due to the quick delivery approach of agile software development makes the task of software testing a bit shallower. Therefore, to mitigate this gap and to strengthen the task of testing, we proposed to combine two different domains to software testing viz., white-box testing and black-box testing in order to generate more effective test cases. Our proposed testing technique is termed as blue-box testing. Experimental results show that on an average blue-box testing is 22.79% more effective than the other considered test case generation techniques.

In future, we plan to verify the effectiveness of BBT using mutation testing. We also extend this approach by adding other test generation techniques such as integration, performance, interface, stress, etc.

References

1. Agile Testing Tools (2021). https://www.ntaskmanager.com/blog/best-agile-testing-tools/. Accessed Oct 2021

2. Bach, J., Schroeder, P.J.: Pairwise testing: a best practice that isn't. In: Proceedings of 22nd Pacific Northwest Software Quality Conference, pp. 180–196. Citeseer (2004)
3. Baumgartner, M., Klonk, M., Mastnak, C., Pichler, H., Seidl, R., Tanczos, S.: Agile: a cultural change. In: Agile Testing, pp. 1–15. Springer, Cham (2021). https://doi.org/10.1007/978-3-030-73209-7_1
4. Dutta, A., Kumar, S., Godboley, S.: Enhancing test cases generated by concolic testing. In: Proceedings of the 12th Innovations on Software Engineering Conference (formerly known as India Software Engineering Conference), pp. 1–11 (2019)
5. Godboley, S., Dutta, A., Mohapatra, D.P., Mall, R.: J3 model: a novel framework for improved modified condition/decision coverage analysis. Comput. Stand. Interfaces 50, 1–17 (2017)
6. Godboley, S., Dutta, A., Mohapatra, D.P., Mall, R.: Gecojap: a novel source-code preprocessing technique to improve code coverage. Comput. Stand. Interfaces 55, 27–46 (2018)
7. Hayhurst, K.J.: A Practical Tutorial on Modified Condition/Decision Coverage. DIANE Publishing, Collingdale (2001)
8. jCUTE (2005). https://osl.cs.illinois.edu/software/jcute/. Accessed Oct 2021
9. Kulkarni, V., et al.: Regression test optimization and automation in agile framework: a review. Turkish J. Comput. Math. Educ. (TURCOMAT) 12(12), 2852–2856 (2021)
10. Mall, R.: Fundamentals of Software Engineering. PHI Learning Pvt. Ltd., Delhi (2018)
11. Pandita, R., Xie, T., Tillmann, N., De Halleux, J.: Guided test generation for coverage criteria. In: 2010 IEEE International Conference on Software Maintenance, pp. 1–10. IEEE (2010)
12. PICT (2021). https://github.com/microsoft/pict.git. Accessed Oct 2021
13. Programs (2005). https://github.com/osl/jcute/tree/master/src/tests. Accessed Oct 2021
14. RERSPrograms (2019). http://www.rers-challenge.org/2019/. Accessed Oct 2021
15. Sen, K., Agha, G.: CUTE and jCUTE: concolic unit testing and explicit path model-checking tools. In: Ball, T., Jones, R.B. (eds.) CAV 2006. LNCS, vol. 4144, pp. 419–423. Springer, Heidelberg (2006). https://doi.org/10.1007/11817963_38
16. Sen, K., Marinov, D., Agha, G.: Cute: a concolic unit testing engine for c. ACM SIGSOFT Softw. Eng. Not. 30(5), 263–272 (2005)
17. Tai, K.-C., Lei, Yu.: A test generation strategy for pairwise testing. IEEE Trans. Softw. Eng. 28(1), 109–111 (2002)
18. Tripathi, V., Goyal, A.K.: Agile testing challenges and critical success factors. Int. J. Comput. Sci. Eng. Technol. 1 (5), 5(06), 632–638 (2014)
19. van Driel, W.D., Bikker, J.W., Tijink, M., Di Bucchianico, A.: Software reliability for agile testing. Mathematics 8(5), 791 (2020)
20. Vilkomir, S., Baptista, J., Das, G.: Using mc/dc as a black-box testing technique. In: 2017 IEEE 28th Annual Software Technology Conference (STC), pp. 1–7. IEEE (2017)
21. Virtanen, T.: Literature review of test automation models in agile testing (2018)

Position Paper

Project Management Issues While Using Agile Methodology

Shariq Aziz Butt[1](✉) , G. Piñeres-Espitia[2], Paola Ariza-Colpas[2], and Muhammad Imran Tariq[3]

[1] Department of Computer Science and Information Technology, The University of Lahore, Lahore, Pakistan
[2] Universidad De la Costa, CUC Barranquilla, Barranquilla, Colombia
{gpineres1,pariza1}@cuc.edu.co
[3] Superior University, Lahore, Pakistan

Abstract. Software engineering has many software development life cycle (SDLC) models to develop a software application and the latest SDLC models have been provided by agile methods. The agile methodology has been introduced due to some existing lacks in software development. Now agile methodology is used to overcome these deficiencies and improve software development. The use of the agile methodology is increased within software industries due to its distinctive features such as enabling change requests from the client at any stage of a project, client satisfaction, iterative development, and client-developer interaction. Another reason for agile adoption is the methods that are being used for agile software development. These methods include Scrum, Feature drive development, Extreme programming, and Dynamic system development methods. However, the agile methodology has some issues for project development and management. In this study, we discuss all these issues which are related to agile methods and individuals (i.e. team and developer). Further, we suggest the possible improvements that need to be introduced in the agile methodology. We believe such improvements is to make the agile methodology more productive for development environments.

Keywords: Agile methodology · Software development · Methods of agile · Challenges

1 Introduction

Software Engineering has principles, SDLC models, and systematic techniques that are used to develop software applications. The agile model was introduced with a complete manifesto in 2001 to overcome some deficiencies from productive software development [1]. Now the agile model is the trendiest and mainly in use model in Software Development. The reason for the popularity of agile is distinctive features such as enabling change requests from the client at any stage of a project, client satisfaction, iterative development, and client-developer interaction [2]. Another reason is agile's methods such as Scrum, Feature driven development (FDD), Extreme programming (XP), Dynamic system development Method (DSDM) [3, 4]. All of them have been presented within the

© Springer Nature Switzerland AG 2022
A. Przybyłek et al. (Eds.): LASD 2022, LNBIP 438, pp. 201–214, 2022.
https://doi.org/10.1007/978-3-030-94238-0_12

umbrella of agile and are investigated in this paper. They have added more productive value to agile development by their characteristics as mentioned in the Table 2 and 3.

Agile also facilitates the client to prioritize the user stories and can give change requests at any level of the project [3]. Agile methods are productive for small-scale projects, small-size teams, requirements welcomed, and group effort estimation for example a planning poker technique [9]. In the agile methodology, the project manager leads estimates the project effort with teamwork [39]. In the estimation, the team assesses the complexity of the user stories.

Agile's most distinctive features and individuals associated properties are productive for agile software development. These individual properties include the developer's capabilities, understanding of user stories, and code writing skills [5]. Although the specifics of all these methods have the same purpose of allowing teams to adjust to changes relatively. Because accommodating changes later throughout the project is costly [6].

Instead of wide use for software development agile methodology still has some limitations that make it less productive due to agile's methods capabilities [3, 7]. This study is identifying the risks associated with each agile's method, as well as with an individual, which are a key part of software project management [8]. Moreover, agile methods usually do not cover some areas of project management like budget and schedule management [10]. Agile methodology is also not pertinently productive for large-scale projects [11]. Therefore, there is a need to make some improvements and introduce new features in agile methodology to support its use for large-scale projects. Some of such features in agile methodology includes SAFe (Scaled Agile Framework), SoS (Scrum of Scrums), LeSS (Large Scale Scrum), DAD (Disciplined Agile Delivery), RAGE (Recipes for Agile Governance in the Enterprise) [40].

1.1 Problem Statement

Agile is the most used model for software development, but still has some issues that directly impact its proficient productivity. The main issues with the development are due to methods used in agile software development [14]. One of the most valuable features is a change request from the client because the client is the owner of the product backlog [15]. In agile development due to small iteration development when any change comes from a client that is not listed initially in product backlog then might increase the cost of a project. Nevertheless, the cost is fixed at the start of the project by the team effort estimation i.e. a cost has decided with the client after the team effort assessment for a project [16]. Normally changes suggested by the client are due to market revolutions [7, 16].

Another limitation with the agile methods is its application only for small-scale projects and for small development teams [4, 11]. Agile also should be applicable for all sizes of projects, large-scale organizations, and large teams. It is because of agile's methods that make it not applicable for the large-scale organization.

Moreover, the agile methodology also has some flaws with respect to individuals i.e. developer and team. All these make agile less productive for efficient software development. Therefore, the agile methodology needs some improvements in its methods to become suitable for all types of projects and needs to introduce a cost estimation process with some new team-based estimation procedure to make accurate estimation [9–11].

1.2   Objectives of Study

This study is to highlights the main issues that directly affect the productivity of agile methodology. Such issues are related to shortcomings in the agile methods and constraints of individuals for proficient software development in agile. On other hand, the effort estimation in agile is also a challenge. The study also suggests some parameters that need to include in the effort estimation technique for an agile estimate. After such improvements, agile will be applicable for all sizes of projects. We can implement these contributions on real projects in the software development industries.

1.3   Significance of the Study

The significance of the study is to improve agile software development for all scales of projects and scenarios. Suggested changes would be useful for the professionals, who are using the agile methodology in their software industries, research scholars who want to contribute scientific methods in the agile methodology. The suggested improvements will enhance agile software development in all diverse areas of development. The project management in agile software development will get a new positive direction.

2   Methodology

We have adopted the methodology for conducting the study and reviewing the related studies of agile software development. For the completion of the study, we have followed an agile development score rating methodology. It contributes to evaluating the depth and accuracy of agile project management specifications, as well as providing a roadmap for experts in identifying flaws in agile development [14].

In Fig. 1 we have defined the steps that followed for literature gathering [15, 16]. In the methodology steps, we defined the necessity of and purpose of study that we mentioned in Sects. 2, 3, and 4. In this section, we clearly explained the study objectives and significance. The second step is defining research questions that illustrate the overall picture of the study. We have developed two research questions that relate to finding the issues with the agile software development and division of these issues according to agile's methods and individuals (developer, team/s). These research questions are mentioned as follows:

RQ1: What are the shortcomings in agile development with respect to agile methods and individuals?
RQ2: How such issues are affecting productive agile software development?

The third step is the searching of literature related to agile software development and agile's methods and issues with them. This step further is divided into sub-steps such as:

2.1   Search Strategy

A search query is used to do systematic searches across the digital libraries including Google Scholar, IEEE, Science Direct, ACM, Springer, Hindawi, MDPI, Sage, and Hindawi [14, 16]. All reputed data search bases are used for the collection of related works.

2.2   Search Strings

We used different search strings to find the agile software development papers within the domain. These strings are ("Agile Methodology" OR "Agile Software Development" OR "Software Development Issues") AND ("Large Development Team in Agile" OR "Agile Project Management") AND ("Factors in Agile Issues" OR "Agile methods positively affects" OR "Issues with key Methods") AND ("Individual Practices" OR "Issues").

The fourth step is application inclusion and exclusion criteria on the searched papers. We used inclusion and exclusion criteria to select studies published and eliminate irrelevant publications. The paper had to match the keywords in the title with the keywords of the study to be considered for inclusion. The first process is to examine the title of every publication and determine if it met the inclusion/exclusion parameters. If the topic of the publication corresponded to key terms within the study objectives, the abstract is examined to check significance using the inclusion parameters. In contrast, we used exclusion criteria when the search strings outcomes did not meet simply a little with the primary terms in our study topic. We have gathered the papers between the years 2014 and 2021, we looked for agile project development and management. Related a total of 60 papers are obtained from the databases described above, and 50 are chosen based on respective titles. The 44 papers that are chosen are then filtered further depending on abstract and keyword, relevancy, getting 39 publications [14, 16].

The fifth and last step is the data extraction strategy, in which after the inter-rater reliability test, there is no conflict after extracting data. Date of study, the title of publication, databases, procedures, strategy applied within the paper for research are all gathered from each scientific publication. We used the reliability test to find the weightage of some topics as mentioned in the Table 1. As stated in the Table 1 P_i represents the topic priority, R_i represents the topic ranking, and W_g represents the weight for every topic [14]. Here the weights are assigned based on the ranks to get a relative magnitude. To rank the validated elements, results of the survey were considered which gave the priority percentage of each element based on its importance in a scope definition.

Fig. 1. Methodology steps

Table 1. Weightage, raking, and priority of agile studies [14].

Topics	P_i	R_i	W_e
T1. Agile methodology survey	2.01	11	2.10
T2. Agile methods surveys	2.91	12	4.02
T3. Agile review studies	3.18	13	5.12
T4. Agile and project management literature	2.14	14	7.52
T5. Agile methods applications	3.20	17	10.72
T6. Agile development limitations	3.78	22	15.30
T7. Agile project management limitations	3.75	25	21.20
T8. Agile methods flaws	3.46	24	21.00
T9. Agile issues with individual	4.42	27	22.10

3   Literature Review

Agile is a well-regarded SDLC development approach and is becoming more well-known and widely used in software industries. The enhancement in agile development becomes well-known. It the adopted in the software houses due to its distinctive features that make agile more productive for efficient software development. Among other SDLC models, the agile method is the most in use model for development due to its unique methods and features [7, 8]. The agile methods include the (i) Scrum: is a much-known approach in agile software development. It enables the product development in sprints and establishes a concept of daily meeting with the team to project updates. (ii) DSDM: is an agile's project delivery process that works with rapid application development concepts and prioritizes the user stories based on user feedback (iii) FDD: is an iterative development process in agile software development and (IV) XP: is an agile process as it takes the development at an extreme level. It is used for small teams and small-sized projects to produce high-quality software products. The agile unique features include client satisfaction, change requests from the client at a time during the project development, user stories prioritized by the client, iterative development. Instead of so much fame and unique features, agile software development still has some issues that are discussed in the next section.

3.1   Factorization of Issues with Agile's Methods

3.1.1 Scrum Iterations Issues
The agile model eliminates many issues from the software development at that time and allows the change request at any time and any level of the project. Scrum teams work in sprints which divide the project into small iterations. These sprints are easy to manage and the software project easily developed. These sprints send to the client to get his feedback. When there is no change request then the next sprints start and otherwise

changes merge with the next iterations. To accommodate the change request is the main in a scrum within the agile model. Ultimately such changes increase the cost and time of the project [14, 15].

Other issues in the scrum are related to the team is daily based meetings for project updates. However, the daily meetings have limitations because not all the developers support the meeting and mostly are non-responsive to meetings. Due to this forced meeting and part of the agile development does not meet the requirements [16].

3.1.2 Extreme Programming (XP) Iterations Issues

eXtreme Programming (XP) has the ultimate objective of completing the project at hand. Exploration, Planning, Iterations to Release, Productionizing, and Maintenance are the 5 phases of the XP product lifecycle. Instead of so much use XP still has some issues that directly impact agile software development. Firstly, XP is not applicable for large-scale projects because it takes development to an extreme level. The reason is that XP does not measure the code for quality and complexity that cause code defects at the initial level. XP is also not feasible for global software development, due to different geographical locations [16, 18]. XP also supports the less documentation that causes defects in documentation, identical defects may arise in the future [36].

3.1.3 DSDM Issues

As agile welcomes the changes at any stage of the project then always the requirements fluctuates while development. Thus in the DSDM primary issue is requirements are not fixed and always add to the product backlog. Due to these continuous adding of new requirements/user stories project's cost and time increased. Cause of direct involvement of client throughout the agile development [7, 19]. Such issues are making the DSDM less productive for agile development.

3.1.4 FDD

Using the FDD in agile development main issue is less documentation. Secondly, it results in a high level of dependence on a single person. The Chief Programmer serves as a coordinator, main designer, and instructor, among other things. Multiple responsibilities in a large project is a problem since it raises the risks of human error. In addition to the aforementioned drawbacks, the structure of this approach is unlike other agile methodology, sprints are not very well described within the process. These are project-specific and adapted to the project's needs. As a result, there is no standardized process for iterations [20, 21].

3.2   Factorization of issues with Individuals

3.2.1 People

A software project might include a wide spectrum of individuals, including developers, testers, and project managers, to mention a few. The final product is frequently required by a client or end-user. Top executives (company managers and development department

Table 2. Comparison of Agile methods.

Characteristics	XP	Scrum	FDD	DSDM	References
Methodology for development	Incremental Improvements are a type of modification	Incremental Iteration	Iterative	Incremental	3, 4, 5
The time between iterations is required	One to six weeks	Two to four weeks	Two days to two weeks	Depending on the method belong to the family	6, 7, 8, 9
Project team	Fewer than 20 individu-als of team/s	All sizes (concept of scrums)	Many people are members of multiple teams	All sizes are available based on the methodology of the family	9, 10, 11, 13
Collaboration inside the team	Regular meetings of team members	Regular meetings of team members	Depends on documentation	Face to face Informal	11, 14, 15, 17, 38
The scope of the project	Small projects	Various types of projects	Projects that are more difficult to complete	Projects of all kinds based on the methodology, could be a member of a family	18, 20
Participation of customers	Involvement of customers	The responsibility to the Product Owner is performed by the client	Customer generated reports	Customers will benefit from incremental updates	19, 21, 23
Project documentation	Minimum documentation	Less documentation	Documentation's Significance	Simple Basic documentation	22, 24
Skills	Refactoring, user stories DD	Scrum master, for example plan-	Diagrams of UML	Family's adaptive methodology	25, 26, 28

Table 3. Summary of agile methods features

Condition	XP	Scrum	FDD	DSDM
Small team/s	Yes	Yes	No	Unclear
Requirements that are very changeable	Yes	Yes	Yes	Unclear
Teams that are dispersed	No	Yes	Yes	No
High ceremony culture	No	No	Unclear	Unclear
Systems with a high severity	No	Unclear	Unclear	Yes
Multiple customers/stakeholders	No	Yes	Unclear	Unclear

heads) are particularly concerned with costs, investment returns, and human resources. In agile development, every one of these has a responsibility [21].

3.2.2 Developers
The developers are maybe the most affected by agile processes. Agile methodologies rely on good programmers who are skilled, experienced, and willing to interact with

clients productively. Developers have to be willing to work as part of a team, be capable to deal with frequent change, and also be innovative in their problem-solving abilities. Agile processes seem to be very flexible approaches that do not require developers to adopt rigorous standards and practices. But it is a problem for a software house as some programmers may not be able to work in an agile environment. In an agile context, the "5" rank of developer shown in the Table 4 would be challenged. "Hand-holding" takes resources even for "4" programmers. As a result, the agile development team's base is made up of the top 3 ranks. Rank "1" programmers may or may not be required for any projects, depending on how rare it seems. Agile Approaches may be challenging to implement within a typically staffed software house due to the high degree of skill required. Highly talented professionals are consistently in demand, and developing a long-term human development approach may be challenging without integrating 4 rank programmers. Long-term projects provide a considerable risk for Agile Methodologies for several reasons [22, 24, 26].

Table 4. Features of developers

Rank	Features
1	Abilities to develop solutions under bizarre circumstances
2	Capable of changing solutions to meet a new, yet previously encountered circumstance
3	programmer capable of implementing functionality, estimating effort, and refactoring code
4	Capable of implementing basic functionality, running tests, and completing tasks
5	Reluctant or unable to collaborate in a team environment

3.2.3 Project Leaders

Project managers and team leads are the two most important Project Leader responsibilities throughout software development. As leadership under such an agile methodology varies from previous approaches, it has its own set of difficulties. This difference is well defined as controlling process resources and leadership effectiveness. A leadership strategy is particularly efficient when agile teams include skilled professionals with significant responsibilities. Team leaders should be willing to provide team members the freedom to take initiative. Rather than using the central command, collaboration is used as a method of leadership. For some, it will be a psychological adjustment, since they will have to share decision-making power. A team leader's responsibility is to make it easier for the team to make decisions. On the other hand, project managers are responsible for monitoring performance and approving business decisions within agile approaches. Project managers must make a more significant adjustment [22, 23].

The attention is on reacting to changes rather than adhering to a strict schedule. It is a problem because they are typically looked upon to provide updates about the project's progress. In addition, project managers play a considerably more active role. In scrum, the project management interacts with the team every day and supervises the daily scrum.

For the agile team, regular team member gatherings are the standard procedure. Rather than emphasizing defining the milestones and contracts, project managers are much more engaged in building and maintaining customer relationships.

3.2.4 Customers

Agile methodologies have a much greater effect on customers as compared to traditional methods. Clients are involved from the beginning of the project, participating with defining the requirements and contract responsibilities, and at the ending, and acceptability testing under relatively traditional techniques. However, under agile methodologies, clients are engaged even more frequently and have more control over user stories [24].

Clients might be unwilling to participate in software development. Clients may be unfamiliar with startups because the market is still to be determined. When using an agile methodology, the presence of client representatives should be considered. In agile clients should be decided to commit, skilled, cooperative, representative, and empowered through the development. They should be aware of the requirements for end-users. Furthermore, as decisions regarding which functionality will be included in which releases should be decided, the representative should have the ability to do so. Agile Approaches may not be applicable including all sizes and types of projects because a client representative might not have been available [28].

3.2.5 Team

The team is important to effectiveness in agile processes because they rely significantly on interaction and coordination. A sole skilled developer, who can't work well together, and a client who doesn't interact with the team all have the potential to undermine a team's feasibility and effectiveness. The chemistry of the team poses a substantial risk for agile development. Another important human aspect to consider within an agile team is turnover. High turnover in a project might result in the loss of key skills if there is no formal documentation. Although code inspections and having developers alternate working on various functional areas can help prevent this, losing the main member of a team can be catastrophic. When determining whether the team is suitable for the agile approach, the project leader should consider this situation. Recognizing that one of the main principles of XP is to keep current knowledge through keeping skilled staff [25, 26, 29].

4 Findings and Suggestive Measures

This section of the study is covering the findings of the research and suggestive measures that can overcome issues in the agile software development and project management mentioned in the Table 5.

Table 5. Findings of study.

Contents	Research findings	Recommendation	Impact of recommendations
Scrum	Daily meetings agitate the developers because they are responsible to update them about their tasks in front of all others	Split the meetings into different sessions rather than arrange them on daily basis The meeting can also be done in the digital environment means online	It will remove issues from the scrum and make the developer and teams more comfortable to update. On other hand, it will enhance trust among them. It will reduce pressure from developers to work productively
DSDM	Requirements are not fixed and also not pertinent for distributed team/s	Defined all the requirements clearly at the initial stage of a project and reduce the level of control of the client on the product backlog but did not remove controlcompletely. Thus, whenever the client gives a change request then the team or chief developer should examine whether do able to or not	Define the project core parameters at the initial stage of a project and fix them to not extend it Digital processes in agile software development will enhance the development and team coordination
FDD	The main issue is less documentation and highly rely on the chief developer for requirement specification and effort estimation	Increase the documentation and make all the specifications clearly defined in the document. Establish a team effort estimation mechanism rather than support the time chief programmer or team lead as in planning poker technique as example	Proper documentation will stop the frequent change from the client because when you defined all the specifications then ultimately the project will develop as per the requirements. In case the client suggested more additional changes than before welcome changes should be validated with the document. Team/s or developer/s individual suggestions about the effort estimation will reduce the dependency on the team lead. Additionally, it will reduce the biased nature of estimation in a team

(*continued*)

Table 5. (*continued*)

Contents	Research findings	Recommendation	Impact of recommendations
XP	Some issues are similar with the FDD like documentation but another issue is not applicable for large projects	Need to increase the team size	Increase the team size and then split the team into 2 parts as per their expertise. Because 2 small groups of the same team will work more productively
Developers	Developer expertise for a user story	Always give a user story to develop who has the expertise for it	It will directly impact on accurate estimation of user stories. It will also eliminate the biased nature of effort estimation from agile. Thus, the estimation technique should be more predictive based and should estimate the user stories by the individual developer rather than follow the process as example planning poker. Estimation by the Indi dual as per their skills and knowledge, team leaders can have the most accurate judgments about the efforts of each developer for the particular user story. This would make the estimation accurate and safe from biased estimation
Client	Control on the product backlog	Document the requirements and then overcome the control of the client on the product backlog	When reducing the control of client from product backlog but supporting client satisfaction, then it will control the changes from the client. Sometimes a client is also ambiguous related to the user stories
Team/s	Team's abilities	As we stated that select developers as per the user story and expertise. Thus, the select team as per their previous project's history and working skills	Selection of team will improve the productivity much more because in the agile team needs to arrange daily meetings, work pressure, and client changes so the team abilities for the current project

5   Conclusion

Software engineering has a lot of models to develop software projects. All models have some flaws and to overcome these from the efficient software development agile models were introduced. Agile methods are more viable for adoption in the software industry. The agile main goal and feature are to support the client who can send a change request at any time and any level of the project. On the other hand, it is a limitation in the agile model. Another limitation in investigated agile methods is that they are applicable for only small-scale projects and do not give fruitful results when use for large-scale projects. We have studied all the factors as categorization for the agile software project's development and management. We have done extensive study on both factors agile's methods and developer, and client, etc. We found that both factors need major improvements to make it more proficient for development. Such improvements precisely regarding the developers, large projects, daily meetings, and client direct much involvement throughout the project. The study's findings and suggestive measures are pertinent for the followers of the agile methodology. These are providing new directions for agile practitioners to amend the agile and introduce some new features. Researchers can improve agile methodology by following the listed suggestions and making the agile method an advanced version for future use.

References

1. Steghöfer, J.P., Knauss, E., Alégroth, E., Hammouda, I., Burden, H., Ericsson, M.: Teaching agile-addressing the conflict between project delivery and application of agile methods. In: 2016 IEEE/ACM 38th International Conference on Software Engineering Companion (ICSE-C), pp. 303–312. IEEE, May 2016
2. Noteboom, C., Ofori, M., Sutrave, K., El-Gayar, O.: Agile project management: a systematic literature review of adoption drivers and critical success factors. In: Proceedings of the 54th Hawaii International Conference on System Sciences, p. 6775, January 2021
3. Trier, K.K., Treffers, T.: Agile Project Management in Creative Industries: a systematic literature review and future research directions. In: 2021 IEEE Technology & Engineering Management Conference-Europe (TEMSCON-EUR), pp. 1–8. IEEE, May 2021
4. Khalid, A., Butt, S.A., Jamal, T., Gochhait, S.: Agile scrum issues at large-scale distributed projects: scrum project development at large. Int. J. Softw. Innov. (IJSI) 8(2), 85–94 (2020)
5. Vishnubhotla, S.D., Mendes, E., Lundberg, L.: An insight into the capabilities of professionals and teams in agile software development: a systematic literature review. In: Proceedings of the 2018 7th International Conference on Software and Computer Applications, pp. 10–19, February 2018
6. Martin, A., Anslow, C., Johnson, D.: Teaching agile methods to software engineering professionals: 10 years, 1000 release plans. In: Baumeister, H., Lichter, H., Riebisch, M. (eds.) XP 2017. LNBIP, vol. 283, pp. 151–166. Springer, Cham (2017). https://doi.org/10.1007/978-3-319-57633-6_10
7. Al-Saqqa, S., Sawalha, S., AbdelNabi, H.: Agile software development: methodologies and trends. Int. J. Interac. Mobile Technol. 14(11), 246 (2020)
8. Fuchs, C.: Adapting (to) agile methods: exploring the interplay of agile methods and organizational features (2019)

9. Gandomani, T.J., Faraji, H., Radnejad, M.: Planning poker in cost estimation in agile methods: averaging vs. consensus. In: 2019 5th Conference on Knowledge-Based Engineering and Innovation (KBEI), pp. 066–071. IEEE, February 2019

10. Noll, J., Beecham, S.: How agile is hybrid agile? An analysis of the helena data. In: Franch, X., Männistö, T., Martínez-Fernández, S. (eds.) PROFES 2019. LNCS, vol. 11915, pp. 341–349. Springer, Cham (2019). https://doi.org/10.1007/978-3-030-35333-9_25

11. Wińska, E., Dąbrowski, W.: Software development artifacts in large agile organizations: a comparison of scaling agile methods. In: Poniszewska-Marańda, A., Kryvinska, N., Jarząbek, S., Madeyski, L. (eds.) Data-Centric Business and Applications. LNDECT, vol. 40, pp. 101–116. Springer, Cham (2020). https://doi.org/10.1007/978-3-030-34706-2_6

12. Tessem, B.: The customer effect in agile system development projects. a process-tracing case study. Procedia Comput. Sci. **121**, 244–251 (2017)

13. Dingsøyr, T., Falessi, D., Power, K.: Agile development at scale: the next frontier. IEEE Softw. **36**(2), 30–38 (2019)

14. Amjad, S., et al.: Calculating completeness of agile scope in scaled agile development. IEEE Access **6**, 5822–5847 (2017)

15. Ruk, S.A., Khan, M.F., Khan, S.G., Zia, S.M.: A survey on adopting agile software development: issues & its impact on software quality. In: 2019 IEEE 6th International Conference on Engineering Technologies and Applied Sciences (ICETAS), pp. 1–5. IEEE, December 2019

16. Abdalhamid, S., Mishra, A.: Adopting of agile methods in software development organizations: systematic mapping. TEM J. **6**(4), 817 (2017)

17. Schuh, G., Prote, J.P., Gützlaff, A., Ays, J., Donner, A.: Fixed cost management as an enabler for agile manufacturing networks. Procedia Manuf. **39**, 625–634 (2019)

18. Raza, S., Waheed, U.: Managing change in agile software development a comparative study. In: 2018 IEEE 21st International Multi-Topic Conference (INMIC), pp. 1–8. IEEE, November 2018

19. Goel, S., et al.: Resilient and agile engineering solutions to address societal challenges such as coronavirus pandemic. Mater. Today Chem. **17**, 100300.(2020)

20. Gablas, B., Ruzicky, E., Ondrouchova, M.: The change in management style during then course of a project from the classical to the agile approach. J. Competitiveness **10**(4), 38–53 (2018)

21. Ratner, B.: The correlation coefficient: definition, DM Stat-1 Articles, vol. 11a (2007)

22. Kuusinen, K., et al.: A large agile organization on its journey towards DevOps. In: 2018 44th Euromicro Conference on Software Engineering and Advanced Applications (SEAA), pp. 60–63. IEEE, August 2018

23. Anwer, F., Aftab, S., Waheed, U., Muhammad, S.S.: Agile software development models TDD, FDD, DSDM, and crystal methods: a survey. Int. J. Multi-Disc. Sci. Eng. **8**(2), 1–10 (2017)

24. Przybyłek, A., Zakrzewski, M.: Adopting collaborative games into agile requirements engineering (2018)

25. Kumar, R., Singh, K., Jain, S.K.: Agile manufacturing: a literature review and Pareto analysis. Int. J. Qual. Reliab. Manage. **37**(2), 207–222 (2019)

26. Patel, A., et al.: A comparative study of agile, component-based, aspect-oriented and mashup software development methods. Tehnicki Vjesnik **19**(1), 175–189 (2012)

27. de la Barra, C., Crawford, B., Soto, R., Misra, S., Monfroy, E.: Agile software development: it is about knowledge management and creativity. In: Murgante, B., et al. (eds.) ICCSA 2013. LNCS, vol. 7973, pp. 98–113. Springer, Heidelberg (2013). https://doi.org/10.1007/978-3-642-39646-5_8

28. Pham, Q., Nguyen, A.V., Misra, S.: Apply agile method for improving the efficiency of software development project at VNG company. In: Murgante, B., et al. (eds.) ICCSA 2013. LNCS, vol. 7972, pp. 427–442. Springer, Heidelberg (2013). https://doi.org/10.1007/978-3-642-39643-4_31

29. Mundra, A., Misra, S., Dhawale, C.A.: Practical scrum-scrum team: way to produce successful and quality software. In: 2013 13th International Conference on Computational Science and Its Applications, pp. 119–123. IEEE, June 2013

30. Correia, A., Gonçalves, A., Misra, S.: Integrating the scrum framework and lean six sigma. In: Misra, S., et al. (eds.) ICCSA 2019. LNCS, vol. 11623, pp. 136–149. Springer, Cham (2019). https://doi.org/10.1007/978-3-030-24308-1_12

31. Habib, B., Romli, R.: A systematic mapping study on issues and importance of documentation in agile. In: 2021 IEEE 12th International Conference on Software Engineering and Service Science (ICSESS), pp. 198–202. IEEE, August 2021

32. Fernández-Sanz, L., Gómez-Pérez, J., Diez-Folledo, T.I., Misra, S.: Researching human and organizational factors impact for decisions on software quality. In: Proceedings of the11th International Conference on Software Engineering and Applications, pp. 283–289 (2016)

33. Khan, R.A., et al.: Practices of motivators in adopting agile software development at large scale development team from management perspective. Electronics **10**, 2341 (2021). https://doi.org/10.3390/electronics10192341

34. Niederman, F., Lechler, T., Petit, Y.: A research agenda for extending agile practices in software development and additional task domains. Project Manage. J. **49**(6), 3–17 (2018)

35. Usman, M., Mendes, E., Weidt, F., Britto, R.: Effort estimation in agile software development: a systematic literature review. In: Proceedings of the 10th International Conference on Predictive Models in Software Engineering, pp. 82–91, September 2014

36. Szewc, A., Karovič, V., Veselý, P.: The documentation in the project of software creation. In: Kryvinska, N., Poniszewska-Maranda, A. (eds.) Developments in Information & Knowledge Management for Business Applications. SSDC, vol. 377, pp. 361–441. Springer, Cham (2022). https://doi.org/10.1007/978-3-030-77916-0_14

37. Przybyłek, A., Albecka, M., Springer, O., Kowalski, W.: Game-based Sprint retrospectives: multiple action research. Empir. Softw. Eng. **27**(1), 1–56 (2021). https://doi.org/10.1007/s10664-021-10043-z

38. Jones, A., Thoma, V.: Determinants for successful agile collaboration between UX designers and software developers in a complex organisation. Int. J. Hum.-Comput. Interac. **35**(20), 1914–1935 (2019)

39. Weflen, E., MacKenzie, C.A., Rivero, I.V.: An influence diagram approach to automating lead time estimation in Agile Kanban project management. Expert Sys. Appl. **187**, 115866 (2022)

40. Kalenda, M., Hyna, P., Rossi, B.: Scaling agile in large organizations: practices, challenges, and success factors. J. Softw. Evol. Process **30**(10), e1954 (2018)

Author Index

Printed in the United States
by Baker & Taylor Publisher Services